ROGER
BLACK'S
DESKTOP
DESIGN
POWER

THE BANTAM ITC SERIES

ROGER BLACK'S DESKTOP DESIGN POWER

Roger Black

BANTAM BOOKS

NEW YORK · TORONTO · LONDON · SYDNEY · AUCKLAND

ROGER BLACK'S DESKTOP DESIGN POWER
A Bantam Book/February 1991

*Throughout this book, the trade names and trademarks of some
companies and products have been used, and no such uses are
intended to convey endorsement of or other affiliations with the
book or software.*

*Published simultaneously in the
United States and Canada*

Bantam Books are published by Bantam Books, a division of Bantam Doubleday Dell
Publishing Group, Inc. Its trademark, consisting of the words "Bantam Books" and
the portrayal of a rooster, is Registered in the U.S. Patent and Trademark Office and
in other countries. Marca Registrada, Bantam Books, 666 Fifth Avenue,
New York, New York, 10103

PRINTED IN THE UNITED STATES OF AMERICA

0 9 8 7 6 5 4 3 2 1

Foreword

It would be fair to say that the art direction of Roger Black has influenced a generation of designers, editors, and even publishers. His ideas, his visual vocabulary, and his emphasis on beautiful typography have become the definition of contemporary publication design.

With *Rolling Stone, The New York Times, Newsweek,* and scores of other magazines and newspapers he has pioneered a style that delights the reader's eye and guides attention across the page. Publications, despite the recent fascination with graphics, maps, and other visual eyewash, are still composed almost entirely of type. Roger recognized that using the type creatively—designing with display headlines, captions, pullquotes, drop caps and the body type itself—was the forgotten secret to making publications lively and informative at the same time.

It wasn't long before editors began to learn the names of typefaces, and the RB look fast became conventional wisdom. Then came the desktop publishing revolution.

Roger was among the first to recognize that this new technology could be used to create high-quality, highly detailed art direction for news publishing. He has led the charge for more typefaces from the foundries, more control in the software, and has even consulted with computer companies about future products. More importantly, he has introduced the technology to a new wave of magazines and newspapers around the world. The creative possibilities of computer-based art direction and production is, because of Roger's lead, spreading around the globe.

Designing on the desktop requires time and study. At first the tools are in the way. Then it gets easier and finally you achieve fluency. If you love type, if great art direction is a personal passion, if you reach an audience and tell the story effectively, if you want to perfect your craft on the computer, then you have the right book in your hands. Roger is the master.

William Randolph Hearst III
Editor and Publisher
The San Francisco Examiner

Preface

This is the first time I've tried to write a book, and having completed it, more or less, I feel certain of retaining my amateur status.

The effort would never have gotten this far, however, without the steady encouragement, if not to say relentless prodding, of Michael Goff, the editorial director of my studio in New York. He literally dragged the thing out of me, and made me organize the material, including the graphics, over a period of many months. If the result makes sense to you at all, it is due to his work.

Michael Roney of Bantam, the most patient editor in the world, has improved the final version enormously, and I am grateful for his steady advice and editorial talent.

Philip Krayna, a wonderfully talented young designer, helped put together the illustrations, and I am grateful for his efforts.

And without Steve Luciani, the director of prepress production at *The New York Times*, I never would have gotten started in desktop publishing. While we were both at *Newsweek,* he got the company to put a PC in my office, and he set up my first system at home. How quaint it seems now, but with this early beginning, I started acquiring enough experience to eventually build an international design studio around the desktop publishing phenomenon. What approximate understanding I have of computers is a result of Steve's tireless tutoring. And when this book was in rough shambles, he kindly went through it and corrected a multitude of technical errors. Thank you.

Finally, thanks to Terry Nasta at Bantam, who labored long and hard on production.

I dedicate this book to Pinkie.

Contents

CHAPTER   11

Image *Magazine*

CHAPTER   12

Desktop *on the Desktop*   265

C H A P T E R   1 3

Newsletters 287

C H A P T E R   1 4

Desktop Design Power 301

Index 313

Diving into Desktop Design

There is no way to learn design from a book.

There is no way to learn to use computers from a book.

So, why a book?

I hope to entice some still-reticent professional designers into using desktop publishing (DTP)—and to entice some nondesigners into thinking design while they are putting the power of DTP to work.

There are many shibboleths and bugaboos about computers and about design. Many designers still draw a distinction between work done with a computer and work done by hand. They will comment that a certain magazine is so good that it doesn't look like it was done on a computer.

But the handicap should go to those still laboriously doing type specs and page pasteup by hand.

Computers must be seen simply as tools, like pencils and X-acto knives. They are only the means. And while any medium—the very paper and ink—constrains communication and shapes aesthetics, computers are already providing the most fluid and transparent access to print, and promise a world where design is almost trivial. The meaning is what should count.

As far as I am concerned, there is no longer any significant differ-

1

ence between the results of desktop publishing and any other kind.

For nondesigners, there is another hurdle: design appears to be an arcane branch of knowledge, like particle physics or the French language—so hard that it might not be worth learning.

Not for Professionals Only

Many graphic designers are alarmed at the spread of DTP because their status as an elite is challenged. They say they fear being overrun by a glut of ugly and disorganized publications. But what really bugs them is the thought that design might actually be easily handled by laymen using some simple computer tools.

The term "design police" has even been heard, especially in corporate environments.

The design fallout from desktop publishing thus far is nowhere near as bad as I thought it might be. As a matter of fact, it has been a nice surprise. No matter how many ugly designs come out of this new technology, taste will still rule what is successful. The public will not suspend criticism just because it is barraged. People will just tune out and turn off, as with television. I have actually found, while judging various design competitions, that some of those new to design are doing very interesting things.

The priesthood of graphic design has perpetrated and perpetuated the myth that design is not something to be attempted at home— that it's something akin to brain surgery. This is hogwash. Simple, straightforward graphic design is something normal people can, and should, do.

Writing is not simply the province of writers—any of us can make competent attempts. Design is the same. Though it is not taught in grade school, there are some basic rules, which people can learn, as with writing. There needs to be an E.B. White of design to make it easier for people to become design literate. This graphic grammarian should give hints like, "Try to make a page with only one typeface."

Not everyone will become a brilliant designer if he or she is armed only with the right rules, just as not everyone becomes a great writer by reading E.B. White. But you can get your point across more quickly and more effectively.

In the late twentieth century we are already seeing an incredible spread of design knowledge. Presumably, your parents didn't teach you about different typefaces, but increasingly, people are coming into contact with type for the first time on their computers. The world is definitely changing when we hear secretaries complain to their bosses about not having enough fonts on their word processors.

The Approach

The number one rule is to be aware, always. If you come from a family which kept books and magazines around, it's likely that you had very clear opinions from a very early age about their appearance. If you were an avid reader as a child, you will remember the smell of books. Sometimes you pick up a magazine, and the appearance will remind you of something—before you've ever read a word. All of design rests upon these associations, deliberate and accidental. If you can evoke the right association in a reader, you are a successful designer.

A good designer has a facility for criticism, and a good eye. With these, you can design something. Or, if you can at least recognize that something is well designed, you can copy it, in style or approach. I am not advocating plagiarism, but awareness.

If someone is composing a song, or writing a short story, he will consciously or unconsciously incorporate elements of his favorites. If you are decorating your apartment, you will start to look for ideas in other apartments or in magazines. Then you can adapt or borrow successful elements. If you are writing, you have favorite writers that have accomplished what you hope for, and you will try to use them. Why not with design?

The Dive

Some of these rules will seem absurdly simple and self-evident, but it is important to think about page design as a process. Some of the most obvious, seemingly simple elements necessitate clear, and sometimes difficult, decisions.

When you face a blank layout, there are no rules. You have to set them. You can start with the pictures or with the text. I usually start with the text. This approach is by no means the only one. Other designers start with the pictures or by laying down a grid.

Most magazines are text-oriented; very few magazines run photographs, or even photo-essays, without some words. And publishers refer to their customers as readers, not viewers.

If you are setting out to make a little newsletter for your company, take your favorite magazine as a model. What are the elements that form its identity? Take a typeface that you have seen used well. *Time* magazine uses Times Roman for text and Franklin Gothic for headlines. They make a good, contrasting combination—safe and mildly classic. If you like them, why not use them?

If you are starting with the text first, there is a series of design decisions which will define your page. The first is the type. Decide which typeface or typefaces to use. The smaller the publication, the smaller the array of type. Once you have a font and point size, you need to arrange the type on the page. Decide how wide to make the margins and columns. Then, when the text is down, bring in the pictures.

And then, inevitably, start again. Modify and improve, or start quickly from scratch. Create alternatives, and choose the best. Note the number of possible ways to design a business card, as shown in Figure I-1. The possibilities for a full page of a publication are endless.

Start by figuring out the associations you want to work with. These initial decisions about the publication determine its basic shape. And, consciously or unconsciously, you are undoubtedly relating the page to a traditional form, a convention in design. This is not a bad thing. If your page recalls a classic or familiar form, a certain amount of the preliminary effort to bridge the gap between you and the reader is taken care of. The reader actually takes newspaper headlines for granted.

He doesn't stop and say, "What is this? The news?" In Figures I-2a–I-2c, note the elements which define each publication. By using the vocabulary of one of these publications, you will create a page with these associations.

Figure I-1
If there are this
many ways to design
a simple business card,
think of the options
for a full page of type,
photos, illustrations,
and headlines

Even the most revolutionary design is only revolutionary in terms of the tradition it is breaking. In this century, successive groups of designers have tried to break new ground in graphic design: the Russian constructivists and their dramatic use of collage (a technique of modern art); the Bauhaus modernists and their machine-age rationalism; the Swiss constructivists who unwittingly ushered in the bland postwar corporate look; and even the punkish new wave designers of the last decade, who brought a sense of humor to the modernist era.

Designers such as the constructivist, El Lizitsky, the Bauhaus leader, Herbert Bayer, the Swiss poster artist, Herbert Mader, or the American new waver April Greiman, rejected the mainstream of Western design and developed a new aesthetic that somehow has maintained a kind of revolutionary energy throughout the century. While the later modernists were no longer in the front lines—their work was inspired by work done before the Second World War—there was plenty of sloppy, slick commercial graphic design to fuel their radicalism. All tried to turn design inside out. But the end result has been a new form of orthodoxy, and we see in 1990s book jackets modernist references as an almost quaint style of the past.

While the revolutionaries were at work, others chose to work closer to the mainstream. At the same time as Bayer was contemplating an entirely lowercase alphabet in Germany, Thomas Maitland

Figure I-2a
Book

F A H R E N H E I T 4 5 1

winged books died on the porch and lawn of the house. While the books went up in sparkling whirls and blew away on a wind turned dark with burning.

Montag grinned the fierce grin of all men singed and driven back by flame.

He knew that when he returned to the firehouse, he might wink at himself, a minstrel man, burnt-corked, in the mirror. Later, going to sleep, he would feel the fiery smile still gripped by his face muscles, in the dark. It never went away, that smile, it never ever went away, as long as he remembered.

He hung up his black beetle-colored helmet and shined it; he hung his flameproof jacket neatly; he showered luxuriously, and then, whistling, hands in pockets, walked across the upper floor of the fire station and fell down the hole. At the last moment, when disaster seemed positive, he pulled his hands from his pockets and broke his fall by grasping the golden pole. He slid to a squeaking halt, the heels one inch from the concrete floor downstairs.

He walked out of the fire station and along the midnight street toward the subway where the silent air-propelled train slid soundlessly down its lubricated flue in the earth and let him out with a great puff of warm air onto the cream-tiled escalator rising to the suburb.

Whistling, he let the escalator waft him into the still night air. He walked toward the corner, thinking little at all about nothing in particular. Before he reached the corner, however, he slowed as if a wind had sprung up from nowhere, as if someone had called his name.

The last few nights he had had the most uncertain feelings about the sidewalk just around the corner here, moving in the starlight toward his house. He had felt that a moment prior to his making the turn, someone had been there. The air seemed charged with a special calm as if someone had waited there, quietly, and only a moment before he came, simply turned to a shadow and let him through. Perhaps his nose detected a faint perfume, perhaps the

4

THE HEARTH AND THE SALAMANDER

skin on the backs of his hands, on his face, felt the temperature rise at this one spot where a person's standing might raise the immediate atmosphere ten degrees for an instant. There was no understanding it. Each time he made the turn, he saw only the white, unused, buckling sidewalk, with perhaps, on one night, something vanishing swiftly across a lawn before he could focus his eyes or speak.

But now tonight, he slowed almost to a stop. His inner mind, reaching out to turn the corner for him, had heard the faintest whisper. Breathing? Or was the atmosphere compressed merely by someone standing very quietly there, waiting?

He turned the corner.

The autumn leaves blew over the moonlit pavement in such a way as to make the girl who was moving there seem fixed to a sliding walk, letting the motion of the wind and the leaves carry her forward. Her head was half bent to watch her shoes stir the circling leaves. Her face was slender and milk-white, and in it was a kind of gentle hunger that touched over everything with tireless curiosity. It was a look, almost, of pale surprise; the dark eyes were so fixed to the world that no move escaped them. Her dress was white and it whispered. He almost thought he heard the motion of her hands as she walked, and the infinitely small sound now, the white stir of her face turning when she discovered she was a moment away from a man who stood in the middle of the pavement waiting.

The trees overhead made a great sound of letting down their dry rain. The girl stopped and looked as if she might pull back in surprise, but instead stood regarding Montag with eyes so dark and shining and alive that he felt he had said something quite wonderful. But he knew his mouth had only moved to say hello, and then when she seemed hypnotized by the salamander on his arm and the phoenix disc on his chest, he spoke again.

"Of course," he said, "you're our new neighbor, aren't you?"

"And you must be"—she raised her eyes from his professional symbols "—the fireman." Her voice trailed off.

"How oddly you say that."

5

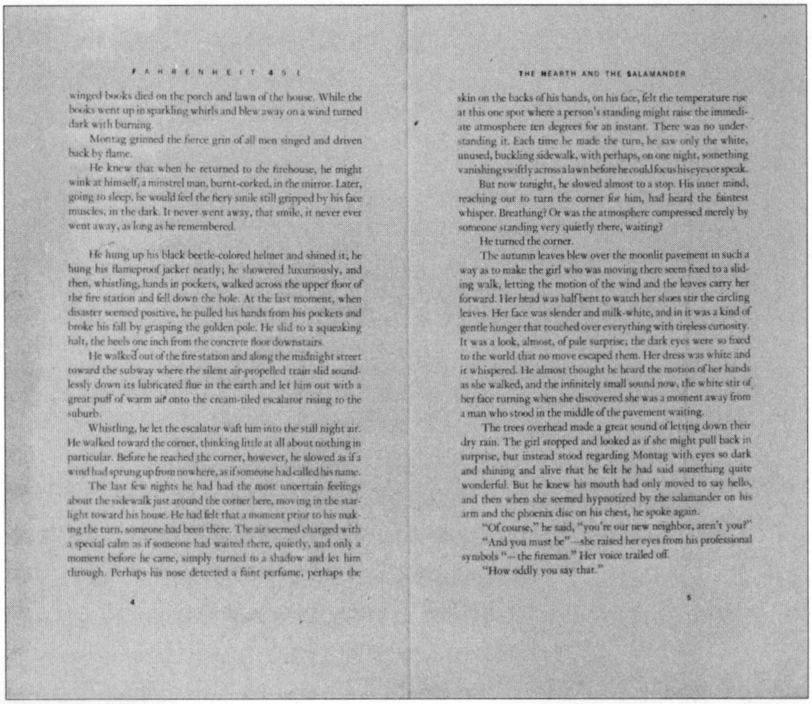

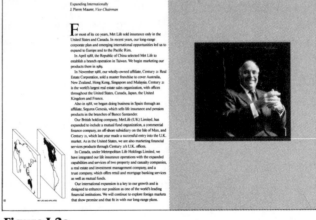

Figure I-2b
Newspaper

EARTHQUAKE EXTRA

San Francisco Examiner

FINAL

5:04 p.m., Oct. 17, 1989

7.0 quake stuns Bay

At least 250 killed
Tremors felt from North Coast to Los Angeles

Terror on the Bay Bridge
Cars slid as if on ice as the span swung & swayed

S.F. Marina devastated
Huge fire leaves 3 dead, buildings collapse

State of emergency

'Impossible, but real'

Expanding Internationally
J. Pierre Maurer, *Vice-Chairman*

For most of its 120 years, Met Life sold insurance only in the United States and Canada. In recent years, our long-range corporate plan and emerging international opportunities led us to expand to Europe and to the Pacific Rim.

In April 1988, the Republic of China selected Met Life to establish a branch operation in Taiwan. We begin marketing our products there in 1989.

In November 1988, our wholly-owned affiliate, Century 21 Real Estate Corporation, sold a master franchise to cover Australia, New Zealand, Hong Kong, Singapore and Malaysia. Century 21 is the world's largest real estate sales organization, with offices throughout the United States, Canada, Japan, the United Kingdom and France.

Also in 1988, we began doing business in Spain through an affiliate, Seguros Genesis, which sells life insurance and pension products in the branches of Banco Santander.

Our British holding company, MetLife (UK) Limited, has expanded to include a mutual fund organization, a commercial finance company, an off-shore subsidiary on the Isle of Man, and Century 21, which last year made a successful entry into the U.K. market. As in the United States, we are also marketing financial services products through Century 21's U.K. offices.

In Canada, under Metropolitan Life Holdings Limited, we have integrated our life insurance operations with the expanded capabilities and services of two property and casualty companies, a real estate and investment management company, and a trust company, which offers retail and mortgage banking services as well as mutual funds.

Our international expansion is a key to our growth and is designed to enhance our position as one of the world's leading financial institutions. We will continue to explore foreign markets that show promise and that fit in with our long-range plans.

10

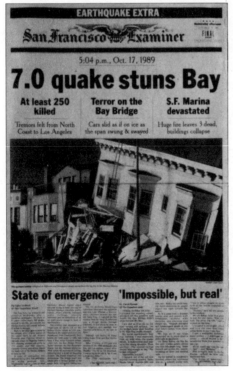

Figure I-2c
Corporate report

Cleland was producing exquisite ads for Locomobile cars. Which looks better today? Oddly, it is easier for us to imitate the Bauhaus than it is to pull off the complex richness of an Old Style design.

One staggeringly talented designer, Jan Tschichold, whose book, *Die Nieue Typographie*, laid down the principles of modern type layout, actually converted to traditional, Old Style design principles later in his life. Tschichold found it finally more productive and satisfying to work on the firm ground laid down by hundreds of years of printing design—standing, as they say, on the shoulders of giants.

Of course, design is largely a matter of fashion; styles change. And while Cleland or Tschichold could build beautifully on classical models, less talented beaux-arts designers created such an enormous amount of pompous, overdecorated nonsense, that is was a great relief to have modernism sweep it away.

The point is to be aware of these forms when designing, say, a newsletter. If the tabloid form is applied to a newsletter or a magazine, there will be big blaring headlines, big pictures, and a fairly horizontal layout. The urgency, popular appeal, and even the cheapness of tabloid papers can be evoked by the newsletter.

The more corporate and straight a publication, the more sparse its typographical diet should be. It will look trimmed down, business-like, efficient, and noncontroversial. Every element will probably be rectangular, and the total effect should be simple and elegant. If color is used at all, it should be muted. Gray, for example!

If your publication is supposed to look fun, you can introduce more typefaces, throw in louder color, and include some sweeping photos or illustrations.

To understand how to use traditional forms in publications, it is essential to know some of the history of magazines and newspapers. Part of this background is presented in Chapter 1, "Some Design History."

Book Organization

This book has a certain split personality. The first half is an attempt to present some of the fundamentals of design for nondesigners. For professionals, there is an exploration of approaches to the computer as a design tool.

In the second half of the book, there are case studies of publications—from small newsletters to national consumer magazines. These should show both nondesigners how to apply the power of DTP and designers how conventional production and design is improved with DTP.

There will be parts that may be a bit over the heads of newcomers—and other parts that are too basic or trivial for the pros. The common ground is desktop publishing, and for all of us this is new territory. Every day there seems to be something new to learn.

The premise is that DTP is the logical next step in the development of the printed page.

A Look at the Chapters

Chapter 1 presents a look at some of the context of contemporary publication design. Spending time with the recent history of magazines, and studying the previous examples is useful because successful design always builds on the past. If you don't know what has worked in the past, you are reinventing the wheel, or worse, the Edsel.

Chapter 2, "Type Basics," deals with some basics of type. This is my own chief interest and starting point for all layout on the desktop. Control over type is perhaps the most important advantage of using these new systems.

Next, Chapter 3, "Reaching the Reader," concerns the root problem of all printing design: getting the attention of readers. With everyone constantly diverted by the pressures and pleasures of modern life, the designer needs an arsenal of what I call reader devices—ways to lift text off the page into a reader's increasingly distracted consciousness.

Color, suddenly made more available by desktop technology, is the subject of Chapter 4, "Color Design, Printing, and Proofing." I have fairly straightforward, if not curmudgeonly views on how color can best be used in print communication, which I'll try to set forth. And there are a number of thorny technical issues involved in using color, which are confounding all of us who are used to letting outside experts do the work. While I can only hope to scrape the surface of these color issues, at least I will try to list them in this chapter.

Chapter 5 addresses the question of images and visual content. Since photography is still, in desktop terms, largely offline—the technology offers only the first glimmer of digital photography and desktop photo editing—this chapter will take on pictures as a basic design problem.

Chapter 6 looks at a publication's most important image and page: the cover.

With these major design considerations under our collective belts, it will be time to go at the array of hardware and software now available for desktop publishing. I don't claim to be a techie, and real wireheads will find much of Chapter 7, "Bits and Bolts: Desktop Systems," obvious, but I'll endeavor to approach the options for platforms and design tools in a useful, practical way.

Once you're up and running with desktop technology, there remain important matters of production and publication management. How to keep track of pages—in a very simple way—is the subject of Chapter 8.

Chapters 9 through 12 are case studies of publications I have designed and implemented on the desktop: *Smart, Trips, Image,* and *ITC Desktop* (now known as *Desktop Communications).* If experience is the only real way to learn design, the next best thing is to hear about others' experience, and this is what I will try to share.

In Chapter 13, there is a general review of desktop design for newsletters, which is, after all, the first thing that many people try to do with this technology. Once barely more elaborate than office memos, newsletters can now take advantage of the same design techniques as consumer magazines—which is why this chapter appears nearly at the end of the book.

And at last, Chapter 14, "Desktop Design Power," is a projection of where all this is heading. This is an opportunity for you to see just how cloudy my crystal ball is. Since the field is moving so quickly, the future may already have changed by the time you read this book. But the excitement can only increase. Desktop publishing represents a merger of print and electronic media, and it's only just begun.

Of course, when you have read this book you will not be a designer or a computer expert, unless you started out that way. But, you may have some new ideas about how to look at design—analyzing the way elements are composed to make a whole. As with anything else, the only way to really learn design is through practice—practice making layouts and practice using your own critical judgment.

Some Design History

Printing was one of the first waves of the industrial revolution. Mass production of books started 500 years ago, and in the nineteenth century another revolution took place. Until then, printing had been done by hand—presses were operated by hand, type was made and set by hand, and even paper was made by hand. All of these processes were taken over by machines, leaving the hands for new innovations and more artistic pursuits.

Magazines are clearly a development of technology. In what became a familiar industrial-commercial cycle, magazines and newspapers prompted the invention of fast color presses, and vice versa.

With the invention of the Linotype machine and the rotary press a hundred years ago, it became possible to print lots of copies cheaply. Handling text was greatly simplified from the days of individual pieces of metal type, and mass periodicals with many pages were possible. New paper manufacturing technology brought great rolls of paper for the new rotary presses. Advertising added the needed revenue. A popular medium was born.

Early History

The first periodicals, the journals of the nineteenth century, looked much like books. The first newspapers were similarly plain, text-driven affairs, with surprisingly small type.

But with the new industrial technology, both forms took off in new directions. By 1892, the influential magazine, *The Century,* was using photographs, engraved photomechanically (see Figure 1-1). The halftone dot was born.

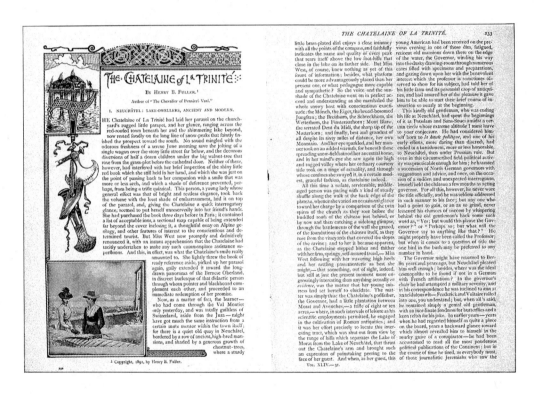

Figure 1-1
The Century magazine,
late 1900s

Daily papers adopted its use in the next few years, and by 1895 there were picture newspapers like New York's *Daily Graphic. Leslie's Illustrated* and *Harper's Weekly* were the first picture magazines, and in England there was *The London Illustrated News,* which was highly photographic. In the United States, some editors saw their mission to be culturally uplifting. Among these publications were *Scribner's, The*

Saturday Evening Post, and *Ladies' Home Companion.* All were fairly high-minded, and by today's taste, quaintly bourgeois.

When pictures first appeared in *The Century,* the printing was remarkable. They printed 90,000 copies, and the quality of the photos and typography was better than any magazine today.

After the turn of the century, the technology proliferated and became progressively more manageable. By 1920, using photos was routine; color was still a big deal.

The New Yorker is the classic magazine of the 1920s. It has remained true to its original form for 60 years, using color photography (with an occasional exception) only for advertising. When it started, the format of *The New Yorker* was not particularly special. But over the years, its restraint (dry text set in Caslon body type, broken only by consistently hilarious cartoons) has served to point to the writing. The reader reacts, "If nothing else is going on, the writing must be good." Lately, its publishers have begun to fiddle with the design of *The New Yorker,* papering over the last survivor of 1920s magazines.

Newspapers were also causing a splash in design in the first decades of the twentieth century. The tabloid zest of the *New York Daily News* and the sensationalism built up in the Hearst-Pulitzer circulation wars was not at first absorbed by magazines, which still were relentlessly middle-class.

The Thirties

In the 1920s and 1930s, all this changed. With the advent of movies, down-market popular magazines like *Photoplay, Screen Romance,* and *Modern Screen* appeared, with a spray of scandal and gossip.

Magazines adopted the form that we are familiar with today—a heavy mixture of photographs and text. Book design, with its highbrow connotations, was left in the dust.

Time (1923) broke new ground, with carefully departmentalized contents, and a mixture of small photos and short stories. *Life,* issued by the same company, was inspired by the rotogravure picture sections in newspapers, but with a new idea: the photo story.

Previously, the daily papers had been running theme pages, like "Crowned Heads of State on Parade." This is symptomatic of the habit of daily news photographers—their aim is to get the best single photo of an event, since only one picture is going to run. When these pictures were grouped on a page, they were still separate, individual events. No attempt was made to thread them together into a narrative. But *Life* was built around the emergence of photojournalism, the idea of telling stories with pictures.

Color didn't really make the scene until the late 1930s. The engraving process was cumbersome and expensive. It took a long time for even *Time* to get color on the cover. If you needed to get a magazine out in any kind of hurry (the usual way), it was hard to get the cover made in time.

At about the same time that color showed up regularly in the magazines, art directors came on the scene. Initially, magazines were creations of editors and writers. Then photographers appeared, and then art directors. Fashion magazines were the first to recognize the importance of art directors and made them equal to other editors. They weren't just flunkies doing layouts. *Vogue,* with its photo and art emphasis, evolved the form it still has today—heavy photo emphasis with ads concentrated in the front.

In addition to fashion books, art directors got jobs on the emerging picture magazines. Alexander Leiberman (now head of Condé Nast) was creating magazines like *Vue* in Paris in the 1930s and 1940s.

The Forties and Fifties

During World War II, there was a hiatus for popular magazines because of war shortages. The photojournalistic efforts of *Life* and *Look* fed a public desperate for information about the war. Then, after the war, the media race continued for the attentions of Americans and for the next technology.

The most significant advance was the conversion of letterpress to photolithographic offset printing, meaning that it was possible to reproduce anything pasted on a piece of paper. The printing plate was a flat photographic plate instead of a three-dimensional relief. It was much easier to reproduce type than to lock it up in chases (steel frames for type) for the presses. The era of the X-acto knife began.

It became possible to do handwriting, lettering, and photolettering. Designers went crazy with it. Look at *Vogue* in the 1940s (see Figure 1-2) and *Mademoiselle* in the 1950s. Actually, the phototype craze started during the war, because all of the lettering artists were off fighting. The U.S. government propagandists ordered headlines from the photolettering company for its posters, and from then on it was the standard.

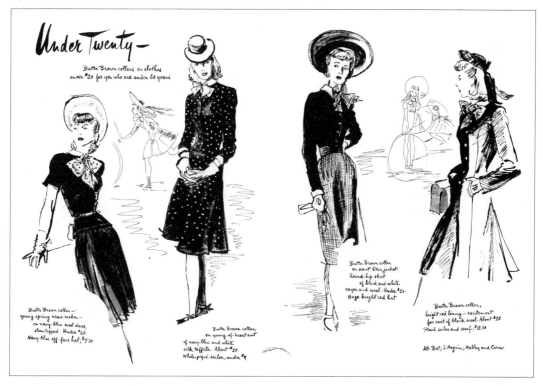

Figure 1-2
Vogue, 1942

The postwar period was the last great boom for mass-circulation popular magazines. *Life* expanded its circulation to 7 million. *Time* ran up to over 4 million, and *The Saturday Evening Post* went up to something like 10 million.

In the 1950s, *Esquire* and *Holiday* started doing some very innovative things within the structure of traditional magazines of the 1920s. They kept the strict departments and quaint little drawings to break up the pages, but they incorporated new features, with splashier pictures, and a large page size. (See Figure 1-3.) All of this set the foundation for the anarchist design movements of the 1960s.

The Sixties and Seventies

As TV arrived, it challenged the place of magazines. Magazines responded by becoming more visual and more narrowly focused. There were more magazines about specific topics.

In Europe, the Swiss constructivist designers divided pages into rectangular units and arranged their layouts according to this grid.

Figure 1-3
Esquire kept the strict departments but incorporated splashier pictures in the 1950s

Look magazine in the 1950s brought these ideas over to this side of the ocean. As though influenced by Mondrian, people divided magazines into little squares. In newspapers, modular layout was introduced. Ironically, this was happening when designers had just been released from the necessarily rectangular structure of letterpress.

Art directors moved to the general magazines from the fashion magazines in the late 1950s. By the 1960s, they were firmly entrenched in magazines like *Esquire,* and even *Time* and *Newsweek* were moving them up the masthead—eventually to the number two position, right after the editor-in-chief.

By the mid 1960s, the "youth-quake" movement had some influence on the mainstream consumer magazines. *Esquire*, for example, reached the pinnacle of its design then, with Henry Wolf as the art director, followed by Sam Antupit. George Lois designed the covers—a series of innovative photo illustrations—including a portrait of Muhammed Ali as Saint Sebastian and a montage featuring Bob Dylan, Malcolm X, Fidel Castro, and John F. Kennedy. (See Figure 1-4.) The inside design at *Esquire* was very clean, with full-page illustrations on the openers opposite a classical type treatment with a different display type (type larger than body type) for each headline.

Magazines like the German *Twen* (shown in Figure 1-5), experimented with incredibly energetic photos and an almost psychedelic use of color. The art was directed by Willi Flechaus. The magazine is considered the quintessential example of 1960s magazine design.

In the United States similar things were happening. Richard Avedon's solarized photos of the Beatles in *Look* signaled the influence of drugs, and rock and roll. Devices like split-fountain colors (where different inks combined to create a rainbow effect) and underground comics were seen everywhere in local underground papers like *The Oracle* in Boston. In 1967 two pivotal magazines arrived, *Rolling Stone* and *New York Magazine,* and the way began to be cleared for the 1970s.

It appeared that special interest (rock and roll) or regional (Manhattan) magazines would have the day, while the big mass magazines

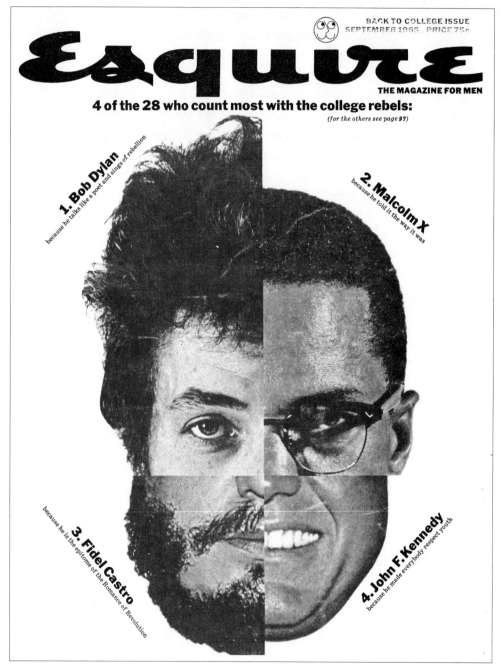

Figure 1-4
Youth-quake movements reflected in *Esquire,* 1965

closed one by one. *The Saturday Evening Post* disappeared in 1969. *Life* closed down in 1972.

At this point, Marshall McLuhan, the Canadian media guru, declared that print was through, that the "cool" medium of television would completely take over.

This view persisted through the 1970s, despite mounting evidence that there were more magazine titles than ever, that more people were employed in the business, and revenues were never higher. In style, the mainstream pop look of *Rolling Stone* was influential, but by the end of the decade the punk-rock, new-wave look, with its confetti and collages, yet another revival of Russian constructivism, became the hot new style.

The Eighties and Nineties

Luckily, by the late 1980s, people were starting to get fed up with new wave and its evil twin postmodernism, in favor of more classical design. And print is far from dead. With the advent of desktop publishing, print began to merge with the electronic media that McLuhan was so fond of.

Even before DTP, publishers were trying micropublishing, directed at a specific geographic, or interest, group. For example, *Avenue* magazine was created for upper-income readers in Manhattan.

In the 1980s, health magazines like *Psychology Today* (see Figure 1-6) and *Hippocrites* gained popularity, and the success was counted on the bottom line instead of in the millions of subscribers.

DTP is a part of this continuity of publishing advances. It is having an impact similar to that of the technical revolution of the 1890s. Ten years ago, few people would have thought of starting a magazine for their company, department, trade association, or church. Now, not only is it possible, they may actually already own much of the necessary machinery.

People have been getting into setting type for the first time. During the first few years of DTP, there was a proliferation of ugly little

Figure 1-5
Twen is the quintessential example of the 1960s

Figure 1-6
Psychology Today

newsletters and hand-outs as people explored uses for the technology. Now, we're seeing this technology applied to high-grade magazines, not only newsletters and startups.

The Constant Form

With the invention of offset printing in the 1940s, a battle began to preserve some of the structure of design in magazines. With the liberation from the locked-up, 3-D, letterpress page, some designers began to lose their sense of gravity. It was as though locomotive engineers, after years of being confined to two steel rails, were suddenly introduced to the freedom of the four-wheel drive jeep. Design got loose, and lines of type started to tilt—sometimes on purpose.

The fact is that 500 years of working within the physical constraints of lead—locking up lines of type in chases—had created a strong and enduring print aesthetic. The technology had changed, but the aesthetic, the tradition of print design, remained in the minds of readers. The fuddy-duddies, the conservatives, and those who yearned for some of the quality lost in phototype, now pasted up from slippery pieces of paper, began to yearn for order. When *Rolling Stone*, for one, adopted some of the rectilinear composition style of the 1920s, the readers responded favorably. (See Figure 1-7.) Perhaps it was only a subliminal recognition, but readers like the familiar. The forms of the past actually establish quicker lines of communication. The evocation of, say, *The Wall Street Journal*, helps create a sense of warm, fuzzy security.

Every time that styles change, something of the old is inevitably incorporated in the new. The fact that you are revolting against something means that you are defined by it. Thus even the most startling graphic revolution of our era—the breakthrough to modernism in the 1920s—now appears quaint. It is so much a part of its time, yet so trapped by its own past, the eclectic, overdecorated banality of the Belle Epoque.

The Bauhaus revolution, which applied the aesthetic of the machine to design of all kinds, shaped books, posters, and magazines by stripping away ornament, including serifs off typefaces. The actual letter forms were rationalized—to become more geometric—rather than following the proportion system dating from classical times. Pages were arranged asymmetrically. "Centered" was out; "ragged right" was in. But 50 years later, it turns out that the mainstream of Western culture is a stronger current than the machine age. Indeed, as mechanics gives way to electronics, designers are returning to the roots of graphic design, just as architects found that there is something that is post modern.

With very few lapses—as when people discovered what they could do with offset printing—there has been an amazing continuity of design. This is despite the best intentions of designers to "do something new every day."

Of course, the newest designs are usually not very popular. It takes about 10 years for anything new to be accepted in mainstream magazines. And then, the changes are rarely seen beneath the surface.

The *Look* magazine of the 1960s, hailed as one of the most innovative, used the traditional typography of early journals—Baskerville

18   *ROLLING STONE, JUNE 16, 1977*

Southside Johnny's Asbury Park rolling R&B revival

By John Milward

CLEVELAND— Some things just don't change. Over a year ago, before the release of their two Epic albums (*I Don't Want to Go Home*, *This Time It's for Real*), Southside Johnny and the Asbury Jukes packed Asbury Park's Stone Pony club three nights every week. Recently, on the first of three sardine-packed nights at Cleveland's Agora Ballroom, the scene was equally charged. And yet Southside Johnny Lyon, sprawled over a chair in his hotel lobby, wasn't quite satisfied.

"When people are up and dancing and generally crazy, the excitement gives you an adrenalin rush that pushes you right through the set, but that high energy fouls up the subtler moments." Some problem.

With the release of *This Time It's for Real*, Southside Johnny and the Jukes hope to expand an already solid Northeast following for their horn-driven rhythm & blues. So strong is their region-

al following that they make a cameo appearance in Joan Michlin Silver's film, *Between the Lines*. The movie's final scene, which finds the shattered staff of an underground paper piecing together their ideals after their paper is bought by a press lord, segues neatly into "I Don't Want to Go Home," the Jukes' song about the ache of failure after "reaching up to touch the sky." Given the Jukes' love for traditional rhythm & blues, their stretch for the big time holds the same perils as those of the young journalists.

"The thing about our music," says Southside, "is that it's honest and every note counts. You can play it till you're blue in the face and it'll still have that honesty and power.

"Our music works because it's good to dance, drink and have a good time to." Substitute "play" for "dance" and you've got a picture of Southside's musically driven youth, which eventually landed him on a bandstand with Bruce Springsteen and Miami Steve Van Zandt.

"When we were kids, my brother and I would go to bed and have to leave the door open

because there was only one heating outlet in the house. And downstairs, my parents would be having a drink and listening to music, and Billie Holiday and Jimmy Rushing would drift up the stairs with the heat."

When his brother brought home a harmonica along with an early Dylan album, Southside started playing the harp, but he looked to the South Side of Chicago for a style, instead of to Dylan. After early teen years spent on doorsteps singing doo-wop and drinking, he began singing with bands.

"Groups would form and break up at the drop of a hat," he recalls, "and in a way, Asbury's Upstage Club symbolized these quick musical changes. For a few years in the late Sixties when the bars closed at 2 a.m., everybody would rush to the Upstage from their other gigs for some serious jamming. We'd assemble a band and put together a set, with some nights coming out real hot and others blowing cold."

Springsteen was the first to galvanize these sessions into a distinct style, and while his success brought attention to the Asbury scene and his hardcore fans gave the Jukes an initial following, his influence also caused the Jukes to be characterized as riding on Springsteen's coattails.

"I can't think in terms of what effect Bruce's career has had on us," says Johnny with an exasperated sigh. "I mean, how can you think of that stuff when he's been your friend for years and has gone through all the same struggles?"

Given Miami Steve's heavy

For real: Southside Johnny (dead center) and his "incredibly non-photogenic" Jukes

involvement (he was a Juke before joining the E Street Band and now manages the Jukes), the Springsteen connection would seem a constant.

The Jukes have been joined on both albums by guest artists,

many of whom Van Zandt met on oldies shows while touring several years back with the Dovells. The Drifters, the Coasters and the Five Satins make appearances on *This Time It's for Real*; Ronnie Spector, who was on the first album (and has released "Say Goodbye to Hollywood," a Van Zandt-produced, E Street-backed single), is currently with the Jukes and doing a miniset within their show.

"After our songs were written," explains Southside, "we realized they fit the particular artists who perfected those forms. So it was natural to bring them into the studio with us. What I was a little wary about was how they would react to us, you know, whether they would look at us as a bunch of white punks copying their style for bucks."

Similarly, Van Zandt sees their participation as acts of respect. "Seeing these guys hooked into shoddy oldies shows was depressing. When they played with us, they could see what they once did was still hip. They didn't have to prove their worth because we already respected it."

So deep are their roots that the Jukes see themselves as part of an R&B rock revival. "Before the first album when we were playing the Jersey bars," recalls Southside, "the excitement was there, but it was hard to get it into perspective. The club audiences loved us but had gotten kind of blasé since everybody at the Stone Pony knew us as Asbury Parkers. But to hit all areas of the country and to find that same drinking/dancing madness, it makes you realize, 'Yeah, we're good, we can make it.'" ♫

New York vetoes outdoor rock

NEW YORK—EVEN IF IT GOES ON AT ALL, the traditional summer-long Schaefer Music Festival in Central Park's Wollman Rink will not rock out with anything heavier than soft folk/pop and easy-listening music.

After 11 consecutive years, the New York Parks Department, Schaefer Brewing Company (which is pulling out as the festival's sponsor after nine years) and promoter Ron Delsener have decided that past episodes of violence, litter, drug dealing and noise were too much of a strain on the small, converted skating rink, park personnel and nearby residents.

"We've almost had to go to court for the last two years to put these shows on," said Delsener, who is reportedly still negotiating with a new, undisclosed sponsor following Schaefer's decision last October to pull out. "But I'm definitely up for trying again—only this time they'd have to start earlier, be less loud, and I doubt if there would be any rock or soul."

Janet Cotton, spokesperson for the Parks Department, agrees that future concerts are possible only if oriented to a "family-type" audience. "In the last few years we've had rip-offs, muggings, near-riots. If we eliminate the more provocative acts we can keep out the undesirable elements."

Outdoor rock concerts in the Boston Common, San Francisco's Golden Gate Park and in other cities have also been restricted recently for similar reasons. —MICHAEL DUFFEY

PHOTOGRAPH BY DAVID GAHR

Figure 1-7
Yearning for order, *Rolling Stone* adopted some of the rectilinear composition style of the 1920s

rather than the then-trendy Helvetica used by the Swiss. The classic form of magazines keeps breaking to the surface. It endures because it works.

Nothing happens to the basic structure. If you look back to the magazines of the 1930s, the 1950s, and today, they all have the same front-of-the-book, middle-of-the-book, back-of-the-book framework. All along, it's been the advertising that has been calling the shots for the dummy, or imposition—the sequence and arrangement of ads within a publication. Advertisers demand that their ads go up front. They always want to have far-forward, right-hand positions, like title pages in books.

Ad spaces have standard sizes. In practice, this means that most magazines must be done in a three-column format and the front-of-the-book section has to be short editorial items to accommodate all the ads. A classic example of this is *The New Yorker's* "Talk of the Town" section. Most magazines have an equivalent section made up of short items to keep advertisers happy. Advertising actually dictates the form of big commercial magazines. Then, whatever the big successful magazines are doing defines how we think about all magazines in a particular era. Magazines in the second rank, even those that don't accept advertising, take design cues from the top few, so they adhere to the same design constraints. People expect to find short items in the front of a magazine, even if it is just an association journal. People always like to have something they can read all the way through in a minute.

Traditional Design and DTP

An important word of caution before you dive into DTP: take it slowly. A newcomer to the computer wants to press every button and use every special device. This is the quickest way to tip your hand as a novice, even if you are a professional designer.

The grossest error is to use the different type styling toys. The crude underscoring, outlining, and drop-shadow effects—part of the Macintosh menus from the beginning—are not things that can be applied automatically. If you want special effects, create them in a separate graphics program, such as Illustrator, and then bring them into the DTP program.

It's the same with expanding and condensing type. Look for typefaces that have been designed as expanded or condensed, rather than stretching or squashing them.

Nothing gives away a DTP document faster than type that has been italicized by simply slanting it or when there is an underline too close to the baseline. This all looks weird, because historically it simply could not be done. With lead type it was never possible to make a close underline, so it looks vaguely fishy today.

If you take the type and track it (adjust the space between letters) so that each letter touches, or if you reduce the space between lines of type, it makes it harder to read and is another one of those things that wasn't possible with lead type. (See Chapter 2, "Type Basics.")

At the beginning, it is better to recall traditional forms. People get greedy when they get all this DTP power in their hands. They try to pull out all the stops in one publication. If you look at some of the most successful design, you will see how simple it really is.

Some of the excesses of desktop publishing come from being faced with the blank electronic screen. The most obvious thing is to play with the toys rather than to use a visual language that people understand.

With the programs and typefaces currently available you can copy almost anything that exists. Again, I am not suggesting plagiarism, but I think a little imitation is better than idiotic experimentation. Use something as a base for your experiments.

And, if you don't have any taste, stop reading right now.

Type Basics

It used to be that most people were unaware there was more than one typeface. Those days are going fast. Now, you are beginning to hear the word "font," and even "kerning" in conversation. "Times" and "Helvetica" are nearly household words. Secretaries are demanding new fonts for their printers.

Executives are increasingly aware of the impact type has on their corporate image. Corporations are adopting house typefaces. Publication designers are relentlessly looking for that special typeface that will set their publication apart from the competition.

In the beginning, it is admittedly hard to tell one typeface from another. The first dawning awareness is that some of the letters have those little feet (known as serifs) on them. Presumably your curiosity leads to further investigation. It appears that there are not only dozens, but thousands of typefaces.

But why? There are only (in English) 26 letters. Why this nervous proliferation of letter forms?

The quick answer is fashion. There are new type designs, just as there are new designs for dresses, or floor tile. But it goes beyond that, because a typeface not only is a statement of style. Each one is a kind of tool that serves a purpose.

Adrian Frutiger, perhaps the greatest type designer of our century, compares the proliferation of type designs to shoes. You can only wear one pair at a time, and yet the stores are filled with different styles. (And some of us have an insatiable need for new ones, like certain wives of certain now-deceased dictators.)

Sumner Stone, the head of type design for Adobe Systems, compares typefaces to spoons. There are many ways to decorate a spoon, but, more importantly, forms change to suit different uses. A soup spoon is bigger; a serving spoon bigger than that. Your grandmother may have had those flat ice cream spoons, a little smaller than the sauce spoons sometimes set on European dining tables.

And then there are ladles.

Mr. Stone, as an exercise, gathered up all the different kinds of spoons in his house and counted 57 varieties. There were differences of style, but also of utility.

So Many Types, So Little Time

Technology has allowed us to accumulate designs in a way previously impossible. At the turn of the last century, a small English job printer might have had just three different type styles: plain, fancy, and Caslon, as shown in Figure 2-1.

Figure 2-1
Three basic type styles: plain (Franklin Gothic), fancy (BeLucian), and Caslon

A small English job printer might have had just three type styles.

A small English job printer might have had just three type styles.

A small English job printer might have had just three type styles.

In those days type was still set by hand from individual bits of lead, all separately cast at a remote foundry. It was heavy, expensive stuff, and it wore it out regularly. When new type was needed, printers seldom went farther than the nearest foundry because of the cost of shipping the heavy metal. In Ohio in 1900, there were fine type foundries in Cleveland and Cincinnati. Few printers would go as far as Chicago for type, and never to London.

The Ohio foundries offered hundreds of typefaces, original designs, revivals, and outright copies. But no printer or publishing house would buy them all, and only the bestsellers were kept in inventory. With mechanical typesetting (the hot-metal Linotype machine was invented in 1886), it became cheaper to accumulate different styles. Nowadays, a commercial typographer might stock 10,000 designs.

So far, only a few hundred of these are available in desktop publishing. But a welter of typefaces is on its way. How do you choose the right one for the job?

Type and Words

Most designers start with the pictures or the structure of a page, and put in the type last. Many say that the type, particularly the body type, is not all that important since most readers are unaware that there is more than one typeface. But is that true anymore? And in any case, is that the way to treat the written content of your publication?

After all, the body type is carrying the basic content, the written content of the publication. Design in books and magazines is not just a package, a cup that contains the liquid—text. It is the molecules of the liquid itself. Type is the code that carries the words. The subtle variations of typefaces have their own, usually subliminal, meanings. The associations called up by type layouts can put the reader in the proper mood.

Connotations and Associations

One interesting typographical and sociological side-effect of desktop publishing is the advent of the typeset letter. At first, people were a little puzzled to receive letters from friends and business associates set in 10-point Times Roman. The first reaction was, "What is this, some kind of form letter?"

Readers must have contemplated the first letters turned out on typewriters with the same bafflement. The complaint was the same: they seemed impersonal. Even today most of us wouldn't think of writing a love letter on a typewriter.

Publishing typefaces suggested mass communication, not individual letter writing. In the days of the typewriter, script typefaces were created to make letters more friendly. Now, with laser printers, some people use Courier, the monospaced typewriter face, so they don't look too corporate or too pompous. People don't want to make the impression that they have spent more time on form than on substance. Compare the examples in Figure 2-2.

This nervousness will pass. Courier, it can be hoped, will be consigned to the same historical dustbin as those hideous typewriter scripts. Traditional printing types, it can be simply stated, are easier to read than typewriter faces, and one might add, most handwriting. The proportional spacing of the letters gives an even, gray tone to the page, eliminating the patchiness of typewritten documents.

There are some new efforts to bring some desirable informality to letters produced on laser printers. The first solution to reach the desktop is International Typeface Corporation's (ITC) Stone Informal, a breezy companion to ITC Stone Serif and Stone Sans (designed by the same Sumner Stone). Another California designer, Zuzana Licko, has created a type called Matrix with the saw-toothed quality of dot-matrix fonts, although it is a high-resolution PostScript font. In the near future, we can expect informal scripts and fonts with "that hand-lettered look" and others that suggest the typewriter typefaces we are reluctant to abandon. Whether these survive depends on how we continue to perceive the problem they've been created to solve. Confronted with some future technology, our descendents may recall fondly the funky roughness of the 300-dpi printers of the 1980s.

There is a lesson in this: always take into account typography's subtle, but powerful, role in connotation and association. Bear in

Figure 2-2
Informal letters:
typewritten, in
Courier, and in
Janson Text

Dear Aunt Mary,

We were having a great time skiing
this weekend in Aspen. The snow here
is great and I am finally learning
how to take the hills. But yesterday
Bob went down the Black Diamond and
broke his leg.

Dear Aunt Mary,

We were having a great time skiing this
weekend in Aspen. The snow here is great
and I am finally learning how to take
the hills. But yesterday Bob went down
the Black Diamond and broke his leg.

                              Sincerely,
                              Judy

Dear Aunt Mary,

We were having a great time skiing this weekend in
Aspen. The snow here is great and I am finally learning
how to take the hills. But yesterday Bob went down the
Black Diamond and broke his leg.

                              Sincerely,
                              Judy

mind that typefaces suggest things to readers—sometimes different
things to different readers. People remember where they saw typefaces
used. Century will always smack of school books. Narrow columns of
Corona inevitably suggest newspapers. If you set up a table in
Helvetica, and box it in with 1-point rules, it will conjure up a grim

tax return. Baskerville, set large and wide, surrounded by ample, classical white margins recalls great books.

The point is to turn these associations to your advantage. Learn the history of a typeface, where it came from, how it has been used. Don't be afraid of trading on a typeface's reputation.

Set Century Bold Italic in caps, in three lines the width of the page, with the first line flush left, the middle line centered, and the last flush right, and—voilà! *The New York Times* on the day the Lusitania sank! (See Figure 2-3.)

Figure 2-3
Century Bold Italic
headline reminiscent
of *The New York Times*

THE LUSITANIA SINKS
SURVIVORS DOUBTFUL
TRAGEDY OF THE SEA

Of course, not all readers will be aware of the specific connotation you are trying to achieve. At best, they may notice that the layout is "appropriate," but that's all you can ask. The effect of typographical design is almost all in the subconscious.

Nevertheless, do not underestimate readers in the matter of taste. Everyone is getting more sophisticated about design in everything from automobiles to watches.

A Type Palette

In a scholarly journal you might want to use just one typeface—Linotype's Janson Text might be the one. You would, of course, need the Italic in the text, but a certain gray elegance would be perfect.

In other situations—a customer newsletter or a popular magazine—one typeface only is just too boring. Headlines, subheads, and other devices (often referred to as the display) are needed, and they must stand out.

The name of the game is contrast. Introduce the bold version of the font, or go to an entirely different face that contrasts in style as well as weight. A good example (if now overused) of combining two contrasting faces occurs in *Time* magazine, which uses Times Roman for text and subheads and Franklin Gothic for headlines.

In a more stylish magazine, you might go for even sharper contrast, farther extremes. The text might be set in ITC Galliard, one of the sweetest, light classical designs around, and the display in Memphis Extra Bold.

If the magazine is filled with advertising, a different palette may be needed, because the ads bring their own extravagant diet of typefaces to the table. To make sure that readers quickly grasp that they are looking at an editorial page and not a paid ad, certain type combinations should be repeated throughout, and new typefaces should be introduced with great care.

However, when you have a clear stretch of pages (say, 20 in a row), each article might have its own typeface, so that you can change the mood to fit the piece.

In general, as with anything else, start modestly. Nothing gives away an amateur as quickly as the use of too many typefaces.

Copyfitting

In the old days (which for some of us are still here) the choice of a typeface was conditioned by how much copy was expected to fit in the given space. Typefaces came in discrete point sizes. It was necessary to count the manuscript (usually done by figuring an average number of characters per line, and then counting the lines). Then the available typefaces were considered in light of the number of characters per pica that could fit in each size. The type foundries published lists of characters per pica (or stated the width of lowercase alphabets), and copyfitting tables for these figures.

Of course, if you made an error in calculating the copy length, it was costly. The type would have to go back to the typesetters to be reset.

With desktop publishing, trial and error is the easiest method. It is faster to style copy that's already on disk than it is to count it. By selecting the entire text, and then choosing the font, point size, and leading, the DTP program automatically reflows it, and you quickly see how long it is. Then you either edit the copy to fit, or change the size, typeface, and/or leading.

With PageMaker and QuarkXPress (page-layout programs), there is a fast keyboard method for doing this that adjusts even very long text with delightful ease.

In mainstream publications, you do not want to change the size of the text and leading from article to article, or it will become inconsistent and patchy-looking. But you can design into the format certain expansion areas, such as introductions or pullquotes, which can be enlarged or reduced to make an article fit. (More on this next chapter.)

Squeezing, Stretching, and Overlapping

The first computer typesetting had just four variables: font, column width, point size, and leading. As the systems developed, each variable took on its own variations. Fonts could be condensed, expanded, slanted, outlined, or shadowed. Column widths could be easily changed, to allow type to flow around pictures and graphics. Point sizes could be adjusted in increasingly smaller increments. Leading (or line spacing) could now be smaller than the point size—negative leading.

And then there is letter spacing. In hot metal, letter spacing was always used to put more space between the letters. Traditionally, typographers would always add space between the letters of words set in all caps, or in numbers, to separate the individual numerals. They felt that without the extra space these words and numbers would stand out, and their goal was to maintain the general even gray tone (or "color") of the page.

Tracking

With phototype, it was discovered that overall letter spacing could be tighter or looser. This is now called tracking, and it is particularly useful in large sizes of type, where normal letter spacing appears to be too loose. (Of course, metal headline types were made for large sizes, and each size came with its own built-in space.)

The ability to tighten the tracking in phototype created an entire typographical style in the 1960s. Even now many magazines set their text so tightly that it is hard to read.

Some designers have recoiled from super-tight setting by running headlines and subheads heavily spaced out. I t   s t a r t s   l o o k i n g   l i k e   t h i s. In general, use looser letter spacing on all caps and nu-merals. Frederick Goudy said that anyone who would use letter spacing on lowercase would steal sheep.

Kerning

Tighter spacing created its own problem: certain letters (like "T" and "o") appeared too loose. Metal text faces were designed to fit evenly, and although some foundries offered special ligatures (Linotype called them "typographic refinement characters"), the fit was traditionally looser than our phototype-conditioned tastes now demand. To alter the letter fit in hot type, you had to actually cut into the "shoulder" of the metal letter. This is called kerning, but it was done only for very fine work.

Computers made kerning easy, and programmers began to draw up "exception kerning tables," or lists of problem character combina-tions. In PostScript fonts, for example, some 100 pairs are included in the font, and if your program allows it, they will be used automati-cally. (In Ventura Publisher and other programs, you simply select "Automatic kerning on" in the type specifications for each paragraph or style.)

With LetrTuck (from Edco), Macintosh font widths can be edited and new exception tables made up. In QuarkXPress, you can make your own exception tables, right in the program.

Most DTP programs also allow "manual" kerning between any pair of letters, which is particularly useful in large display type. The global kerning and tracking is usually fine for text, but the larger type gets, the more kerning pairs are needed. The computer sign-making systems, such as URW's Signus, use as many as 10,000 kerning pairs!

This would slow down desktop publishing to near stop, so while we are waiting for faster computers (and someone to create these huge, aesthetic kerning tables), we can go in and kern manually in the big headlines.

Spacing Rules

It is good to keep in mind some of the traditional rules of spacing in type, and to remember that the background is just as important as the actual letter. In general, letters have two shapes: straights (like an "H" or an "l") and curves ("S" or "a"). Representing straight letters as an "I" and curves as an "O," there are three possible combinations. (See Figure 2-4.)

Figure 2-4
Letter spacing rules:
the two straight are the
loosest; the two curves
are the tightest

II
IO
OO

Note the letter spacing is handled here by the set widths in the font, and not by exception kerning. The two straights are the loosest; the two curves are the tightest. That's the way it should be. Note what happens in Figure 2-5 when we forget this norm.

Similarly, negative leading is useful in headlines and large type. But

Figure 2-5
These three lines of
type demonstrate no
kerning, exception
kerning, and bad
kerning

AVATAR
AVATAR
AVATAR

the use of these controls will occasionally cause letters to touch serifs, or ascenders and descenders to knock together. (The latter seems to happen with maddening regularity.) The descenders on one line seem to reach out and try to grab the ascenders of the line below, even if, as is the case in Figure 2-6, there is only one descender in the top line. This eventuality was first noticed by the German designer, Eric Spiekermann, and is known as Spiekermann's Law).

Figure 2-6
Descenders and
ascenders

admittedly
hard to tell

Many are annoyed by these collisions, which could never happen in metal type. If you are seeking a traditional look, avoid them by all means. In more informal work, where tight spacing is desired, you may be forced to live with them. Some designers don't mind them at all, and one type designer, Gerard Unger, has actually built them into the set widths of a new typeface. (In his Swift type, not yet available on the desktop, the lowercase "r" and "t" always will touch at normal setting.)

Condensing and Expanding Letter Forms

More drastic is the ability in desktop publishing to condense and expand the letter forms, now possible in most high-end DTP programs through the Horizontal percentage control. See the results of this feature in Figure 2-7.

These distortions can ruin a type design very quickly. When a letter is condensed noticeably (say, more than 5 percent), the vertical strokes are made thinner, while the horizontals remain the same. This creates

Figure 2-7
Using the scaling tool
distorts type and ruins
the integrity of the
type design

Distortion

Distortion

Distortion

weak, spindly type with thickish, stubby serifs. The proportions of Roman type (like classical architecture) require that horizontals be thinner than verticals, and if you condense so much that the verticals are thinner than the horizontals, a hideous weightlessness sets in. Conventional wisdom says this is worse on monoweight types, like Futura, but it doesn't do any design much good.

Expanding is easier to get away with, since the vertical strokes get thicker, and thus bolder.

Is It Really Italic?

Slanting happens on the Macintosh every time you format some type italic without having an Italic companion font for the face already specified. When the printer can't find the real Italic, it often tilts all the verticals seven degrees. Occasionally this may be necessary, but if you have the real Italic, use it. Figure 2-8 provides a comparison.

Other Crude Styles: Underlining, Outlining, and Drop Shadows

Other style controls in DTP are too crude to use at all. The underlining on the Mac always puts the line too close to the baseline, although

New Baskerville

New Baskerville

Figure 2-8
Real Italic versus computer italic, which simply slants the roman type at a 7-degree angle. Note the differences in the design of particularly the "e" and the "a"

this distance can be changed in Ventura Publisher. Traditional typesetting never uses underlining for emphasis.

The outline command on the Mac gives you a fat outline that cuts into the face of each letter, as well as building on the outside of it. (At the same time, the machine automatically increases the letter spacing quite a lot.) The Mac shadow effect is even worse.

Outlines and drop shadows are really special effects, and seldom are needed in text. There are some special effect programs, like Letraset's LetraStudio and Broderbund's TypeStyler, which apply more elaborate special effects. These can look a bit soupy if you don't watch out, but are really useful as logotypes.

The best way to get outlines is to create them in drawing programs like Adobe Illustrator or Aldus FreeHand. In PostScript, the standard page-description language for DTP, letters are mathematically defined as outlines—lines and curves that are filled with black. But this basic outline is simply a boundary for the fill, and has no thickness or color. In Illustrator or FreeHand, it is a simple matter to add a stroke—of any weight—to the outline, and incidentally change its color, or change the color of the fill.

One thing to watch out for: stroking in these programs always builds both ways on the edge of the letters. Simultaneously, it is making an inline and an outline. If you want to preserve the face of the letter, copy and paste a solid, unstroked version of the type on top of the stroked version, and the result will be a true outline.

Small Caps

Caps and small caps type has been a recent fad in magazine design. But sadly, most of the small caps you see are just reduced big caps. As a result, they are lighter in weight, and generally create a patchy effect. So, steer away from them, unless you have one of the Adobe "Expert" fonts, which contain true-cut small caps. These are heavier and a little wider than regular caps. Other foundries, such as Monotype, are also now producing expert font character sets. As in setting all caps, it is a good idea to apply letter spacing to caps and small caps a little. (With 12-point type, an extra point between characters gives a refined, old-style look.)

Note in traditional typography, names of people, when used as signatures at the end of text or on business cards, were always set in caps and small caps.

X-heights, Ascenders, and Descenders

In choosing typefaces, many have recommended paying a lot of attention to the "x" height. That is the height of lowercase letters (like "x") that have no ascenders or descenders. In text type designs in the same point size (more or less the distance from the top of the ascender to the bottom of the descender), a design with a larger x-height will be more legible. It will appear to be bigger. Times New Roman proved this point over 50 years ago. And in the last 15 years, many of the types produced by the International Typeface Corporation have consistently had a high x-height, as compared to traditional faces like Garamond and Baskerville.

There is a limit to this wisdom, however. ITC faces seem to require extra leading in small text, which obviates the issue. In large sizes, typefaces with longer ascenders and descenders can be set with negative leading, to create the same size and impact as a "contemporary" typeface.

Fashion, of course, plays a role here, and after several years of big x-heights, designs with exaggeratedly long ascenders and descenders, like Bernhard Modern and Cheltenham Old Style, are back in vogue.

Hyphenation and Justification

When PageMaker was first introduced, there was justification, but no hyphenation. Thus words could be spaced out to fill a line and square off a column. But the words could not be broken into syllables when necessary to avoid big gaps in a line.

With every release, DTP programs have improved "h & j" controls. Ventura Publisher was the first to allow users to specify word spacing controls (expressed as optimum, minimum, and maximum), and adjustments for the use of letter spacing if word spacing was not enough.

In Europe, letter spacing is never used to fill a line. Europeans regard the use of letter spacing to justify a line as another barbarism of the New World. Americans seem to have gotten used to it by seeing it done in newspapers every day.

But a good typographer tries to avoid letter spacing on the grounds that it emphasizes the line for no reason, and thus reduces readability.

Hyphenation is handled by a set of logical rules, which allow, for example, hyphenation between two consonants. Such algorithms are supplemented by an exception dictionary. It now appears that the desktop algorithms work as well as those in the expensive "front-end" systems like Atex. But the dictionaries are not as big, and that makes a major difference in the quality of the typesetting.

In any case, most h & j systems work on the fly, as they go. Unlike the human Linotype operators in the hot-metal composing room, they can't make one line slightly looser in order to avoid a really loose line later. They can't rework a paragraph to avoid a widow (a very short line at the bottom of the paragraph).

The human operator still has to do that, and publication typography is vastly better if the time and skill is devoted to fixing loose and uneven hyphenation during the proofreading process.

The easiest way to spot sloppy typography is the number of widows. Purists will actually go back and rewrite the text to avoid widows, and will kill anyone who leaves a widow at the top of a column.

The problems with justification can be avoided by setting everything ragged right. Some theorists claim that ragged right is easier to read, since all the word spaces are equal. (The opposite is also held—that the even width of justified lines is easier on the eyes.) People definitely notice, and most Americans seem to prefer justified text, as appearing more finished, complete, and "typeset" rather than typewritten. Ragged-right type is seen as a signal of informality, something which can be capitalized on. *The Washington Post,* for example, sets its bylined, first-person columns ragged right, to clearly distinguish them from news stories.

In general, ragged right seems more modern. Justified type is more traditional.

PostScript

The role that PostScript plays in desktop typography cannot be exaggerated. This page-description language, created to be machine-independent, allows the same file to print on a wonderful diversity of output devices from low-resolution plain-paper laser printers to high-resolution film imagesetters.

PostScript fonts are an integral part of the language. They are described as Bézier (a kind of mathematically-generated curve) outlines, which can be scaled to any size, and printed out according to the resolution of the printer.

While phototype machines and digital typesetters eliminated the need for separate fonts for each point size, these devices usually could not set type bigger than 72 points. With PostScript, 400-point type is easy. So is 399-point type. Or even 399.75-point type! And it is still just as sharp as the resolution of the printer.

Moreover, the generally open architecture of PostScript has brought many players to the field—in fonts, as well as drawing programs.

Monotype and Linotype fonts could be mixed in the metal era, along with foundry types from all over the world. But with photo and digital typesetters, each manufacturer's fonts worked only on its proprietary hardware.

Publication designers can once again mix types from different foundries. And to their bafflement, the manufacturers find that their rivals' fonts are running on their own equipment, and vice versa. This can only be good for the customers.

The remaining problem is the delay while the manufacturers convert their old libraries to PostScript. Within the year there should be more than a thousand top-quality PostScript fonts available, from the major vendors: Adobe, Bitstream, Compugraphic, Linotype, Monotype, and Varityper. The competition is bound to bring the price down, making it possible for individual designers to own their own libraries.

In the meantime, it is possible to roll your own, using programs like Altsys Fontographer, or to commission independent type designers to create a new typeface for you.

All in the Family

If nothing else, the awareness of associations may make it easier for you to choose typefaces. But with potentially 20,000 of them to choose from, you need another way to get a handle on them. Somehow you have to sort them into styles and shapes. There are obvious styles of typefaces, like roman and italic. Generally, you can say that Roman types are upright, and Italic types are slanted. Many typefaces are now available in some basic variations, such as light and bold.

About a hundred years ago, type designs began to appear in "families," that is, a basic design with several variations. The first families were small, with just three members: roman, italic and bold. There are still plenty of typefaces that are only available in these three styles.

"Roman" refers back to the letters of the Romans, which were actually all capitals; the small letters (lowercase) emerged as corruptions of the caps. We now think of roman as the basic form of each typeface, closest to the ancient model, although some designers have substituted the words "normal" or "regular."

Italic goes back to the beginning of type, and, obviously enough, was modeled on the elegant cursive handwriting of the Italian Renaissance. Aldus Manutius, the great printer in Venice, introduced Italic type in the late fifteenth century, but at first it was used by itself, as its own typeface. Within the century, however, printers found that an italic word stuck in among roman text worked well for emphasis, and the practice has continued. By the time of William Caslon (1692–1766), type founders were designing a special italic to go with each roman typeface.

It took until 1860 for a foundry to come up with the idea of a companion bold type—that is, a companion roman typeface with the strokes fattened. This was Antique No. 7 at the Scottish foundry, Miller & Richard, which was made to accompany their Old Style. The design became widely popular, and now exists on its own, under the name Bookman, which, curiously, has its own bold and italic variations.

At the end of the nineteenth century, the pantographic engraving machine allowed type founders to quickly produce different sizes of each typeface, which previously all had to be cut by hand. From the time of Gutenberg, type was cut on the end of a hard steel punch, exactly to the size desired. Considerable skill was needed to cut a tiny 6-point "e." The punch was then driven into softer brass, which was then shaped into a matrix (or mold) into which molten lead was poured, and type was cast—all of this by hand.

Now, a set of large wooden patterns became the master font. With the pantograph, various sizes of matrices could be made directly, then placed in casting machines. This process made it easier to introduce new styles, and bring them all out at the same time. By resetting the gears of the pantograph, the operators could quickly change the width of a type, to condense or expand it, much the same way that today you do this at will by changing the Horizontal percentage control in, say, QuarkXPress.

Cheltenham (American Type Founders, 1901–1920) was the first major typeface to be issued as a full family. (ITC Cheltenham is a useful version, albeit redrawn without the very small x-height that gives the original its idiosyncratic charm.)

With Univers, designed by Adrian Frutiger for Deberny Peignot in 1957, type families became tribes. With his Swiss sense of order, Frutiger planned a family so large that individual designs had to be numbered rather than named. The Italic designs are all even numbers, Romans are odd—and so on.

More recently Linotype redesigned and reorganized the Helvetica family along the same lines. As the typeface became the most popular design in the postwar era, the family had grown in a higgledy-piggledy way. Variations were adopted, like Helvetica Compressed, that did not look like they were carrying the same genes as the parents.

New Helvetica solves these problems. (See Figure 2-9.) There is an almost Teutonic order to the family, and inevitably some designers will insist on going back to the original funkier designs produced by Max Medinger and the Haas foundry in the 1950s.

Figure 2-9
Variations on the
Helvetica design

Helvetica
Helvetica Bold

Helvetica Compressed
Helvetica Extra Compressed
Helvetica Ultra Compressed

New Helvetica (No. 55)
New Helvetica Medium (No. 65)
New Helvetica Heavy (No. 85)

With current computer technology, type designers can simply make a light and a bold design and the computer will extrapolate a number of the intermediate weights in between. (This can be done with any two outlines electronically with the Blend tool in Illustrator 88.) The designer can then choose the variations he likes, do a little editing, and produce a family.

Hermann Zapf (the designer of the dingbats, as well as Palatino), had *twenty* weights, not just three or four, run up for two new typefaces at URW, the German digital foundry that invented the process of type design interpolation.

This should be enough for any family.

Type Classes

Some designers still pick typefaces like they pick out colors from the PMS book—on whim, like the young couple in the wallpaper department. To use type effectively and intelligently, you have to put them in categories. You must classify them some way.

Even the terminology can be confusing. For example, "antiqua" simply means roman in Germany, but "Antique" traditionally meant slab serif in England. Meanwhile, Americans call slab serifs Egyptians. Gothic means sans serif, not black letter. The English call sans serifs Grotesque. And so it goes.

While it is easy to understand the differences between the roman, italic, and bold versions of any typeface, it is something else to get a handle on the differences between designs. One distinction is between serif types and sans serifs. But that is not enough; as you get closer to the subject you realize that there are a myriad subtle differences in structure and form.

The French designer Maximillian Vox tried to sort them out in the 1950s with a system of nine basic classifications.

- Humanist
- Garalde
- Transitional
- Didone
- Slab Serif
- Lineale
- Graphic
- Glyphic
- Script

The names of the classes are a bit odd, since some of them were coined to avoid the confusion of the old nomenclature. It is an imperfect system, with only one group for all sans serifs, but it is the most widely accepted system, and sensibly, it is based on history.

Humanist

The first great roman typefaces were designed in Venice, and were based on the humanist letter forms of the scribes in the monasteries. The Renaissance effort to revive classical letter forms was part of the humanist movement, and so Vox called his first classification group, Humanist. Goudy Old Style pictured in Figure 2-10 is an example.

Figure 2-10
Humanist

Goudy Old Style

A B C D E F G H I J K L M N O P Q R S T U V W X Y Z
a b c d e f g h i j k l m n o p q r s t u v w x y z
1 2 3 4 5 6 7 8 9 0

Nicholas Jenson's type from 1470 was one of the first and the best of the era, with the capital letters based on the monumental inscriptions of classical Rome. The lowercase was derived from the handwriting reforms initiated by Charlemagne 400 years previous, and called by scholars, the Carolingian miniscule.

It is rather astounding that Jenson's type, appearing only 30 years after Gutenberg and the Western invention of movable type, was so good. The model has survived to this day, with twentieth century classics like Cloister based directly on the Humanist letter form. On the desktop, the purest Humanist example is Goudy Old Style (1925).

A more faithful revival, Bruce Roger's beautiful Centaur (1915), is available from Monotype in PostScript format.

Garalde

Early in the first century of the printing explosion, a second style appeared. Vox called it Garalde (see Figure 2-11), after its most prominent advocates, Claude Garamond of France, and Aldus Manutius. Aldus came first, in Venice, and his type was immediately perceived as more sophisticated and graceful than Jenson's. He was the first volume paperback publisher, and the first to produce books in Italic. (On the desktop, Poliphilus and Baldo Italic from Monotype, and Aldine from Bitstream, are derived from the Aldine types.) His image has already made it, however. It is Aldus Manutius' profile on the screens every time you fire up PageMaker or FreeHand. (Monotype's Bembo, a superb revival of one of Aldus Manutius' typefaces, is due out soon.)

In France, Claude Garamond took up the style in the 1540s and his types for the Imprimerie Royale became the typical French letter form.

Figure 2-11
Garalde

Stempel Garamond

A B C D E F G H I J K L M N
O P Q R S T U V W X Y Z
a b c d e f g h i j k l m n
o p q r s t u v w x y z
1 2 3 4 5 6 7 8 9 0

It is too long a story to tell here, but most of the typefaces called Garamond are actually based on designs of his seventeenth century successor in Paris, Jean Jannon. In the 1920s many foundries produced Garamonds that should properly have been called Jannons, among them Garamond Old Style by the American Type Foundry (available on the desktop from Bitstream as American Garamond, and from Linotype as Garamond 3. The ITC Garamond, the corporate typeface of Apple Computer, is an updated Garamond Old Style, a revival of a revival, with ITC's characteristic big x-height. (More on this later.)

Stempel Garamond from the foundry in Frankfurt (available from Linotype and Adobe) was the first attempt in the 1920s to revive a true Garamond, instead of making another Jannon. More recently, Adobe Systems, the people who invented PostScript, have set up a strong type development group lead by Sumner Stone. In the last year, after extensive research and design work by Robert Slimbach, they have produced Adobe Garamond, which has the distinction of being the first desktop-publishing typeface with real small caps.

The first great English old style, Caslon, is another Garalde. In fact, the ever popular Times Roman really belongs in this class also. This, the most durable of all twentieth century romans, doesn't look much like Garamond, but it is a worthy descendent.

Transitional

It took 200 years for the next wrinkle in type design to appear: the Transitionals are so called because they form a bridge between the "old-style" Humanist-Garaldes and the "modern" Didones to follow. (See Figure 2-12.)

Baskerville is the most common example, with more pronounced thicks and thins than earlier types. ITC New Baskerville, is quite a faithful rendering of it, and available on the desktop.

The recent design by Adrian Frutiger, Centennial, is a stylish and useful 1980s Transitional. It's available from Linotype.

Didone

In the late eighteenth century, at a time of great political ferment and neoclassical revival in Europe, there came more startling experimentation with letter forms. In France, Didot, and in Italy, Bodoni (hence, Didone) produced new designs with a striking contrast between thick and thin strokes. The thins had become nearly hairlines, and could just be printed on the finer paper and more precise presses emerging at that time.

Of the original Didones, only Bodoni Book is ready in desktop format, as yet, and it is useful only in small sizes. The thin strokes just aren't thin enough above 24 points. There is a 1970s Didone, ITC Fenice (see Figure 2-13), designed by Aldo Novarese, which is remarkably stylish and useful for larger (or display) sizes. Fenice was released in PostScript format by Compugraphic.

Figure 2-12
Transitional

Baskerville

A B C D E F G H I J K L M N
O P Q R S T U V W X Y Z
a b c d e f g h i j k l m n
o p q r s t u v w x y z
1 2 3 4 5 6 7 8 9 0

It took a century for the Didones to become popular, and as that happened a new force was at work influencing the shape of type: the industrial revolution.

Newspapers and advertising posters called for bolder, heavier typefaces, and about 1800 the first "fat face" appeared—a superbold type, perfect for announcing horse sales and the like. Poster Bodoni (from Linotype) is a sturdy survivor of this style.

Slab Serif

The fat face was such a sudden development, after 300 years of slow evolution, that type founders rapidly spun another new style, the slab serif, originally called Antiques or Egyptians. These were Didone types, but with thickened thin strokes, and squared-off serifs. (See Figure 2-14.)

Starting in about 1810, the slabs proliferated in weights and widths. As printing became part of the commercial rather than the literary world, quality was sacrificed for quantity and impact, and the slab serif types could survive cheap paper and long runs much better than the delicate Garaldes and Transitionals.

Figure 2-13
Didone

ITC Fenice

ABCDEFGHIJKLMN
OPQRSTUVWXYZ
abcdefghijklmn
opqrstuvwxyz
1234567890

Figure 2-14
Slab Serif

Clarendon

ABCDEFGHIJKLMN
OPQRSTUVWXYZ
abcdefghijklmn
opqrstuvwxyz
1234567890

There are no revivals of the early robust slab designs on the desktop yet, but there are several useful twentieth-century versions including Memphis, Haas Clarendon, and Glypha.

Lineale The sans serifs arrived as early as 1815, and quickly took over as the journeymen of typography, doing all the utilitarian work of the industrial era: the railroad timetables, the classified ads. (See Figure 2-15.) Lineales were never considered for fine book work until the modernist movement at the time of the Bauhaus.

Helvetica (designed by Max Medinger and T.K. Hoffman in 1957) is the heir of that movement. It is a standard on all laser printers, and the first global typeface. In form, Helvetica traces back to the very first Lineales, called Grotesques in England. Sadly, this fine Swiss design has been so influential it has become commonplace and taken for granted.

Futura, which appears to be drawn with a compass and pen, and is therefore a "geometric" Lineale, survives as a contemporary of that era.

Figure 2-15
Lineale

Helvetica Compressed

A B C D E F G H I J K L M N
O P Q R S T U V W X Y Z
a b c d e f g h i j k l m n
o p q r s t u v w x y z
1 2 3 4 5 6 7 8 9 0

In the U.S. one of the most popular "grotesque" Lineales has been Franklin Gothic (which owes nothing but its name to the great American printer, Benjamin Franklin, who predated the type by 100 years, and actually used Caslon and Baskerville, and corresponded with Didot and Bodoni.) Available on the desktop is ITC Franklin Gothic, a useful type with several weights, although none of them matches the original.

Graphic

We all know about Gutenberg (c. 1450) and the invention of movable type 20 years before Jenson, but few long for his typefaces on the desktop. They were all black letter, with the encrusted, pinched letter form of the Dark Ages. (See Figure 2-16.) Vox grouped these true Gothics with the Graphic category, since they are based on drawn, or "built-up" lettering, as opposed to the Humanist letters, which could be written with free, simple strokes of a pen. (One modern example available for desktop publishing is Bitstream's Cloister Black.)

Germany continued to use these archaic, weighty, hard-to-read styles until Hitler threw them out, in favor of classical Romans.

Figure 2-16
Graphic

𝕱𝖗𝖆𝖐𝖙𝖚𝖗

𝕬 𝕭 𝕮 𝕯 𝕰 𝕱 𝕲 𝕳 𝕴 𝕵 𝕶 𝕷 𝕸 𝕹
𝕺 𝕻 𝕼 𝕽 𝕾 𝕿 𝖀 𝖁 𝖂 𝖃 𝖄 𝖅
𝖆 𝖇 𝖈 𝖉 𝖊 𝖋 𝖌 𝖍 𝖎 𝖏 𝖐 𝖑 𝖒 𝖓
𝖔 𝖕 𝖖 𝖗 𝖘 𝖙 𝖚 𝖛 𝖜 𝖝 𝖞 𝖟
1 2 3 4 5 6 7 8 9 0

Glyphic

Glyphic means carved, and Bitstream's Latin Wide is a good example. Matrix, a new offering from Adobe, is a new-wave send-up of this old idea.

Script

Scripts are "fancy" typefaces from different times and places, and have never been near the mainstream of typographic use. (See Figure 2-17.) There are several Scripts available on the desktop, including ITC Zapf Chancery (with the look of calligraphy) and Kauffman (from the 1940s). Neophyte printers (desktop and traditional) are often drawn to Scripts because they are so obviously different. But they quickly become tiresome, if not used with discretion.

Figure 2-17
Script

Kuenstler Script

A B C D E F G H I J K L M N O P Q R S T U V W X Y Z a b c d e f g h i j k l m n o p q r s t u v w x y z 1 2 3 4 5 6 7 8 9 0

Revivals and Revolutions

Type design, like all cultural history, is a series of revivals, punctuated by revolutions. It becomes difficult to sort out every individual design into the nine categories. Sometimes a typeface owes more to its own era than to the forms it is attempting to revive. There are hybrids, such as Gill Sans. It's a Lineale, but the letter forms are derived from the first Romans, so it is classified as Humanist-Lineale.

Memphis, a slab serif which came out after the Bauhaus' impact on typography, can be called a Geometric-Slab Serif. But perhaps Vox's structure will help sort them out.

To conclude, Figures 2-18a–2-18e below give examples of some recommended PostScript typefaces, together with contrasting companion type. An asterisk indicates that the face works well for body type. The faces are all shown in 24-point type.

Figure 2-18a
Humanist

Goudy Old Style*
Monotype Centaur*

Figure 2-18b
Garalde

Stempel Garamond*
Adobe Garamond*
Janson Text*
ITC Galliard*

Figure 2-18c
Transitional

Caslon 540
Centennial*
Century Expanded*
Century Old Style*
ITC Cheltenham
ITC New Baskerville*
ITC Stone Serif*

Figure 2-18d
Lineale

Frutiger 55*
Monotype Gill Sans*

Figure 2-18e
Contrasting
companion type

BeLucian Demi

Bureau Grotesque

Caslon Open Face

Cooper Black

Eurostyle Bold

ITC Franklin Gothic Heavy

Frutiger Ultra Black

Helvetica Ultra Compressed

ITC MACHINE

Memphis Extra Bold

New Caledonia Black

ITC Stone Serif Bold

ITC Stone Sans Bold

ITC Stone Informal Bold

Weiss Extra Bold

Reaching the Reader

Perhaps once, a long time ago, there were those who had nothing better to do than curl up with a good magazine. Just give them lots of text (all in 9-point, with some headlines in, say 24-point) and they'd start from the beginning and read right through to the very end.

But today, millions of good Americans are jogging when they ought to be reading.

They're working out. Or else they are sitting, nearly comatose, watching some ball game on TV. Their magazines are piled up in the corner, neglected, with their cats sleeping on them. When they do pick up a magazine, their attention span is short. They are constantly distracted.

The phone rings; or the kid demands to be taken some place in the car; the dog wants to be let out. And there is always the seductive remote control unit on that coffee table, beckoning—for them to change the channel, or to switch on that new CD, the VCR, the cassette deck.

How do we get them reading again?

Well, of course, we could hope for better writing, but we might as well hope for honest politicians. Assuming you are not a writer and more or less have to take the stuff as it comes in, what can be done to make it less leaden? Less deadly gray? More readable?

Put in pictures—photos and illustrations. That has been the quick fix over the years. But as people have become jaded to images in a visual age, this no longer works the way it did. People now expect lots of pictures in their reading material, and tend to browse through publications, checking out the "artwork" and skipping the text.

Clearly, something must be done with the type. It has to be made more legible, more inviting, even compelling. At the end of the day, it is not the type that readers should consider, but the *words*.

Type is more than the gray rectangular area designers like to "greek" in (see Figure 3–1a), with the side of a pencil. Your treatment of the different elements of that gray area make the difference between an invitation to read and an invitation to skim (see Figure 3–1b). If we are to capture the attention of people who are constantly being distracted, we have to shove those words at them—get them interested, get them started reading, make the text easy (preferably delightful) to read, and hold their attention. Sadly, this effort is doomed. People have only a finite amount of time in their lives and can't be expected to read every article in every magazine, or even every word of just one article.

"Tricks" for Grabbing the Reader

A publication should serve up enough information outside the main text so "readers" feel they're getting their money's worth.

What follows is a list of typographical tricks. Don't use them all at once. In some cases—to combine clichés—pictures are worth a thousand words, but you can have too much of a good thing. If you pull out all the stops you'd end up with a typographical blizzard that can bring on a kind of reader snowblindness, if not nausea.

The Big Initial

Fifteen years ago, big initials were not in fashion, stripped out of printed pages by the urge to make clean, modern, unornamented design. Now, they're everywhere. There are drop initials (where the

Figure 3-1a
Layout with
greeked-in type

Figure 3-1b
Finished layout

letter extends below the line of text it belongs on), and there are raised initials—some call them stick-up initials—where a larger first letter rests on the first line, rising up into white space.

Obviously, drop initials take less space. They are also more traditional, and date back to before the invention of type, to the days of hand-copied manuscripts. Scribes embellished their pages with elaborate, illuminated initials. Sometimes they incorporated illustrations, but often the work was purely decorative. Early books imitated these initials, and developed square block initials to make them uniform, as shown in Figure 3–2. Some of these are beginning to appear in desktop clip-art libraries.

Figure 3-2
An illuminated
manuscript letter

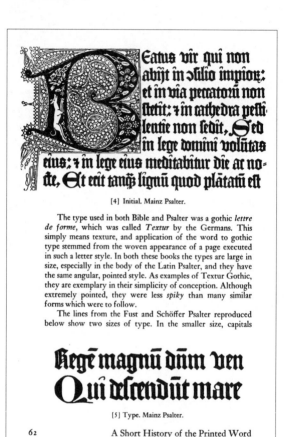

Typographers found it easiest to simply indent the first five lines or so of a story, and put in a big letter. And desktop designers are following suit.

In most DTP programs, there is some provision for drop initials, but it is never completely automatic. Ventura Publisher, for example, allows you to incorporate a "big first character" into a paragraph style. This is a delightful feature, and easier than anything provided by competing programs, but it still can be tricky. The hard part is to get the initial to line up exactly with the adjacent text.

In general, you want the cap height of the initial to align with the baseline of the first line of the text indent, and you want the baseline to align with the baseline of the last line of the text indent.

With PostScript, you can scale the initial to fit exactly in most desktop programs. Even then, it can be a real hassle. While some programs provide automatic drop initials, be sure to check alignment.

In any case, whenever the initial is big, the shoulder (the built-in white space) on the left side of the letter prevents it from lining up with the margin. In Ventura you can just "kern" it over. In QuarkXPress it still won't fit exactly unless you actually make two text boxes—a transparent one for the initial, and an empty, runaround text box to repel the body type.

Without PostScript, you should limit the number of lines indented to fit the font sizes you have. If you are printing most publications on an H-P LaserJet, it is worthwhile to invest in Bitstream's Fontware, and generate the exact size you need. (There are also bitmapped initials available on bulletin boards, such as Drop Cap from Prograf.)

The bother of all this may lead you to raised initials, which take more space, but can somehow look more modern, and seem more appropriate with ragged-right text. All the desktop-publishing programs automatically align different sizes of type on the baseline. But be careful about the leading. The raised initial may cause extra leading below the line it is sitting on, or it may overlap the text above.

Some magazine designers have gotten to putting big and drop initials on things that are extraneous to the main text, such as pullquotes. This may get people to read the pullquote, but you don't want them to stop there.

For some reason, writers always seem to start paragraphs with an "I" or a "T," rectilinear letters which don't add much to a page and can get repetitious in a hurry. Try for variety, but watch out for "Q" and "J," which in some fonts have tails that stick down below the baseline and will require a different indent.

In general, the initials should mark natural breaks in the narrative—either chapter titles or smaller divisions. The more there are, the smaller they should become. Generally, you want the initials evenly distributed through the text. Figure 3–3 shows examples of big initials.

Usually, the initials are in the same typeface (or at least the same family) as the display type on the page. Alternatively, they can be the same type as the body text. Try to achieve contrast, either in size or color. If the headlines are in Bodoni, and the text is in Century Schoolbook, avoid big Century drop initials, which are too close in style to Bodoni to provide contrast. Some designers will introduce a third typeface for the initials. This can be made to work, but contrast is something between two things, two styles. Three styles gives variety, and variety is much more difficult to manage than contrast.

Really talented typographers can get away with this, but most manage to produce a muddle. Keep it simple.

Whatever you do, do not spell out secret messages with the drop initials. It has been done.

Large Text

In the old days when type was three-dimensional lead, large type was used sparingly. The old slug-casting machines were great for regular text sizes, but above 14 points the matrices were expensive, and hand-set foundry type was time-consuming, and there was never enough type.

Computers don't care what size type is. This whole book could have been set in 48-point type, and the computer would have been perfectly happy. (The book would have been rather heavy, and you and the publisher would have been dismayed at its cost, but that is another matter.)

We've had computer type (phototypesetting and its digital successors) for many years now, but text continues to be confined to its 9-point cage. Let it out! Try a full page of 24-point text for a real feeling of liberation.

Figure 3-3
Three possible
initial caps

DDY was determined to see *Cats* this time. Every body else had seen it, so why not Eddy? Or maybe he would see the new Doc Simon. He had not seen a Simon in ten years. Maybe the man had come up with something. What did he have against Doc Simon? He would use either *Cats* or the new Simon as a means of getting back to the theater. Then maybe he would see a ballet or try one of the new Thai restaurants instead of letting the whole city go to waste. He thought of this on a Thursday,

DDY was determined to see *Cats* this time. Every body else had seen it, so why not Eddy? Or maybe he would see the new Doc Simon. He had not seen a Simon in ten years. Maybe the man had come up with something. What did he have against Doc Simon? He would use either *Cats* or the new Simon as a means of getting back to the theater. Then maybe he would see a ballet or try one of the new Thai restaurants instead of letting the whole city go to waste. He thought of this on a Thursday, the night before he was scheduled to go in. But already the pressure of the visit was starting to get to him. He tried out the idea on Julie, who was reading a mystery next to the fireplace. She sat at the other end of the large living room, which they

DDY was determined to see *Cats* this time. Every body else had seen it, so why not Eddy? Or maybe he would see the new Doc Simon. He had not seen a Simon in ten years. Maybe the man had come up with something. What did he have against Doc Simon? He would use either *Cats* or the new Simon as a means of getting back to the theater. Then maybe he would see a ballet or try one of the new Thai restaurants instead of letting the whole city go to waste. He thought of this on a Thursday, the night before he was scheduled to go in. But already the pressure of the visit was starting to get to him. He tried out the idea on Julie, who was reading a mystery next to the fireplace. She sat at the other end of the large living room, which they had once wanted to design as the lobby of a small rooming house, with bachelor friends

Or start out an article with big text—to make it easy for the reader and to create a vigorous graphic texture.

And, consider using large body text for a special piece. After reading pages and pages of 9-point type, 12-point is like having it read to you.

When the type gets bigger, its style becomes more apparent to the reader. With larger type, the text becomes more of a design element; the texture and feel make the page look "designed." The connotations of different typefaces, as discussed in the previous chapter, are also more apparent.

If you or the editor say the words are too important to cut for large type, get more pages or start with a bang, by blowing up the introduction in a huge point size, and then going back to the conventional size. (See Figure 3–4.)

Remember that most of the typefaces available on the desktop were designed for text. As they get bigger, you should track tighter (-1 or -2) by adjusting the kerning in your program. Global automatic kerning becomes more essential.

Quotations

Pullquotes, panel quotes, readouts, decks, windows—whatever you

Figure 3-4
Layout with
descending
type sizes

call these words pulled from the text and used as design elements—are another, if more conventional way to use large type.

Skillfully extracted from the piece, these devices allow a reader to get an idea of what a story is about before taking the cold bath of actually reading it. You can't really expect everyone to read everything, and a pullquote, as shown in Figures 3–5a and 3-5b, will help people get something out of an article they only glance at.

Figure 3-5a
Layout without
pullquotes

Figure 3-5b
Layout with
pullquotes

These are type tricks from magazines, and the editorial joy of magazines is the assortment of information that is brought together. The word *magazine* originally meant storehouse. For this serendipitous juxtaposition to be enjoyed by readers, they have to get at least a smattering of the content of every piece. Of course, the tricks of magazine designers are useful in other publications. The desire is the same: make the reader not want to put it down.

The only drawback to pullquotes is that some writing definitely does not deserve to be excerpted and served up in beautiful blocks of type. The answer to this recurrent problem is the precis. Rewrite the stuff. Summarize it. Make little lists. A good designer never lets a bad writer get in his way.

An easy trap to fall into, especially under editorial pressure, is using pullquotes to make editorial space. A short quote, even in larger type, takes up less layout space than a relatively small graphic or photo. While they understand the need to break up a full page of type, editors become squeamish when they realize they may have to cut parts of a sacred story. A story this sacred may deserve big, bold pictures or graphics. If the editor wins out and a brilliant story is cramped with text, it will never get the audience it deserves.

On the other hand, if there are too many pullquotes, the story becomes hard to follow and begins to look fragmented. The same goes for quotes that are too long. The reader should not have to figure out whether something is a separate sidebar, or only a huge block of text which he will read again in the course of a story. Watch out for the placement of the quotes as well.

If you go through a number of layout revisions, watch out when juggling the quotes for design purposes that they do not intrude at the wrong point in a story. If a pullquote appears too early, it can steal the thunder of a story—too late, and it is boring. And don't give away punch lines!

One other alternative to pullquotes is to turn information in the text into graphic elements such as charts and tables. Lists and summaries in the margins not only highlight specific points in the story, but also serve as design elements and novel ways of bringing a reader into the piece. Tables are all the vogue in magazines at this point. Every other article incorporates a "scorecard" distilling the narrative into neat boxes. These devices may not be as prevalent in a few years when the novelty has worn off, but they will always have appropriate uses.

Captions

After headlines, captions are the most common reader typographical device. At first there wouldn't appear much to say about them, but that is the problem. Captions tend to be taken for granted by designers and editors, and are usually left to the last minute.

As with everything else in a magazine, editors are so close to the subject that they sometimes think the picture so obvious that it needs only the most cursory caption—if it needs a caption at all. This explains the terseness of many captions, and the bafflement you must have felt when you looked at a picture and wanted more explanation, but found a caption didn't exist.

This throws away a great place to provide information. Readers are so used to captions that they automatically look under every picture for one. The caption can then be used for more than just the details about the picture; it can become a pullquote or a summary of the story.

In some cases the caption can be the whole story. When there is a great picture that doesn't require a piece to go with it, run it alone, with a narrative caption set in a special style, with its own headline, and maybe a drop initial.

Even with normal captions, there is no reason to be bound by convention. Why not make captions bigger than the text? Captions often have two parts—a lead-in, and then the description. Why not run them on two lines?

What Does He Mean, Slugs?

Well, that was one just then, a subhead between paragraphs that helps organize, or at least break up, long text. They should carry some information (another reader aid), but I'll let you in on a secret: they don't always have to fall at a natural pause in the story—just read any newsmagazine.

Slugs can be big or small. They don't even have to take their own line—they can start on the first line of a paragraph, in type that's bigger, bolder, or both. (In that position, they're often called subheads.) Figure 3–6 provides some examples.

Figure 3-6
Layout with slugs

Slugs aren't meant to slow the reader down, but to add a sense of pace, and typographical accent in gray text. Well-written slugs titillate, promising something new and exciting down the line. Just as many people scan headlines on the front page of a paper, they scan subheads in an article to see if there is going to be something interesting or just more of the same.

And, on the off-chance that a section is boring, the reader can find a logical place to jump back into the story for something different.

Boxes and Sidebars

The most frequently used type device in magazines is the box, a short bit of text separated from the main story by a ruled box, and inevitably filled in with a tint background.

Readers do like boxes, if only because the box serves up a smaller amount of reading matter, an amount they can hope to get to the end of. And usually the box signals a tidbit of information that is special in some way—it's funny, or it adds a different perspective.

Thus the box is a signal, and it is important to use it as one. Just filling up a box with "more of the same" does nothing for readers, and they quickly will learn to ignore them.

In a tight layout, a box is a good way, also, to squeeze in a tiny illustration or photo—which would be lost amid the main text.

Note that boxes don't have to be enclosed by thick rules, or any rules at all. White space can serve the same purpose, combined with a different width of text. (For example, the main text can be set on a three-column grid, while the boxes are on four columns.)

A color tint background (warm gray or beige, or even a very pale yellow), can set the box off. But, watch out for the screen tint of black. In low-resolution printing, with, say, a 60-line screen, the dots are lethal to legibility; they fill in the counters (the interior white spaces within the letter), and ruin the text letter forms. There is also something cheap about a 10-percent black fill in a box, perhaps because it is reminiscent of tabloid newspapers.

Headers

Take a lead from book design. Headers are the little headings on the top of the page, called "running titles" by some. These labels add a bit of finish to a page, and supply useful information—the chapter title, section titles, or topics. By running them larger, they can become miniature pullquotes. Headers are a great way to establish the identity of an article for those perverse readers who start at the back and flip toward the front—undoubtedly more than half the population.

The header doesn't have to be the complete title; it doesn't even have to be part of the title. It can be used to signify different sections. When repeated at the top of every page, it becomes even more of a design element and less text-like.

Rules

Column rules made a comeback some time ago, but now magazines are replete with Oxford rules (a thick and a thin), Scotch rules (thick, with a thin on either side), and Bendays (there really was a man named Ben Day, who foisted screened rules onto the publishing world), and even dotted leader rules. My rule is: take them all out and see if the layout is any worse for it.

The wonder of DTP programs is that at last we can get column rules straight, and once they are down we can change them to an infinite number of permutations. If you feel like you must use them, or if they are necessary to divide radically different concepts—editorial or design—experiment with different weights to find the least intrusive and most effective. (See Figure 3–7.)

Figure 3-7
Layout with headers and rules

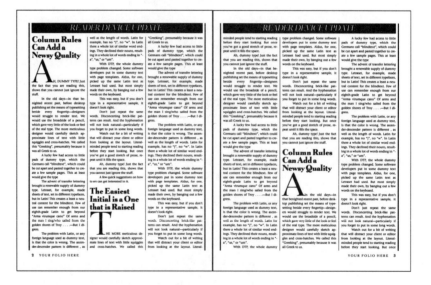

Rules can also be used effectively when combined directly with type. An Oxford rule above a subhead (or slug) in running text can add emphasis and a little class. This can be useful when the type is a normal weight, and does not stand out enough from the color of the page to do its job.

However, you don't want to interrupt the reader, just keep him going. So it usually works better to have a bolder rule (Scotch, Oxford, or whatever) above the subhead, and a thin rule or none at all below. The rules can be cut off to align with the actual text in the subhead, or they can be a uniform width. Ventura Publisher handles these text-rule combinations very well, and moves them around automatically when the copy changes.

Ornaments

If rules are difficult, ornaments are impossible. There are artists who make these fleurons (flowers) accent the page, and blend perfectly with the type, but I am not one of them.

If you don't watch out, ornaments will make a layout look canned, like the prepackaged clip art that has proliferated with desktop publishing.

However, you may be great with these things, so give them a try. Figure 3-8 shows some examples. An interesting selection is ITC's Zapf Dingbats, which assigns a different ornament to each key on the keyboard. Fleurons work most effectively if they are used in the context of the story, like type.

Ah...! White Space

If editors are afraid of type, they abhor white space. They can't stop thinking of all the words they could get into those "holes."

But for readers these holes are a godsend. It's the needed oxygen in a magazine. A page packed with type is forbidding; it looks hard to read, or dull, or confusing. Judiciously used, white space can invite readers into a story.

There are other kinds of space needed in typographical layouts— space between lines, and space between characters. But for now, why don't we just consider type as the figure, and white space as the ground? You can't have one without the other.

White space needs to be planned out just as much as any photo or headline. It should not just be whatever is left over. There is nothing

Figure 3-8
Ornaments and
fleurons from Adobe
Wood Type 2 and
Adobe Caslon

as unprofessional-looking as uneven blocks of white space at the bottom of columns or at the end of stories. This implies that the designer either couldn't think of how to use this space on the page or couldn't be bothered. The beauty of DTP is that you don't have to waste a huge amount of time pasting something up only to find that there is space at the end. Incorporate this space earlier with nicely framed pullquotes, spacious subheads, or extra breathing room around a photograph.

The basic concept is not to forget about white space as a tool. Correctly used, white space gives more emphasis to a certain aspect of your design than a big painted arrow across the page.

Reader Devices

A few years ago, *Newsweek* introduced a new format in which the typical text space was cut 10 percent to allow room for bigger headlines, subheads, sidebars, and white space. Writers were not too happy about this, but readers responded with enthusiasm. The editor of the magazine, Rick Smith, wanted to find ways to get more information to the readers—even if they didn't read through every piece. The idea is that a publication should be worth the cost and should inform readers, although they might just flip through it.

Figure 3-9
Page from *Novedades*

Figure 3-9
Page from *Novedades*

This is looking at the big picture. It is very hard in a magazine (or in a newsletter for that matter) to get the needed impartiality to do what is best for the reader, which, of course, ultimately, is what is best for you. As the writer, it is painful to be forced to realize that most people just aren't as interested in the subject as you are.

In a magazine situation, editors tend to side with writers (they used to be writers themselves). But the readers always look at the pictures first, the headlines and special type treatments next, and then, finally, the body type.

There are learned journals, and special-interest newsletters where the content is so important and compelling, it could be put in as uninterrupted dot-matrix print-outs and subscribers would still read it. But nowadays the publishers of the most technical and arcane publications are becoming aware of the competition for their readers' time.

The reader devices discussed here are increasingly essential to any publication, just for survival. Somehow, information (or just entertainment) must be lifted out of the basic text and offered to readers in forms that can be quickly and easily absorbed. The trick is to martial these devices in an intelligent way, to design them so that there is a logical system and style in a publication.

For example, in the newspaper *Novedades* in Mexico City (see Figure 3–9), the same typographical configuration is put to a number of uses. Basically the device is a caption set in Janson type with a bold Franklin Gothic Condensed preamble, or lead-in. Above the bold type is a thick rule, in black or in color.

This is not an original device. But the trick at *Novedades* was to use it not only for captions, but also for pullquotes, subheads, and even section headings.

This may be carrying a good thing too far, but every publication needs an array of reader devices. Making them work well together is the heart of publication design.

Color Design, Printing, and Proofing

In the beginning, everything was black and white. At least on the desktop. For all intents and purposes, DTP could produce one color; with typical laser printers and typical copy paper, that meant black "ink" on white. There were a few crude ways of putting color into DTP documents using transfer foils—hardly worth the effort. Or, you could put colored paper into the laser printer. Still, the early desktop world was monochrome.

But now, everything is going color in the computer market. Color monitors are coming down in price, and the quality of color printers is improving dramatically. All the major graphic and design programs are now in color. While the first applications focused on color charts and diagrams, or simple color rules on a page, now attention is turning to color photography. Color scanners are bringing pictures into the desktop, and the quality is good enough to suggest that soon there will be no difference between desktop publishing and just plain *publishing*.

Recent developments in digital page-description technology will make it possible to produce acceptable (the word is used advisedly) four-color printing directly from DTP files. But technology, sadly, seldom brings taste along with it. And in the enthusiasm to try out new tools and toys, we sometimes get carried away.

Color Design

Ultimately, color should be an integral part of a design, and a color page should not just be a colorized black-and-white page. Nevertheless, a well-designed color page usually looks good in black-and-white—because its underlying structure is good. It's like "good bones" under a beautiful face.

Much has been written about color theory, psychology, and philosophy. In terms of psychology we are told, for example, that red is alarming. Blue is supposedly soothing; brown is masculine; green is the color of nature—and so forth. Again, association plays a major role. Colors remind people of things they've seen, in printing or in the larger world around them. You are more likely to evoke emotions by playing on these associations than by using some kind of psychological color theory. For example, black borders suggest death notices in some cultures, and yet, in the United States, black is the color of choice in the fashion world.

Taste is the key.

A Colorblind Layout Tip

It is very tricky to design things in color and expect them to work. Even within the 256-color gamut of an 8-bit monitor, there is plenty of room to get it wrong. However, the basic structure of a design can always be seen in black and white. When you print out a color page on a black-and-white printer, you can see if the structure is good. It is like an x-ray cutting through the distractions.

Through most of my design experience up to now, I have been forced to work in black and white, using photostats or copies of color pictures to play with the layout. The color was added later, sometimes not until the page hit the press. Yet this discipline or limitation was largely positive. The maximum contrast obtainable is between black and white. A page that you may think looks marvelously subtle, with intricate overlays of color, can turn into a muddle in monochrome. The black-and-white proof makes you think twice, and question whether the reader is going to see a confusing mess or some delightful colorful array.

Don't allow yourself to be blinded by color. Set up the skeleton of your design in black and white. Then add the color very carefully, when you are already happy with the foundation. (See Figure 4-1.)

Figure 4-1
The black and white skeleton of a good color layout always looks good in monochrome. Note color specs in margins.

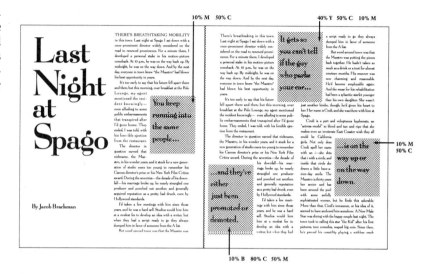

You may want to stop soon after you start. A little color goes a long way. Color is much better used as an accent, particularly if you are not an accomplished color virtuoso, and few of us are. Implement some of the rules for color. Take a black bar under a headline, at the bottom of a page, or on a border, and turn it to red. Beware of tinting broad sections of the page. Play around a bit and run a color proof if you can, just to be sure you aren't overdoing it.

Think very carefully before actually running type in any color. Typically, novices rush to make colored headlines. Color invariably reduces the contrast, and thus the legibility. The association you evoke with color type will be closer to packaging than journalism. Often, the subheads will look better in a color than the big headline.

The best way to look like an amateur is to indiscriminately splash a lot of color over a page. It takes a lot of experience, following proofs through the final printed page to learn how to use color naturally and authoritatively.

The Second Color— Turning Red

When color was introduced into medieval manuscripts and early printing it was often a simple second color. While we all have seen the elaborate illuminations produced by feverish, cloistered monks, these were usually isolated bright spots, and all the more effective for it.

With the need for mass production and the decline in ranks of monks, color became mechanical. The hand touch was given up in favor of more, cheaper, copies. Color was used more sparingly.

But from the first books onward, the first additional color, the "second color" after black, was invariably red. Red, white, and black have been the brightest, and most useful combination in 500 years of printing. Why? Tradition, perhaps. Red ink may have been easier to mix, and it printed well. And some say that there is an instinctive reaction to red, since in nature red is usually a sign of danger. It took thousands of years for the first human to eat a tomato, for example, because red is often a signal of poison.

That may explain why it can be so striking. But I use red because I like it. (See the *Type 90 Report* newsletter in this chapter's color section.)

Look at the alternatives. Blue doesn't have much contrast with black. Yellow is too light for type, and too bright in any quantity. (There is the venal association of yellow journalism.) Green, in my experience, is seldom pleasant in printing; perhaps it has something to do with the dyes used in ink. Purple and orange seem garish with black. So, start with red and maybe stop soon thereafter. (But, beware of screen tints of red, unless you want pink.)

The best use of red is as an accent, for drop initials or in graphic elements, particularly rules. Try a 4-point red rule parallel to a black hairline, at the bottom of a text column or above a headline. Red is loud, so use it sparingly.

Adding More Colors

For a third color on your palette, try something more subtle: beige or cream or warm gray. These milder colors can be splashed over larger areas, such as the background in a box that contains some type—a "tint box." The tint helps separate the contents from the rest of the page, and the color can add a bit of warmth.

If you are ready to use all three colors at once, try a thin hairline red rule around that box. A virtuoso touch is to pick up the paper color, too. For example, "reverse" the headline in the box to white. The result is really four colors: black, red, beige, and white.

This palette can be produced in three distinct colors, usually called out from the Pantone Matching System (PMS), and defined as individual plates—separations—in your program's color menu. Or it can be created from the standard four printing colors: cyan (bright blue), magenta, yellow, and black. CMYK, for short (the "K" is used instead of "B" for black to avoid confusion with blue).

If you are ready to use four-color photos on your desktop system, concentrate first on the pictures, leaving the paper white and all the type and rules black. Remember that your task is to convey information. The color photos are always the first things that a reader looks at. The best solution may be to leave the type and rules in black, and let people focus on the pictures.

Choosing a Palette and Sticking to It

If you are choosing colors from the nearly infinite choices of four-color processing, it is not a bad idea to choose a limited palette. Choose a few nice shades and then set them in stone for the whole issue or publication.

If you decide that your colors are black, red, and gray, it keeps you from going crazy when it comes time to add color to a page, and from producing nausea in the reader. A specific color palette provides welcome continuity, holding your publication together visually.

Picking these specific colors is, unfortunately, a matter of experience. Forget art school. Be very careful about applying somebody else's knowledge of color to your own work. Remember, you can't make up absolute rules for color; it is all a matter of taste.

Instead, consider color connotations and associations, as you do with type (discussed in Chapter 2, "Type Basics"). For example, a red border around a cover suggests *Time* magazine. I have no quarrel with the fact that red used vividly like this suggests urgency. There have been studies, in fact, that have shown red to attract attention, like the red in front of a bull. But, red doesn't always indicate urgency in every shade and design.

What I am saying is that colors do not have neat prescriptions for use.

If you are new to using color, experiment and show your results to a few friends before you actually print anything. And don't forget about white. A typical beginner forgets white and covers every square inch with ink.

Using Tints and Fades

It rarely works to put type in color, or to paint swatches of color behind blocks of text. In both cases, the color tends to distract the reader's eye from the reading instead of drawing it into the story. For that reason, the tint background can be useful for small boxes and sidebars.

Fades—some call them degradés—are very popular right now (see Figure 4-2). Before DTP, they were created by having an airbrush artist make a painting of the dark-to-light fade and then shooting a halftone of it. It's certainly not a new trick; lithographic posters a hundred years ago were full of fades. On the desktop, there are a number of ways of getting them.

Figure 4-2
Fade box from
Smart magazine

Aldus FreeHand can automatically create blends and fades. In Adobe Illustrator you have to do it manually, using the Blend tool to create a pattern that can be used to fill type or illustrations. Or you can pick up canned fades from the Collector's Edition, a library of various images and effects.

You can get pretty good DTP fades, but they are limited by two primary factors. First of all, they are essentially made up of separate horizontal strips of gradually lighter shades. These distinct fields are visually blended together using coarse halftone dots. (See the discussion of halftones in "Color Photos on the Desktop" below.) Secondly, the resolution of your output device limits the number of shades you can use: the higher the resolution you make the screen, the fewer color levels you can reproduce. This is because each colored dot in a field is made up of several pixels—points on the computer screen that can be turned on or off, or displayed in red, green, or blue (RGB). With higher resolution, a larger number of dots have to share a finite number of available color pixels, resulting in fewer pixels for each dot, and less control over color. (For illustrations of the color cell and fades, see this chapter's color section.) The key is in finding the balance between color control and resolution.

Color Proofing

To get the right color, you need a way to check your results as you go. The screen, with its video color beaming into your eyes, may be deceptively bright. New color printers provide a higher resolution proof, and it is now possible to print out on the paper you plan ultimately to use. Finally, when the page is sent to a film printer, a proof can be "contacted" from the films, giving you the closest check you can get before the page hits the press.

The problem here is that at each stage the technology is different, and each proof may be disconcertingly different. Only when you have followed the process all the way through a few times, can you learn to judge what each proof indicates. In a publication, experience builds up with each issue, and you can compensate for color problems with some certainty. With a one-shot project, it is essential to obtain the best proof possible before press time, and then work with the professionals at the press to make sure that everyone agrees on what the color should be.

Color quality control requires vigilance at every step: the original color range of the pictures; the accurate reproduction—or compensation—at the scanner; the calibration of the color monitor; adjustment of the color printer so that it approximates the final high-resolution film; control of the film itself; and finally, personal supervision at the press for a "color okay." Indeed good color can not be achieved without checking quality and making adjustments at each stage.

PostScript Color Printers

Printers that use Adobe's PostScript page-description language are certainly good enough for color layouts and presentations, and buying one is probably worthwhile if you produce a volume of color work. The cheapest ones (without PostScript) are several thousand dollars—double the cost of a laser printer.

The QMS ColorScript was the first color PostScript printer with an output resolution of 300 dpi. It sends special paper back and forth four times, and uses heat imaging, involving big sheets of color foil that run out quickly and cost a lot.

Another presentation printer is the Du Pont 4Cast digital color imager, which at $75,000 delivers 256 different hues and what appears to be almost a continuous-tone image. Actually the resolution is no greater than the 300 dpi of the QMS printers, but Du Pont uses a dithered imaging pattern that almost looks like the grain of photography. The resulting prints are glossy, and ideal for advertising comps.

Now Canon is selling a PostScript interpreter for its Color Laser Copier 500, effectively turning that machine into a color laser printer. The quality is quite good (with 400-dpi resolution), and it has the advantage of printing on plain paper. Thus, a newspaper designer can feed newsprint into the machine and get a better idea of how a final color page will look when printed. But it will cost. The copier itself retails for about $49,000, and its PostScript device may cost an additional $30,000.

Others—including EFI, the color technology company started by the founder of Scitex, Efi Arazi—are expected to offer less expensive PostScript interpreters for the Canon copier.

At this high end of PostScript color printers, we are no longer on the desktop. (The Canon CLC sits on the floor.) And at this price level, one starts wanting more than a comp or presentation proof—one wants a real proof that shows the color as it will appear on the press.

Until the Canon CLC, the best way to get real proofs from desktop files was to go to film and pull color keys, Cromalins, or match proofs. This leads us to decide whether to use desktop technology as a fully integrated color production system. It's the obvious next step, but this decision can only be made in the context of all the other hardware and software you have or want to get (explored more fully in Chapter 7, "Bits and Bolts: Desktop Systems").

True Colors— Color Calibration Issues

The color you see on the screen and the image you see printed out on the QMS printer will each be different from your final color. It can drive you nuts. Calibrating the colors of various display and output devices is one of the major problems of color DTP.

How you bring an image to the screen (or create color graphics) is the first variable that effects calibration. Each scanner (whether it uses light or laser) has its own limitations of imaging. And consider the scanner's resolution—how many pixels are recorded to the inch, and how many different pixel colors can be scanned. The scanner is really only "sampling" a photograph.

Moreover, each software program has different values set for the colors; even the "standard" PMS colors look different in different programs.

On the screen, colors are translated into video color—red, green, blue, or RGB. Unlike four-color printing which is done by printing with the four "process" colors (cyan, magenta, yellow, and black, or CMYK), video color is only made up of three. Thus, even the most perfectly tuned monitor will not display the same hues as printing colors.

A desktop color printer produces three or four CMYK colors (some do not bother with the black). But, the colors will be off again, because the color is created with foil, waxy pigments, or granular toner, not ink. If you're using a Cromalin proof of the films you've created, that's yet another, still less-than-perfect rendition of the final inking.

When you're finally on your own paper with your own ink, and the press is working at top speed, the output will be something totally different. If you work on a publication using the same suppliers, month after month, you can learn the relationship between proof and final printed colors—through sometimes brutal experience. For example, the QMS printer version is much darker than the video screen image.

There are a number of products on the market that claim to maintain color calibration between your display and your proofing device. They help, but are not totally reliable, and offer very little assurance for calibrating what you see now with your final press run. Your best tool in this area is still experience.

Color Printing

A year ago only a few brave souls had ventured into color separations and film production using desktop technology. But suddenly everyone seems to be interested in the game. There are two directions: coming from the top, high-end systems, such as Scitex, Crosfield, and Hell; and coming from the bottom, developers like Adobe, Quark, and others making it possible for a publisher to produce good color from the desktop. As with everything related to computers, there are significant price-versus-performance trade-offs. But if your goal is to create a complete desktop system that combines design, photo editing, typesetting, and prepress production, the tools are rapidly being made available.

Most of the DTP programs that write PostScript can easily separate colors in final output. Take QuarkXPress, for example. If you decided that a bar should be tinted 100-percent red and 30-percent blue, it comes out reddish purple. Assuming the rest of your document is printed in black, QuarkXPress divides it into three screened colors for the final output. The PostScript imagesetter (such as a Linotype L-330 printer) then makes films of the separate colors, with the halftone screen resolution you have specified.

Before you start experimenting with color, be aware of your program's color limitations. Each program has different methods for bringing in color—particularly four-color pictures. For the most part, the separations must be made in separate software (such as Spectre-

Print, Aldus PrePrint, or Adobe Photoshop), before being brought into the DTP program.

Desktop Color Problems

Sadly, PostScript has not been perfectly adapted for four-color processing yet, although the just-released upgrade, PostScript Level 2, gets much closer. The problem goes back to the halftone screens: the pattern of dots which make up the color layers, when superimposed, must be rotated to avoid undesirable "moiré" patterns in the image. (See this chapter's color pages.) The name comes from the silk that has a wavy pattern produced by engraved rollers. The same effect happens in screened film by overlapping two transparencies on angle.

It turns out that the four-color angles that have, after years of experimentation, been perfected in conventional color lithography, are difficult to achieve in digital separations because everything is made of pixels in the digital world, and these are aligned rectilinearly. An angle of 45 degrees is easy to make, but try to draw a line in Mac-Paint at 70 degrees, and you quickly see the jaggies that confounded the developers of digital color. One major color supplier, Dr. Hell (which sounds a little bit like a character in a James Bond movie until you realize that _hell_ means light in German—the full name is Dr.-Ing. Rudolph Hell, AG, of Kiel, Germany,) had the foresight to actually patent their method of achieving these angles for a digital imagesetter.

Hell licensed this technology to the other major color scanner and film recorder manufacturers, but so far there is no license to the PostScript developers. With the release of PostScript Level 2, Adobe has come up with improved formulas which should lessen the problem somewhat.

In lower resolution, the angles are less critical. The _Dallas Times Herald_ production people found that they get pretty good results on newsprint by just printing all the colors on the same angle! The Spanish firm, Anaya Systems, went around the angle problem altogether by coming up with what has been described as a dithered dot pattern. This separation technology is now available from The Color Group, of Richmond, California.

Screen angle problems are being solved, but there are a number of sophisticated techniques developed in digital color that will not easily be brought down to the level of desktop printing. For example, Hell and Scitex systems actually change the shape of dots, as well as the size, to improve color quality.

In QuarkXPress you can quickly change color contrast and brightness, as you might on a TV set. In Photoshop and Color Studio you can create masks, and adjust color balance and hue within tonal ranges—such as shadows only. As soon as you get deeply into these programs you become aware how little you know about color technology. The expensive training and experience of scanner operators and color retouching specialists becomes more valuable. And with the explosion of color in publishing, there are not enough experts to go around. One source of talent is the color photography printing labs. First you have to know color, in any case.

Another problem is the sheer amount of information needed to render any color picture with great fidelity. A single color slide (a 35-mm transparency) contains some 30 megabytes of data—which would swamp the RAM of any PC. Fortunately, many of the current desktop color manipulation programs, including Photoshop and Color Studio, use the computer's hard disk as simulated RAM or "virtual memory" when dealing with large color files. File transport problems are solved with various compression schemes.

While waiting for our computers to get bigger and faster, and for the technology to be brought down in scale and cost, DTP color is a difficult subject. But already, desktop-publishing technology can handle small pictures (or larger photos at low resolutions, such as in newspapers). For high-end uses (magazine covers, for example), you may want to use color on the desktop just for design. Then, you can send out for final separation to be done according to your layout, but using conventional methods. Or your files can merge with the bigger systems, using Scitex Visionary, Crosfield StudioLink, or Hell Colorscript. (See Chapter 7, "Bits and Bolts: Desktop Systems.")

As color PostScript technology matures, more people will experiment with four-color separations. Professional color separation houses will survive as skill resources. But they will become service bureaus, and the most alert of them have already set up channels to the growing desktop-publishing market. People will feel confident enough to use desktop color capability when the software is so smart that it separates pictures for them, and when adjusting the color is like fiddling with the knobs on a TV.

Color Fouls   Meanwhile, the importance of good taste (and design talent) will never go away. Though using subtle colors can evoke sophistication and dignity, it can also backfire. A typically amateur combination is to use very creamy yellow paper with brown ink. The net result, however, is often not the subtle, sophisticated one hoped for, but a rather boring lack of contrast. In addition to the color of the ink, the color of the paper is important. Go to any quick printing shop and you will see a hundred invitations that were done with the yellow paper and brown ink combination. The contrast of the type is effectively softened to the point of being corny.

Poor uses of colors are rampant on modern newspapers that have just installed color presses. You find editors who are traditionally in charge of newspapers and who don't have a feel for color. They've never had color in their lives before and probably don't even watch color TV at home. They apply color like a neophyte at Mardi gras. They go nuts.

USA Today is actually a very controlled example of what newspaper men think color can be used for—essentially everything. For a real treat, try midsized regional newspapers. You get pages that are almost like confetti, with every graphic element, box, illustration, and four-color picture strewn around it until it no longer looks like news at all. One exception in this sea of poor taste is the Spanish newspaper, *El Sol*, which is produced in full color totally on the desktop. (See the illustration in this chapter's color section.)

If you find yourself in the situation of using color for the first time, be very careful. Walk softly. Maybe your four-color printing capabilities should be reserved for four-color pictures only. Remember to design everything in black and white first. Then change elements to color. You are going to be in much better shape if you don't color every rule line, tint every box, make every headline red, and run every photo in four color.

Paper Grades and Colors

Typically in magazine production, paper is not a design decision—primarily, or even secondarily. It is an economic one. At a commercial magazine, you are primarily interested in making advertisers happy. So you work to find the cheapest possible paper that prints the ads well enough that the advertisers don't demand refunds. Luxury magazines, like the big fashion books, get fairly good paper, because the advertisers are willing to pay for it. Most magazines can't afford it, however. If you print a large run, paper can be the single most expensive item in your entire budget.

All paper is described by standard characteristics, including size, weight, finish, color, bulk, opacity, and grain. Combinations of these factors are expressed as grades. Deciding which grade to use depends upon the specific nature of your design and the publication's purpose.

The paper grade affects the quality of the printing in two ways. First, the different grades have different reflective qualities. A grade three paper is much whiter than a grade four and therefore all the colors are much brighter. Secondly, it is easier to print on better grade paper because the surface holds the ink better. The coating on paper is key here. Smooth clay particles are applied to the paper at the mill to enhance printing quality. Coated paper is described as either glossy or matte. The glossy stock takes color the best, but it can appear too slick for some uses. Expensive annual reports are often produced on luxurious matte-finished paper, like Warren's Cameo Dull. For most large publications, these points are moot because the paper is chosen on the basis of cost.

On the other hand, if for a relatively small newsletter, paper cost is not a huge concern. Paper choice should be whatever you like, or whatever your printer likes—and printers are the best practical source of information about available paper.

Increasingly, people want to use recycled paper. In addition to the trees required for new paper, there is the process: paper mills are among the worst polluters. So far, there is no top quality recycled stock, because the recycling process results in shorter fibers which create weaker, flakier paper. More "lint" comes off and gums up offset presses. What is more, the process of clay-coating paper is itself an environmental hazard. Kaolin, a rare earth used in coated stock, is actually carcinogenic. The low demand for recycled stock makes it more expensive than an environmentally-oblivious equivalent. You have to accept costlier, lower-quality paper if you want to use recycled stock. It is a question of values. But the paper mills are, as every industry is, increasingly catering to environmental concerns—and even more to customer demand.

Local paper merchants have consultants who will be happy to send samples of paper, if they can tell you are a serious potential customer. The merchants will also make up dummies in blank paper in the format of your project to show how different stocks will look and feel.

In design schools there are whole classes about paper grades and treatments, so you can learn about standard sheet sizes, reflective qualities, tensile strength and flexibility, and how the length of the fibers affects printability. But then, you go to the printer and you want only 2000 of something. What are you going to do? Make a special order of something that will take a month to arrive and that will cost extra because there is a minimum quantity? Or, do you look around in the back of the shop, forgetting everything you learned, and find a pile that is good enough—at the price.

A fairly good rule of thumb when choosing paper is to keep it as simple as possible, like your design. You want to call attention to the content, the words, and the pictures. Don't overshadow the content with extravagant or gaudy paper.

Newsletter designers should be particularly careful of the urge to use "linen-finish" or "pebble-finish" or "cockle finish" papers. They always look, to me anyway, incredibly cheap, like contact paper or vinyl tile that looks like marble. Go for something plain and smooth.

One way to distinguish your publication is to choose a heavier paper. Look into getting a slightly heavier weight than typical letterhead paper. This is especially effective if you are just doing a four-page mailer. Heavier paper goes through the mail better and will be significantly more impressive. Moving up one paper weight usually won't move you up to the next postage category, so it's probably a good investment. To add dignity to your publication think about using off-white paper—what they call natural (since in order to be printed on at all, pulp has to be heavily bleached and processed). If you are doing an elegant newsletter, it is well worth it to spend some time researching the right paper. It can make or break the design.

And above all else, remember that for four-color printing, the whiter the paper is, the brighter the colors will be.

Visual Content

People see before they read. They see pictures—photos, illustrations—and even the general shape of a page—the layout—before reading a single word. A reader's immediate reaction to a page determines whether he will devote some time to the story or if he will get up to make a sandwich.

The images come across the reader's threshold first. Readers go to a bigger picture before a smaller one. They go to a color picture before a black and white one—before a headline, before anything. (Consider Figures 5-1 and 5-2.)

Indeed, visual images remain the quickest, the most natural, basic form of communication. They clearly represent the real world, without much interpretation or participation from readers.

If you accept this, you obviously want to include pictures in your publication. To use multiple clichés again, a picture is worth a thousand words, but it's easier said than done. For one thing, other people are involved—researchers, librarians, interviewees, editors.

With text alone, you can just write it, lay it out, and change typefaces at will, without even talking to anyone else—especially if you use a desktop-publishing system. But these are skills enough, and it may be stretching it if you expect to be a good photograph editor as well.

A Promise Fulfilled

Maine's Department of Education uses automated report generation to keep a campaign promise

BY CLAY ANDRES

Desktop publishing may not help balance the budget or lower taxes, but it did help Governor John R. McKernan Jr. of Maine keep his platform promise to give the voters more and better information on the status of their public schools. In his inaugural address McKernan called for a "report card" on Maine schools. Like so many campaign promises, the Governor's vision lacked a strategy for achieving it. He certainly didn't realize that there were serious technical barriers to overcome.

The task of developing a report card for each of the nearly 300 school administrative units fell to Maine's Commissioner of Education, Eve M. Bîthes. She created a task force of about 20 people, headed by the deputy commissioner, Richard Card, and including Jim Watkins, the director of management information. The group met monthly for most of a school year and turned over its recommendations to Watkins.

By the time Watkins's data processing manager, Dale Elliot, found someone who could produce the report, there were only two weeks left in which to complete them. But, as you will see, this story ends happily. Before McKernan took office, the state had been preparing an annual set of about a dozen four-page tabular reports comparing each school unit statistically. "We had a lot of data on our Burroughs minicomputer and were able to do some analysis using COBOL programs," said Elliot. "We made lists of facts and figures, but had never put it in a graphic form."

LIVER AND ONIONS

The reports would have to convert dry, sometimes unpalatable data into fare for mass consumption. Tables of numbers—meat and potatoes for the statistical-minded—are liver and onions for the average voter. "We had a diverse readership for the report card, technical educators and administrators, as well as the public with interest in the school budget," said Watkins.

"It had to be self-explanatory, avoiding overly technical statistics, while still addressing the audiences without compromising the quality of the information. We knew that to communicate to the man on the street, we had to do it graphically."

At the task force's final two meetings, the group discussed how the material should be presented.

"They were trying to design it in an IBM environment and couldn't," said Christopher Lyons, senior planner with the state of Maine. "They wanted to switch to Macs, and I was one of the few people in the department with expertise." A contract was

JIM WATKINS
Director of Management Information

"It had to be very self-explanatory, avoiding overly technical statistics, while still addressing the audiences without compromising the quality of the information."

DALE ELLIOT
Data Processing Manager

"We believed that with new graphics technology becoming available, we should be able to do it, somehow."

38

ITC DESKTOP : No. 5

Figure 5-1
Images impact before text

This is the point where the original notion of desktop publishing gets pushed into the professional arena. To bring photos in, you have to hire photographers or research the stock photo agencies, and you've moved beyond the desktop. In smaller publications, the designer often must function as a photo editor.

Most desktop publishers send their PostScript files for high-resolution proof to a service bureau, and there are photo service bureaus, as well—agencies that represent photographers and sell their stock.

Photography is the last area to yield to desktop technology. While many illustrators are happily learning how to use new tools, photographers are, for the most part, trapped in the analog world.

There are digital cameras now. Cannon and Sony make still video (SV) systems, priced from under $1,000 to more than $10,000; however, the key word here is video. The resolution is no better than the current U.S. standard, NTSC. Some newspapers have started giving their staffers this equipment, and their ability to bring live news photos in on deadline justifies the cost. But the quality is still not

Figure 5-2
Photo layouts with
a large and a small
photo work well
as stages of entry
to the text

much better than television, and an SV picture enlarged much bigger than three columns in a newspaper starts showing the video scan lines.

With high-definition video, we can expect quality much closer to 35-mm photography; but different standards are being developed in the United States, Japan, and Europe, and it is unlikely that we will see much better SV technology in the next few years.

It should, however, get cheaper. It is expected that consumer cameras like the Sony Mavica will be priced at affordable levels in the next year or so. And this will encourage weekly and monthly publications to get into still video.

The whole joy of this is that there is no more darkroom! No money is wasted processing and printing pictures that will never be used. Just as DTP eliminated the photostats, SV eliminates the prints or slides.

The software allows you to see all the contents of a disk and quickly chose what you want to save.

For small pictures such as a one-column mug shot—even in color—the quality is adequate now. A publication like an employee newsletter could put still video to good use right away.

Stock Versus Assignment

Before assigning a photographer, you should decide if perhaps it makes more sense to find photos through stock sources. You never know what a photographer is going to come back with until you see it. Is it more practical to get a photograph that has already been taken in another context than to send a photographer out to get a picture of the subject? Yes and no. It depends.

If you want a photograph of a movie star, a stock agency may be the only way you can get it. The *Nuts and Bolts Reseller News* may not be able to attract Paul Newman's attention long enough to take his picture. But at the same time, if *NBRN* wants to do a story on the newest bolt factory, it may be easier to send a photographer than try to make do with existing pictures.

When you ask for stock photographs, you pay for the research. In the old days you could request photos to peruse at no charge. No more. Now, there is typically a $50 research fee just to look at a bunch of color copies. You may never get the originals, even if you decide to buy the right to use a photo, because the shots of certain photographers are too valuable to risk loss.

For a journalistic look, it is a good idea to work with the big agencies, like Sygma, Sipa, or Gamma, rather than commercial stock houses which have slicker pictures, oriented for advertising. If you're using more than one picture, try to stick with the "take" of one photographer. This will automatically give you some consistency, and the results will be closer to your own photo assignments. For consumer-interest magazines—travel, for example—there are often surprisingly good takes that have never been used, just lying in files, because the publication that originally assigned the "shoot" killed the accompanying article.

One last hint is: don't lose any of the shots sent by a stock agency. You will have to buy them, and a typical cost is $1,500 per transparency. You will be set back quite a bit if you lose a whole sheet of twenty photos, so be sure to keep close track of everything. A common mistake made by new publications is not logging in photos. Treat them like cash, and apply the same bookkeeping methods, or you may pay for it in the end.

The Right Photographer

There are more and more photographers, agents, and stock houses with various photo books—annuals or showcases—advertising their work. (These showcases are usually for sale in art supply stores.) Assigning photographs and finding appropriate existing pictures comes under the general heading of photo editing.

As with everything else in design, keep photo editing simple. In the last chapter we said the most intelligent choice of paper is the one that works at your printing house. It makes sense to stay with a paper stock that your printer has experience using. This also goes for photographers. You may have favorite photographers that you have seen in books and magazines, but calling up Herb Ritts or some other current star photographer to do a photo for your newsletter probably won't work. He or she might do it, but also may charge you $30,000 and still not get what you want.

When looking at a photographer's portfolio, you cannot assume that on assignment he or she will get a photograph equal to any in that portfolio. Those photographs are selected out of all the failures. They could have been taken on assignments that had nothing to do with the subject. They may have been accidents. Choosing the photographer is largely a matter of taste—for photography and for people. If you like the photographer, and think you'll get along together, that is a good sign. (If the assignment is a portrait, then personality is critical. Charming, outgoing photographers tend to be better portrait photographers, because they can warm up their subjects.)

Study the photographer's "book" for assignments that are similar to the one you have in mind. Beware of portfolios that contain only original prints and transparencies. Ask for tear sheets, which will show how a real assignment came out. It is one thing to be able to take good pictures occasionally, but another to complete an assignment under time and budget constraints.

There are famous photographers that I have tried to use, who seem to produce beautiful photographs for other people and other magazines, but who just don't work out with me. Perhaps they aren't the right photographer for my assignments, or maybe I'm not giving the photographer enough information. Whatever the reason, I've learned not to bank on what a photographer has done elsewhere.

Once you have the right photographer, you still have to expend a significant effort to communicate the assignment correctly. In many cases it is effective to work with the photographer's agent or rep, who serves as business manager as well as salesman since his commission is dependent on the successful completion of the job, and photographers (like other creative people) tend to be a bit sketchy about the details. There are individual agents, and then there are photo groups like Magnum or Sygma (the largest, with some 2,000 photographers represented). These agencies also handle the back files, or stock, keep them indexed by subject, and provide a research service.

Sadly, none of the agencies are yet equipped to handle their stock in a digital format, ready for desktop publishers. The Associated Press started transmitting news photos in a digital format, and over the next year plans to replace all of its old analog wire-photo receivers across the United States with digital darkrooms. The AP opted to use a proprietary system, based on Leaf scanners, and the Leafax receiver. But soon newspaper photo editors will be able to browse through incoming pictures on a screen.

Accompanying the pictures will be a caption (in ASCII format) and a header that will allow the picture to be sorted properly into the paper's photo database. The choices will be sent through networks to layout desks, where the pictures will be cropped and scaled, and incorporated into the pages. Ultimately, the first time the photos will hit paper will be when they are printed on newsprint.

We can expect that AP will offer, through its Wide World stock photo service, some kind of digital retrieval of file photos. And eventually perhaps, nonsubscribers will be able to call up a digital photo library through their modems, and do some online photo research.

Anaya Systems in Spain has developed a digital photo desk that runs on Macintoshes and is used by the Spanish news agency, EFE. Using the Hypercard-based program Browser, you can quickly sort through photos. But someone has had to enter all the data in the header to make the database work. Considering how many pictures are taken a day, you can understand that the conversion to digital is a mammoth undertaking—never mind all the pictures lurking in dusty photo morgues.

The agencies like Sygma that service magazines are struggling with the decision about how to go digital, in part because it is not clear how many magazines are ready to receive pictures in digital format, or who could afford to pay for the creation of the database. But all recognize that it is inevitable, just a question of time. Meanwhile, most photography remains offline.

In any case, you have to be certain that the photographer understands what you want him or her to bring back for you. Spell it out clearly. Many visual-minded people tend to atrophy their verbal ability and vice versa. As the designer, you need to preserve a bit of both sides, especially if you are putting it all together electronically, where more of the process is in your hands.

Once the assignment is in and you are happy with the results, plan to work with the photographer on the next similar project. Building a track record is essential.

Visual Content

Almost everyone will agree with the premise that people see photos before they see words and text, but they turn right around and ask, "Can we get a picture to go along with this story?" Why should the words always take precedence over photos, when pictures have stronger immediate impact?

There are two reasons. The first is historical. Journalism was invented by writers. There were newspapers before there was photography. Secondly, writers are (one hopes) verbal people and tend be more persuasive in the everyday political give-and-take of a publication office than their hapless, tongue-tied visual colleagues. So they tend to run the place.

This hierarchy is true in almost every publication except the fashion magazines and *National Geographic*. Generally, an article is assigned or received, and then pictures are found to go with it. Photography is considered to be illustration, to be secondary, to fill out the point, to demonstrate the fact of an article, to add a little credence. A photograph is used as a device to make it slightly easier for people to understand what is going on in the text.

From a writer's point of view, using photos to supplement a story is natural. But from the publication reader's point of view this is meaningless. We call them readers, of course, but they tend to absorb magazines in a kind of holistic way—all at once. Pictures and text blend together in a reader's consciousness. They don't start at the beginning of each article and read all the way through; they skip around, taking a bit of this and a bit of that.

Haven't you—at least on one occasion—actually read an article backwards, a couple of paragraphs at a time?

Bring in the Pictures

Even a well-chosen mug shot can add to a story. People want to see what the guy in a story looks like. If it's George Bush, maybe not.

But perhaps you can find a picture of Bush that has a bit of twist, and one that advances the story. And perhaps you can find a sequence of pictures that not only advances the story, but tells the story.

With the launch of *Life* magazine, the evolution of the picture story (see Figure 5-3), and the picture magazine was steady, progressive, and fascinating. Editors and photographers continually came up with new adaptations for visual images in magazines—until the invention of television. As Americans turned to TV, the visual energy went out of

THE BACK OF BEYOND

TRIPS

At round-up time, you're in the saddle before daybreak and until dusk fourteen hours later. The exhaustion shows.

Aboriginals, whose ancestors lived for thousands of years off some of the most hostile land on earth, have used their local knowledge to become expert stockmen.

It's the end of the day at Bradshaw station, dinner is going to be a steak, like it has been every night for the last three months, and nobody is going to ask you to look dressy.

136   No. 1 : Spring 1988   No. 1 : Spring 1988   137

Figure 5-3
Photo content: pictures should tell a story and give a firm sense of place. (*Trips* magazine.)

magazines, and editors, generally more interested in the words anyway, by and large did not try to lure readers back with good pictures.

The fact that still photographs have some advantages over moving pictures has been ignored. The images on television are ephemeral; the viewer has to be there at the right moment to catch them (or tape the program). The apparatus is cumbersome, lacks detail, and must be plugged in. Broadcast and cable TV programs tend to be expensive enterprises, with so many people involved that creativity is sapped. Magazine articles can be created by individuals—an individual photographer, for example, travelling without elaborate crews.

What is ironic is that television remains extremely verbal. If you turn off the sound during most programming, you can't understand what is going on. TV is not taking full advantage of the visual media. What does this mean? If people respond so strongly to images, why do we have so much difficulty producing and manipulating them, and why do publications shy away from using them? The answer is that it is hard.

It takes real planning to come up with photos and text that actually work together. Photos should provide one part of the story and text should provide another.

Because images are harder to work with than text, it takes more people. During the heyday of *Life* magazine, there were 100 photo editors and assistants, and 25 staff photographers. Most magazines today don't have even one staff photographer and the art director may have to double as the photo editor. In many cases, there is no thought as to the importance of photo editing.

Increasingly, magazines are not even assigning many photo shoots. The picture stories that make it into print tend to come from books-in-progress or work that a photographer has done in his free time. I'm not saying these aren't good or valid, but the commitment to strong visual content has slackened. You hear this all the time from editors talking about "accompanying photographs." In their minds, the story is the content, and if the photos don't match the story, then they do not qualify as content and should not be run.

Photo/Text Balance

There are times when pictures can run on their own. There are times when pictures can run without captions. There are even times when text should run uninterrupted. Don't be afraid to run some stories that are just text and some stories that are just pictures. If you have decided to run only photos for their visual content, this idea is obvious—only use photos that are going to add something.

The balance of photos and text should be determined by the demands of the story. Some stories will lean heavier in one direction than another. For example, highly cerebral stories may not lend themselves to photographs, so don't use any. The other extreme, obviously, is the photo-essay in which the photos tell the story and the text only fills in the little that is missing.

In the second issue of *Trips* (see Chapter 10, "*Trips:* A User-Friendly Magazine"), we included a 12-page story with only text and a 19-page photo story that was almost exclusively photos. This was the right thing to do in each case. The photo-essay was about the immediacy and intensity of Peshawar. The photos were good enough that they needed little text support. The 12 pages of text was a story of romance in Florence. Adding pictures might have distracted the reader from the feeling and vision created by the writer.

The narrative photo-essay in magazines is all but dead. Pictures aren't used to tell a story anymore. What you find are unrelated collections of photographs, an anthology by one or more photographers, a gallery show. The shots are connected by a certain place or story, but there is no particular connection between the pictures. This shows laziness on the part of the photo editor, the inability of a photographer, or, lamely, a conscious desire to present a collage rather than a coherent or narrative story.

What we did at *Trips* was to get closer to the narrative photo-essay. The effect in the end was something like a collection of random scenes from a movie. While the photographs worked together and were by one photographer, they did not tell a story. An equivalent in writing would be a character study told in one voice, but without a plot—not completely satisfying.

My prescription is to bring in visual content the same way you bring in written content. Both efforts should be made at the same time. First, an idea originates with you, a photographer, or your colleagues. Then you figure out the visual angle. But, don't wait for the story to come in to figure out how to use photos with it.

Examples of photos which do not add content to a story are in almost every business magazine. The way the editors assign photos is to have the business person being profiled pose in eight different situations. They put him on his horse, at the plant, with the board; they put him in his car, with his wife, in the back yard, his favorite restaurant. At *Manhattan Inc.* magazine they actually run all of the pictures. But they don't add up to much.

In the 1950s, *Fortune* magazine used to do wonderful photo-essays. They would send a photographer to explore a distant industry like the oil fields of Saudi Arabia. They would show the plain ground and the sand. Then they would show the drilling crew, the rig, and the drilling. Then, the oil shooting up, and the Christmas tree valves, and the pipeline. Finally, there would be a shot of the depot and the ships. The story would be called "How We Get Oil Out of Saudi Arabia." Sometimes there would be text accompanying, and sometimes it would be just photos, but always it was effective in showing a place or a process the reader might not know.

You don't even need a huge amount of space for a picture to tell a story. At *Rolling Stone*, we sent a photographer to Panama for a single photograph of the Panama Canal to accompany a story on the transfer of control. We only had room for one big photo, and it was obviously going to be of the canal. So what is the story? The picture needed to show how the canal works. The obvious boring shot of a boat in a narrow channel just wasn't going to cut it.

The photographer came back with a masterpiece. She had the little tractors on shore pulling a big boat through the narrow locks. She caught both levels of locks, and in the background, included palm trees, water, the bay full of ships waiting to pass through—in one picture. We ran it very big. It said it all.

A surprisingly good place to find examples of effective visual images is between the stories in your favorite magazine—the advertisements. Ad-men and -women are the most successful and consistent users of strong visual images these days. The most effective advertising is the most visually enticing, and people are almost always included. (More on this in the next chapter, "The Cover.")

The Decline of Illustration

Readers usually get more facts from a photograph than from an illustration. It may be illogical, but most people trust a photograph. "Pictures don't lie." (Readers don't think about cropping, electronic airbrushing, set-up photos, etc.) But, they will not immediately accept an illustration. This is no reason not to use them. Illustrations can create emotions or just moods, add excitement or humor—often where photographs cannot.

Every day I see editors accept photo layouts and make changes to ones with illustrations. They think that once you take a photograph it is done, and it's expensive to hire someone to retouch it. But, with an illustration, you just call the artist and have him add another arm, leg, or whatever you want to the drawing. Illustrations are mutable in that way.

The place of photography and illustration in publications has changed dramatically in the last 50 years. Because of the relative ease of getting photographs taken and reproduced, they're plentiful now. One hundred years ago they were nonexistent. Magazines were filled with illustrations, woodcuts, and etchings.

The first halftones were done at the turn of the century. Now they're everywhere. With desktop scanners, everyone is incorporating them. Illustrations still have to be done by hand, so there is a horrible law of economics at work.

When *The Saturday Evening Post* paid Norman Rockwell $20,000 per cover in the 1940s, being an illustrator was an attractive profession. A kid on the farm in Iowa would dream of going to New York and painting or drawing for a magazine. It was especially glamorous when there was no television. A magazine was the most glamorous thing that ever came into your home. Illustrators were extremely well paid, and all the famous ones—N.C. Wyeth, Rockwell, etc.—had estates, and yachts, and cars, and penthouses.

Now, you don't find many illustrators over 30, except the very few successful ones, the few survivors. Most illustrators try their luck in their 20s, starve to death, and go away to do something else like investment banking. It is almost impossible to make a good living in illustration. It has become something like a third-world spiral; since you can't make a good living in the field, it doesn't attract good people, so designers rarely end up using illustration. I am still convinced that there is a role for illustration, however.

There are still plenty of illustrators around. However, if you are try-ing to do a magazine on a reasonable budget, it is difficult to bring in a famous one. But check the local art schools, and see if there is an art directors' club or graphic design group that has competitions that include illustration. Or survey local publications (including the daily paper) and look for art that you like.

Typically, all the young illustrators copy the styles of the successful older ones, but it's a start. It's hard for them to do original illustration or anything with an edge to it, and hope to make a living from it.

Be aware that illustration takes time, something most people in publishing just don't have. You can't hope to fill in last minute holes in your layouts with "quick drawings." The holes will be filled in, but you probably won't be happy with the results.

One new sign of life for illustrators has been desktop publishing itself. It represents both a new market and new tools.

Some accomplished artists, particularly newspaper staffers, have found that their work is really enhanced by the paint and graphic programs on personal computers. They have been using Adobe Illustrator in ways that go far beyond that lady golfer illustration used in the early promotion for the product. What Illustrator (and FreeHand or Corel Draw) give the artist is the ability to edit. Whether they start from a sketch that is scanned in and used as a template, or by plunging directly in on the screen, the finished artwork can always be changed.

This makes editors and art directors deliriously happy, because they always want changes. Some artists have learned the hard way to never give the designers their source files, because the control of the art can be taken away from them.

Perhaps the most powerful part of this new market is information graphics. While started well before the use of computers, newspaper graphics always had technical, or diagrammatic, style, and they were easily adapted to computers when the first painting and graphic software became available. We've seen some changing in the style. Artists at *Time* magazine—tired of the sterility of technical drawings used for news, and of the unavailing boredom of plain pie charts and bar graphs—turned to cartoons. The bear market was suddenly depicted as a circus bear sliding down a chute, with the data cleverly tucked into the drawing. *USA Today* took this style to the daily world, and now we've seen so much of it that it has become a bit goofy. Some news artists are now turning to a more realistic style, and perhaps we can say that the news graphics are coming of age, and that traditional art styles are merging with computer graphics.

Canned Art

Another source of images for desktop publishing is electronic clip art, advertised in the back of magazines like *MacUser* and *Publish*. These are the successors to the clip books or swipe books that infested cheap ads in newspapers and the *Yellow Pages* over the years. I've never had much use for these things, on the theory that even a bad original drawing or photo is better than a generic image bought off-the-shelf. However, if your work calls for symbols and frequent use of different graphic shapes (and whose does not?), you may want to invest in the Adobe Collector's Edition, which has a number of shapes and patterns in editable format.

Role of Wit

Increasingly, it is hard to find anybody with a sense of humor who can also write. Newspapers have segregated their humorists into rigid columns, implying that there is no place for humor in the rest of the world. This attitude mirrors a stylistic change in writing—toward the more serious.

The New Yorker used to have serious stories that still managed a dry, witty edge. They approached everything with the lighthearted view that the world is essentially an insane place, so to avoid cracking, we can't take anything seriously. Their wry point of view used to pervade the entire magazine.

In the late twentieth century, people—particularly writers—are forgetting the importance of humor and satire. It thereby falls on the designer to lighten up overly serious editorial matter. If you can't get the writers to be funny, try to get the illustrators to be funny, or even the photographers.

A side note of caution here: photographers have a hard time being funny because they take themselves almost as seriously as writers. Half of them, it seems, live in Washington, D.C.—a very serious city. The other half are of the roving "cowboy photographer" variety. Also very serious. This second group continually says things like, "Damn, I missed Afghanistan completely. Maybe if I go to Managua something will happen there."

You need to bring in some humor when a story is serious and boring for no apparent reason. The readers will thank you. Most are not as serious as editors. In the first issue of *ITC Desktop* (see Chapter 12, "*Desktop* on the Desktop"), we assigned a story called "And by the Way, It's Fun!" (See Figure 5-4.)

It was supposed to explore the idea that an important part of DTP is the play time on the machine. People get distracted and have fun with the video game aspect of it. Unfortunately, when the story was turned in, it was mildly entertaining, but not hilarious. What it needed was some funny cartoons to go with it. I found Patrick McDonnell, a Krazy Kat-inspired illustrator who came up with a hilarious little guy peering querulously at his computer screen. Above the scene is a dark cloud. The machine had bombed on him.

This illustration saved the story. It changed the way readers would read the story, and it gave some relief to the other purposefully serious stories in the rest of the magazine.

Cropping

The directive below sounds dumb, but I actually had it printed up and posted when I was at *Newsweek*.

Look at the picture before cropping the picture.

The most important rule of photo layout is to consider the forms in the pictures. Work your layout around the shapes and subjects inside

KEEP THE RIGHT WORK WITH THE RIGHT PERSON

You're asking your staff to learn how to use new tools. Don't make the mistake of asking them to learn a new profession. Writers aren't designers. Designers aren't typesetters.

With today's software, it's easy for responsibilities to become blurred. Word-processors, essentially writing tools, include type specification capabilities. Page layout software, basically a design tool, includes text editing features. It's too easy for your people to wind up spending their time trying to perform tasks beyond their capabilities.

Take a good look at the responsibilities of each member of your staff. Be aware of the areas in which they overlap so that you can coordinate their activities to make the most of the expertise of each member of your team.

One designer I know was horrified to discover that a newsletter produced on the desktop publishing system in another department in his company bore no resemblance to the corporate look he had spent three years developing. His solution: creation of design guidelines stored as templates in the system's software so that the other department could produce a newsletter that properly reflected the company's image.

Give your people time to master their new tools.

EDUCATE YOUR STAFF

Give your people both adequate training and sufficient time to master their new electronic tools. It's not as easy to develop desktop publishing skills as many of the ads would have you believe. Too often, tens of thousands of dollars worth of equipment lies idle for want of the expenditure of a small fraction of that amount on proper training.

Take a look at the responsibilities of each member of your staff. Coordinate their activities where they overlap.

ITC DESKTOP : No. 1

61

Figure 5-4 Use humor to get the reader into the story

the borders. Don't make the photos fit your arbitrary layout. Move the pictures around before you start to change them.

If possible, you want to preserve the photographer's mental cropping when he took the picture. If the pictures are good, change the layout to fit them. Don't change a 35mm shape into a square. Similarly, don't change a square photo taken with a 2.25-inch format into an oblong rectangle. The photographer's image should be preserved. Obviously, occasions come up when a picture calls for judicious cropping to get rid of a big blurry section that shouldn't be in there. But look first. Sometimes you want the blurry parts.

Cropping is much more important when you are trying to impart straight information. News photographs are often taken under conditions that don't allow the photographer to practice photography as an art. The photographer is just trying to get the picture. In this case, the photo editor will crop out the extraneous details. In very bad reproduction situations, crop liberally. Close in on the essential information in the photo and make that as big as possible.

When I started at *The New York Times,* Lou Silverstein, the great art director who changed the whole newspaper in the 1970s, looked over my shoulder and said, "Well, I see you don't know how to crop a photograph for a newspaper." I was a bit put off because I had been cropping photos for years, and said something to that effect. He told me to crop it more. Because reproduction in newspapers is so bad (and the same might be said for low-resolution desktop scans), Lou gave me this rule: "Crop intelligently…then crop another half inch off each side."

In the 1960s the fad was to crop faces tightly. After Kennedy was assassinated, the government issued a stamp in his honor where the top of his head was cropped out, a sort of official recognition of a style that probably owes a lot to TV closeups. Some flat-earthers, especially in newspapers, don't think you should ever crop a head. I even heard there was an editor at a San Francisco paper who issued an edict that he would never run a photograph larger than his hand. He didn't want big pictures in his newspaper. But these arbitrary rules ignore the fact that impact can be increased by good cropping.

Suppose you have four pictures on a page. Rather than forcing them into a uniform grid, choose the best of the four and make it big, make it the focus. Then arrange the other three, subordinate to the big one. Or, consider using only two or three. Look for shapes and lines in the pictures and line them up or point them at each other.

An excellent comparison is *Newsweek* and *Time*. *Time*, although more informal now than in the past, tends to keep to a grid, and makes the photos fit the format. Typically, *Time* designers pair photographs—either two matching pictures, or contrasting ones. *Newsweek* is less rigid, and tends to overlap a number of pictures in interesting combinations. *Time*, more formal, pushes pictures to the top or bottom, or stacks them in the center on top of each other. These stacked pictures tend to start vibrating when you look at them, and you really don't see either. By overlapping photos and running them in different positions and sizes, *Newsweek* comes up with a more dynamic layout and one which can be adjusted to work with the forms in the pictures.

Photographers hate overlapping photos, called "mortising" in the newspaper business (see Figure 5-5). They hate having a little corner taken out of their picture. In some respects you want to humor the photographers so that they will do a good job for you the next time. But there are times when mortising will save space—and allow the pictures to be bigger.

Most magazines seem to stack pictures in grids now. If the photos are mainly horizontal rectangles, they put in four horizontals and that's that. For a nice change, notice the two-page spread (shown in Figure 5-6) from *Schweizer Illustrierte* magazine in Switzerland. It features four people and their new minitel, a phone which is like a computer terminal—with a keyboard. You just type your message right into it. One nice aspect to notice is that the editors did not crop the pictures. The photographer obviously thought about how he was framing them in the camera.

In the course of a recent redesign project, this spread was done again, but this time the focus was given to one picture.

A surprising tactic to use when there is little quality in a photo is to run it huge. Bad photographs look better big. Good photographs can survive being run small. A mediocre photograph that is run huge with an important story actually looks dramatic. It is amazing what you can

The Art of the Deal

Congress and the administration finally agree on a budget package. But Bush's plummeting approval ratings could drag down GOP candidates.

Figure 5-5
Photographers
hate mortised or
overlapping photos

Figure 5-6
Minitels from
Schweizer Illustrierte

baldly get away with by running bad photos across two full pages! People forgive the big picture and they think the photographer may be doing something artistic. Naturally, it would be better to run a good photograph big, but pragmatically, the day will come when you are forced to run a less than brilliant image—blow it up.

Photos on the Desktop

A publication's photos used to be screened and "stripped" into the printing film by hand. Now, DTP technology allows us to digitize photos with a scanner and then import them into their final positions on a page. This method is quite reliable for black and white, but it is still to be perfected for color.

Scanning Pictures on the Desktop

True desktop design, therefore, requires some kind of scanner. You simply cannot design a page unless all the elements are in front of you. If you paste in stats or photographic copies of pictures after you have laid out the rest of the page on the machine, you are in danger of reducing your system to a typesetting machine. (For a full discussion of scanners and accompanying software, see Chapter 7, "Bits and Bolts: Desktop Systems.")

It is enticing to be able to scan in a picture, manipulate it on the desktop using any number of different software programs, crop it and scale it on your design program, and then print it out, camera-ready, with the rest of the page. But you can't expect beautiful halftones, in color or in black and white, to come out automatically. You have to consider scanning parameters, scanning quality, the characteristics of color and ink, the capabilities of your output device, and the quality of your paper.

This requires not only knowledge and skill, but also hard-won, old-fashioned experience. The best way to pick up this experience is through trial and error. In regular periodicals, you can eventually learn all the variables and test all the controls the system offers.

Scanning Parameters, Dot Gain, and Other Quality Issues

You can maximize your print quality by getting the best photos possible—bright, and with good contrast and color. Then, with your scanner, adjust the resolution of the image to be brought into the system. Remember that finer screens on output reduce the range of color that each dot can be, thereby negatively affecting the resolution of your image. Also consider your target output: if it's 300 lines per inch, then it won't do you much good to bring in 6000-line scans, which the Nikon scanner is capable of making.

One of the ways to make the picture smoother is to reduce the line screen in the page setup menu of your DTP program. If you are producing laser output, reduce the screen to around 40 lines per inch. If your final target printer is capable of 2,540 dpi or more, go for the highest resolution output, but for most desktop scans, keep the halftone dot size coarse—to around 85 lines per inch. While this will give you grainier pictures than you might want, the colors will be reproduced more faithfully, because there will be a greater range of color levels available for each dot. (In most newspapers, you probably can't print much finer than a 100-line screen anyway, although newspaper printing is improving all the time.)

You also have to consider the quality of your paper. For example, when printing on newsprint, the printed image will be altered from the film image. First, the color of newsprint is at least a 10-percent yellow-gray, so the contrast range is cut. No matter how good your halftone is, you cannot get a good white. Then, because the paper absorbs ink, you can never get 100-percent black. The ink spreads when it is absorbed and cuts down on the sharpness of your image. This is known as dot gain.

On newsprint, this spread is significant because the paper is so soft (see Figure 5-7). The ink easily spreads out through the fibers. So, if one of the dots that makes up your photo has a value of 60 percent, it will become nearly a 70-percent dot—under the best conditions, assuming no dot gain. A 10- or 15-percent gain is the best you can hope for. With poor printing, it can be much worse. Printing on better paper—coated paper—with heat-set presses will reduce degradation of the image. But the same variables apply.

Figure 5-7
The broadest range of lights and darks makes for the best printing on newsprint

There is software help available. Some programs, including Aldus PrePrint, have controls for dot gain and other paper/press compensations.

Creating
Duotones

In the early days of printing with colored ink, designers realized they could achieve some of the richness of an original photographic print by putting down a solid tint block and printing the picture on top of it—called a duograph. But the highlights were thus filled in, and the overall contrast and tonal range of a picture reduced.

With duotones, two halftones are adjusted so the second color carries a particular tonal range, usually the mid range and shadow, leaving the highlights white for full depth. The screen angles for each color layer are adjusted, as in four-color printing. (For a duotone example, see this chapter's color section.)

When you add another color behind the black in a picture, the black gets richer. The shadows become deeper because you are using literally more ink. Orange as the second color can create beautiful sepia tones. Blue can give a steely quality. Warm gray can get closer to a good black-and-white photo print. And some printers actually use two blacks—one to carry shadow detail and the other to reproduce highlight detail.

In desktop publishing there are no simple provisions for duotones, but it can be tried by taking two of the plates from a four-color separation, and printing one in a custom color. Or, you can place the image on two separate pages, applying a different screen frequency and angle to each image, then printing out the pages, one as the black plate and one as the color plate.

With the new color software, Adobe Photoshop or Letraset Color Studio, try some duotone experiments. If you're planning a periodical, and setting up a regular schedule with suppliers, you have the chance to learn how a proof turns out on the final printed page, under repeatable conditions. This is how experience is built, and experience is the only way to learn about color printing, desktop or factory-sized.

Color Photos on the Desktop

Scanning and stripping color photos (or any continuous-tone image) is still at the frontier of DTP technology. Attempting anything more than color layouts and presentation proofs has been very daunting.

Now, however, several manufacturers and software developers are rushing to develop complete color systems based on Adobe System's PostScript page-description language and standard computer platforms. (For a full discussion, see Chapter 7, "Bits and Bolts: Desktop Systems.") The interest from publishers is intense, and it is all because of the cost. A complete PostScript color system can be assembled for as little as $200,000—something like ten percent of a more traditional high-end system. Swallowing hard, publishers are risking quality problems—just in order to have color at all.

Some Color Basics

Printing photos in full color requires that an image be separated into its four process color components: CMYK. Software (or in the old days, a big camera) essentially filters out three colors at a time—leaving one for each separation. The same halftone screens that make black-and-white pictures in every newspaper (whether created physically, with glass or acetate, or digitally by a computer) are put to work screening each color into little dots; the bigger the dot, the darker the color. At, say, 100 percent blue, the dots are big enough to bleed together and fill the area. At, say, 30 percent, the dots are too small to touch one another—the resulting space between them lessening the color saturation.

The fineness, or resolution, of the picture is determined by the frequency of the dots, expressed in dots per inch (dpi) or lines of lines per inch (lpi). In a typical halftone, you might get a resolution of 60 lpi, or a 60-line screen (see Figure 5-8). Magazine color is usually made with a 133-line screen. The highest quality color sometimes uses 200 lines or more, but again, as mentioned above, it is easier to control the color with fewer dots. Often a 200-line color image will seem flatter than one screened at 133 lpi.

After screening, each color layer is overprinted on the press. The inks are transparent, so they blend to create the impression of the original picture.

Future Desktop Photo Technology

Desktop photo development is going to be intertwined with advances in digital photography. The first example of this technology was at

Figure 5-8
Macintosh
halftone

President Bush's inauguration in 1989. While Mr. Bush was being sworn in, an Associated Press photographer used a digital camera to take a picture and transmit it over the wire seconds later. It was like television—literally "still video"—except that the picture was picked up by print editors and run in newspapers all over the country. Later in the day, Associated Press followed up with conventionally produced pictures, but many papers went with the first shot. The quality was good enough to run—and make the next edition.

On the desktop level, there are simple Sure-Shot-like still video cameras on the market (priced at around $1,000) from Sony and Canon, that are great for small color pictures, at the quality level of, say, newsletters. Better quality can be bought from the same companies' professional SV cameras that cost around $10,000. High-definition television will give more detail in these live scans. Film will eventually go the way of zinc engravings for halftones. And quite soon afternoon newspapers will be out before Dan Rather can bring you the story with the same pictures.

Designing on the Screen

At first, it is cumbersome to do photo layouts on a DTP program. But if you have a decent (flatbed) scanner, and a good-sized monitor (at least a 16-inch), eventually you may find it preferable to conventional methods. A large photo book is hard to do on a PC, and photo editing is still easier off the system (if only to avoid all the scanning). But the design of normal magazine articles, a combination of text and pictures, is what desktop publishing was invented for. The most important feature is the ability to size and resize, over and over, up and down, until you're happy with a photo. When designing by hand, you continually have to get up and go to a copy machine which reduces or enlarges, or send out for a photostat. If you decide to change the size, you have to start over. But with DTP, you just push some buttons. This saves time and money.

If you have a good idea of how you want to proceed (perhaps after making a thumbnail sketch), then you can simply import the TIFF files, (TIFF is generally the most flexible format for gray scales and color), and place them on the page, making some minor adjustments to perfect it.

But, photo layout is obviously more difficult the larger the page, and the more pictures involved. The analog method was to simply lay the pictures out on a table, size the pictures to fit your gird, get some preliminary stats made, and start messing around with them. With desktop publishing you can do much the same thing. After scanning the halftones, make a separate file that I call a catalogue. Put all the scans into the catalogue at a convenient size, getting six or eight on a page. (Some programs, like Ventura Publisher, do not allow you to open more than one file at a time, so put the pictures on an extra page at the beginning or end of your chapter or document.)

Then copy and paste the pictures onto the appropriate page in your layout. From there, it is a simple matter to adjust the size. Look at the pictures in relation to each other. Find a logical sequence of events, or a connection between the forms and subjects in the photos, rather than a random geometric pattern. The pictures should tell a story.

Don't simply make a bunch of rectangles and fill them in with pictures. Especially in QuarkXPress and Ventura Publisher, which are based on rectangular forms, this may be an enticing, easy way out.

Captions

As a general rule of thumb, always put a caption under a photo. People automatically look for captions there. Putting them on top of photos doesn't work as well. And never run text in interior-page photos. This is a matter of taste, but I've always preferred a rather church-state separation. Put the heads on the white paper—in inside pages. In the old days it was not a trivial thing to superimpose type and illustration. You had to think about it, and the engraver had to spend some extra time. And so as a printing tradition, the pictures were usually separate. With all photo layouts, simpler is better.

The Cover

The most important page of any publication is the cover. If the cover is attractive and suggests interesting content within, people will pick up the publication and take a look inside. If not, it may sit there forever, unopened.

With the pressure to get, say, 50 pages into a magazine, designers sometimes forget how important the cover is. Given two weeks to get the work done, the designer will try to do five pages a day, and then rush to finish the cover in the last few minutes. A wiser use of time is to spend a full week on the cover—half the allotted time—and then work double-time on the inside pages.

The Cover Image

To get attention, there is no better way than to use a picture on the cover. Pictures work faster (and color pictures work faster than black-and-white) to attract the eyes of the readers, and to quickly convey information. And the bigger the picture, the better the response.

People and Props

People are more interested in people than anything else. This is not, of course, an original thought, and if you look around at the covers of best-selling magazines, you see people on almost every one of them.

If you can use a person on the cover, the reader on the newsstand has an immediate link. The subject of a cover story may be new, or intimidating—or, worse, heretofore uninteresting. But if there is a human being involved, the subject is easier to relate to.

The conventional wisdom in consumer magazine circulation departments is put a recognizable celebrity on the cover, and it will sell. It is not enough, however, just to put, say, Tom Cruise, on the cover—it has to look like Tom Cruise.

But, most publishers are not putting out *People* magazine, and a celebrity may not be a logical option.

For example, with *Desktop* magazine (see Figure 6-1 and Chapter 12, "*Desktop* on the Desktop"), you'll notice there are people on the cover, even though no one has ever heard of them. On the first issue there was an executive from Dun & Bradstreet and in the second issue, a vice president of MCI Communications. The editors were not deluding themselves that readers would know these cover "personalities." The idea was to present a success story—someone who has benefited from desktop publishing—as a way to a point of access for readers. We wanted to say, "You can do this, too." In any case we knew we did not want to do "graphic" covers, with meaningless geometric shapes and confusing symbols. And, since the market for *Desktop* is the business DTP user who may or may not be a computer enthusiast and a publication expert, we wanted to avoid the strangely somber back-lit photos of computers seen on most of the big PC magazines.

The notion of using people can work for any magazine. At *Pig and Cow Barn Monthly,* for example, you can show a real live contractor in front of a barn. The person fosters a better link between the reader and the subject than a simple picture of the barn, or just a big headline.

The context is important if the personality is not well known to the audience. *Business Week* could attract readers with a good photo of Carl Icahn—by himself. But on the cover of *Newsweek,* it would be intelligent to have a TWA airplane in the background somewhere, so readers would think, "Oh, yeah, this is the guy who controls the airline."

Figure 6-1
Desktop

Putting an anonymous person alone on your cover just won't do it, however. As in the case of *Pig and Cow Barn Monthly,* the photographer needs to include a picture of a barn with the contractor, so that it is semirelevant. It never hurts to remind your photographer that you are looking for a cover shot that tells a story involving this person. Tell him you want a person and a prop. The context and the prop give meaning to the picture of the person. (See Figure 6-2.)

Figure 6-2
New York

In the 1950s, every cover of *Time* magazine was a realist portrait with some kind of contextual backdrop, often painted by Artzybasheff. The portraits were slightly stylized and the icons in the background would define the issue—like a big globe for a statesman, or belching smokestacks for an industrialist.

If you can't find a success story, or an appropriate representative to introduce the cover subject, then try a more generic person. Any farmer would work in the case of *Pig and Cow Barn Monthly*. Now, of course, you can have real problems photographing normal human beings. They tend to be shorter, fatter, older, and balder than the people we see delivering TV news. They may stand rather stiffly in front of the camera, and sweat a little before their portrait is taken, and the result may drive people away, rather than attracting them to your magazine.

This is the time to start thinking about hiring a model. Working with your photographer, go through the books of local agencies. For a few hundred dollars, you can hire someone who looks like an executive (or a pig farmer), and is photogenic to boot. It is surprising that models are not all young plastic studs ready to pose for Calvin Klein underwear ads. There are women who have the authority and poise of big-time business leaders, and men who simply look real.

As with other photo assignments, rely on your photographer to mastermind the shoot. Spell out clearly what you want, and if you like, make some sketches. But it is usually not necessary for an art director to supervise the photo session, and sometimes disastrous. A good portrait is the result of the relationship between the photographer and the subject, and this relationship is not necessarily improved by someone off to the side kibitzing and waving his or her arms.

Alternative Covers

Still, there are some magazines where a photo of any kind won't work. Right now there is a fad in trade publications for graphic covers where color and quirkiness are more important than relevance. A recent DTP magazine featured a Monopoly game board on its cover—not a particularly original concept. But, it was colorful.

Others are turning to information graphics—bar graphs and fever lines—that are quickly produced on PCs and can be very effective if the chart shows a dramatic new trend. More often, these charts are so much eyewash, or when they get too complicated, more like eye surgery.

Similarly, an infrequent all-type cover (see Figure 6-3) might have been interesting five or 10 years ago. But now, so many people are doing them—big paragraphs of type which fill the cover—that it's become just another generic option.

Figure 6-3
New West

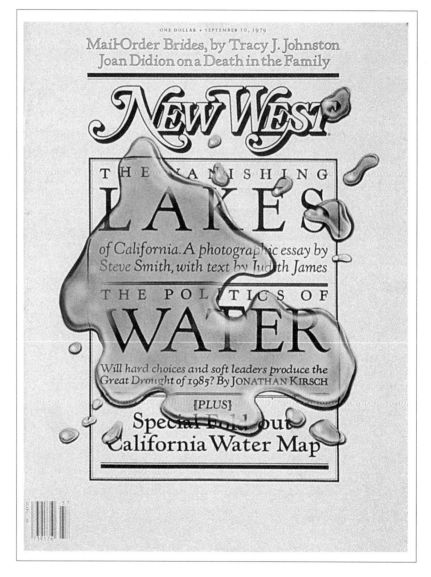

Recently, photo-illustrations have been showing up on covers again. These are ideas that normally would be handled as a painting—something that does not exist for you to send a photographer out to shoot. Figure 6-4 shows an example. In the 1960s, this was a hot idea. *Esquire* ran delightful covers, building elaborate sets or employing squads of retouching artists.

New York magazine ran a cover for a story called "Living in Tight Spaces"—about the apartment squeeze. Two models crouched in a tiny living room—all put together in the photographer's studio.

Newsweek recently ran a cover story on the best U.S. cities to live in. They could have run a photo of one of the cities, but this wouldn't have communicated the point of the article. So they constructed a photo illustration. Their art department built a sign post with arrows for each of the cities, and then they shot a picture of it. It was obviously contrived, but it got the point across. The focus was the names on the sign boards, so it *was* essentially a type cover, with a twist.

With computers, we are beginning to see a new kind of retouching, where photographs are so heavily altered that they might as well be illustrations. We are seeing just the beginning of a whole new medium. The results are so effective that it is hard to tell what is "real" anymore. Journalism professors are filled with consternation that these new techniques will be used to dupe the reader, and of course, there are troublesome ethical issues for newspapers here. And there are copyright questions for all of us. You simply cannot use a photograph as the basis of a computer illustration (done, for instance, on Letraset's ImageStudio) without obtaining permission.

In the 1950s, all covers would have been illustrations. Sadly, illustration has lost much of its currency, mainly because editors prefer photos. They are under the impression that photographs are more credible, more immediate than drawings and paintings.

This is a self-fulfilling pronouncement. If readers see only photographs, they get used to them, and people tend to like what they are familiar with. Meanwhile, there is a smaller market for illustrations, and fewer artists can stay in the business—so art directors have a harder time finding good artists.

Figure 6-4
Photo illustration

I think readers still like illustrations. They like the idea that the cover of this book was painted, handmade, specifically for this. It's an original. It's art.

The bottom line is that doing a good cover is difficult and takes time—no matter which technique you choose. It is still possible to design a great type cover even though now the idea is slightly overused. It takes just as long and just as much effort to do a good type cover as it does to do a good photographic cover. The big mistake is deciding on a type or graphic cover as an excuse, as a last resort. A type cover never works well when it's the last resort—used to make up for a lack of good photos or illustrations. Think ahead and make contingency plans. Whatever your plans for the cover, always have a backup.

Poster Principle

Think of the cover by itself. It's just like the dust jacket of a book, which is often designed by a different person than the rest of the book and produced in a more urgent style, with bolder type and a compelling title treatment. The whole point of a cover is to attract readers' attention, to tell them what's inside, and to get them interested in it. In America, it's all marketing.

Once you accept this, it's obvious that it's not essential for the cover to have any of the trappings of the inside—the margins, the typeface, the paper. The cover can be an entirely different object. It may or may not be graphically related to the inside matter.

Think about the cover as a poster. Both covers and posters have to attract attention quickly, offer quick information, and most importantly, sell. A poster that doesn't use a single strong image, like many art museum posters today, doesn't attract any attention—though it may be fun to pore over. Remember this when you think of cover images. Keep it simple, bold, and direct.

Using a big photo of a person fits this poster concept. The more you reduce the size of the person on your cover, the more you lose the poster quality. The big consumer magazines have all gone to close-ups—just the face. A full-standing figure is just too small. The big consumer magazines go for eyes, and they try to get the eyes as close to the top of the cover as possible. Take a look at *Elle* magazine, which has been running beautiful, sharp, and sexy covers. It is the eyes and the face that count, that reach out and demand attention.

What Is Worthy of a Cover?

If you liked "Look at the picture before cropping the picture," here is another dictum.

> ## *If you don't have a cover image, you don't have a cover story.*

These words were first uttered by A.M. Rosenthal, the legendary editor of *The New York Times.* Do not be deceived by the disarming simplicity of the idea. It seems obvious, but it escapes most magazine editors. The newsstands are plastered with covers that don't make much sense, in part because the story chosen as the cover subject does not translate well into a visual idea.

The story you put on the cover must be made into a poster. If you can't think of a quick, visual way to relay the point of the story, it should not be on the cover. In other words, you have to be prepared to change the story on the cover if there is no picture that goes with it. Think about cover images before accepting or deciding on a cover story. Some stories are extremely difficult to illustrate, which leads the designer to a hopeless graphic or type cover when he or she should be looking for another cover story. If there is no person to represent a story, and no metaphorical illustration to commission, pick another story. Once again, if there is no image for a story, then it is not a cover story.

Bear in mind that cover placement is not a comment on the ultimate quality or importance of the story, only on its preeminent appeal. Many editors are unwilling to understand this. Literal-minded as only editors can be, they will insist, "This is my most important story." Or, "But think what we paid for this!"

It is worth repeating: always have a backup, a contingency cover. And do some reconnoitering before committing to the cover subject. If you are going after a success story, say the most productive farmer in Iowa, try to get a photograph of the subject before you make a photo assignment. Then you and the photographer can think about the options for a cover image. Always be prepared with at least one or two other farmers in case the pictures get lost, or it turns out that the first guy looks mean and ugly. If it rains that day, you don't get wet. Keep your options open for the cover. You need to have a number of different stories with a number of different images for each of them.

Cover Forms and Elements

Many Sunday magazines are not sold by themselves. They don't have separate subscriptions, yet they often adhere to basic cover forms so readers associate them with the popular newsstand magazines. (*Parade* is good example.) Newsstand magazine covers have the biggest circulation, and thus set the forms. Working within the newsstand conventions can help your cover communicate more quickly to readers.

Though the cover image usually illustrates only one article, the cover as a whole must stand for the magazine. You want to reflect the personality of the whole magazine. Some of this weight is carried by the logo and general style of the cover elements. Content in the rest of the magazine can be covered in secondary headlines.

This presents a conflict. If you want your cover to be poster-like, then you want to use fewer headlines, which diffuse the central image—unless of course, you are deliberately trying to evoke a circus poster or nineteenth century playbill with the headlines stacked up. *Harper's* and *Reader's Digest* both have very old cover forms which stack headlines, like the contents page of a book. It can occasionally be applied to other magazines.

Once at *Rolling Stone* (see Figure 6-5), I used the playbill idea in an attempt to enliven an incredibly bland picture. I used part of the cover

Figure 6-5
Rolling Stone

to create a miniature Victorian theater poster using different typefaces and colors for the stacked headlines.

More cover lines are sometimes better than fewer. They add urgency and give a clue about the articles not related to the cover image. Use between two and five. If you have more than five, they get too small and start competing with each other. If you use only one, you exclude readers who may not be interested in the one cover story. The definition of *magazine* is *storehouse*. It's supposed to include a lot of different things, not just one—that would be a book. Some effort, of course, is needed to make the headlines work together. Confusion results if each headline is structured differently—one long, one short, one with a kicker, one with a subhead.

The best-funded magazines hire specialists to work on the cover headlines. On most publications, cover lines are often written in committee, and sometimes some of the brilliant ideas are rejected at the beginning. Good writing cannot be done by committee, but a certain amount of brainstorming can be useful. (In headline-writing sessions, never reject any idea instantly. The most stupid suggestion can trigger a brilliant line.) One person must make the final call and trust his or her instincts rather than the immediate consensus.

When you sit down to write these cover lines watch out for labels. Don't write "Food Issue," when you can describe something meaningful about the contents, like "Beach Barbecue Bonanza." Often the slug used internally for a story finds its way to the cover of the magazine. The editors and artists have always called it the "Food Issue," and they forget there is no information and certainly no energy in the name. Specifically, it is good to adopt the old newspaper headline rule to use verbs in headlines. The cover is your ad. Tell the reader what to do instead of presenting flat information.

Stickers and Starbursts

Newsstand magazine ideas, like little stickers that say, "Special Issue" seem slightly cheesy and consumery, but can be used effectively for unrelated purposes on other kinds of publications. These devices give some of that newsstand urgency, dazzle, or cheapness.

Experienced magazine marketers, will tell you that certain labels are actually very effective sales tools when used in conjunction with descriptive cover headlines. "Special Collectors' Edition," or just plain "Collectors' Edition" seems to sell.

Desktop (see Chapter 12, "*Desktop* on the Desktop,") put "Special Première Issue" on its first issue. "Première" is used often, even if a magazine has been around for a while and just wants to inaugurate a new section of the same old magazine. *Memories,* a nostalgia magazine started in 1988, used "Inaugural," "Première," and "Charter" as labels on each of their first three issues.

Stickers and starbursts can contain a lot of information, they don't compete with the other headlines, and they use only a small amount of space. Even small stickers (like the one on the issue of *Smart* (See Chapter 9, "*Smart*") that read, "Absolutely nothing about Woodstock in this issue") can draw the readers in and make them pick up the magazine. These work best when they are done in contrasting colors and are slightly tilted. You can see the wide variety of these devices at your local newsstand.

Watch out for doing the same cover design every issue. It's like the old saying that you don't bump into your own living room furniture when you're walking around at night. You want readers to feel comfortable, but with no sense of déjà vu. *Newsweek* uses a yellow sticker above its logo every week. It's gotten to the point where it seems like part of the logo. I suspect no one reads it anymore.

DTP and Covers

Though the DTP process for covers is the same as for other pages, it is especially useful because the cover is so important. You can manipulate and create proofs quickly, which means you have the luxury of trying many more cover possibilities.

If you have a big screen and you are using color scans, you can quickly mock up a cover on the screen. Then it is a simple matter of trying different colors, typefaces, and treatments. Before you even shoot out a proof, you can get a second opinion of the image on the screen. The covers at *Smart* (see Chapter 9, "*Smart*") were done almost entirely on the screen. In the case of the Keith Richards cover shown in Figure 6-6, compared to three other colors we looked at on the screen, the four-color separation of a black-and-white original won out.

After experimenting at the screen stage, you can make color proofs on the laser printer and see a number of variations side by side. To an old timer, it is a luxury to be able to line up eight cover variations in a matter of minutes, compared to mocking up all the covers by hand. When you finally decide on a cover, no further

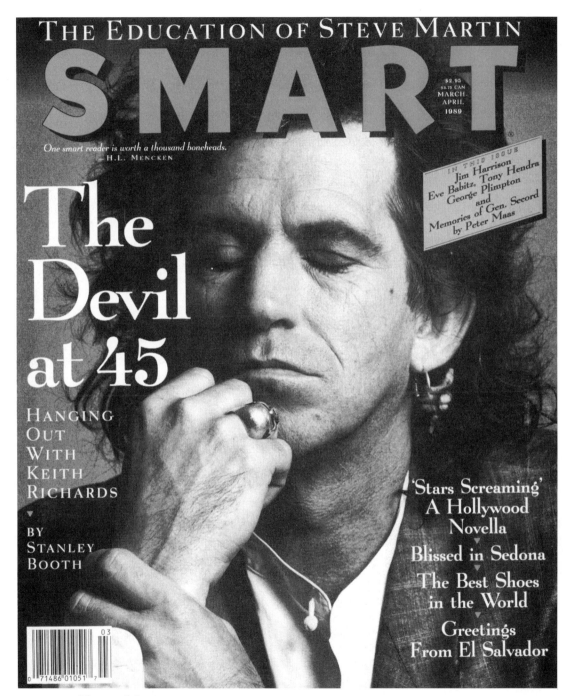

Figure 6-6
Smart

work is needed. You simply save it as final output and it's off to the printer. Mercy.

Typically, the cover is almost always done in a hurry, although it may have been planned since the beginning. A better picture is always "on the way," and the cover lines "aren't quite right." With the *Smart* cover mentioned above, we started with the cover line, "The Devil at 45," about Keith Richards, and then we had grave second thoughts about it as too much of a downer. We also thought Keith wouldn't talk to us when the Rolling Stones go back on tour because it would get him angry. Finally, we realized he would probably like it, and that it was a vastly better headline than anything else we could write. Of course, all of this was going on during production of the rest of the magazine. We did on-screen experimenting with the cover before we did anything else, but it was the last page printed.

Logo à Go Go

Logos aren't headlines. And just as any spelling of any word starts looking strange if you stare at it too long, the letters in any title start looking awkward if you scrutinize too much. Obviously, a logo should withstand much scrutiny, but the letter forms in any typeface were designed for average combinations, and aren't guaranteed to work perfectly together in any single word. With a logo, you are looking for a relationship between the letters, an identity for the whole unit. Just as the cover is separate from the magazine, the logo is independent from the magazine's typography. It does not have to be, and perhaps should not be, set in the same typeface as the rest of the magazine, or even the rest of the cover. It stands out on its own.

The word *logo* (from the Greek *logos,* for *word*) comes from the typographical term for letters that have been joined together. In the early days of printing, anytime a word was cast as a slug, it was called a logotype. They were made of metal, like type, but later engraved zinc cuts were used.

With DTP you can customize combinations of letters using one of the drawing programs like Adobe Illustrator or Aldus FreeHand. These programs allow you to modify and manipulate any image, including type. (The programs Altsys Metamorphosis on the Mac or Corel Draw on the PC can give you a head start; they create outlines from PostScript Type I fonts.)

Take the *Smart* logo as an example (see Figures 6-7a and 6-7b). It started out as a simple typeface, Bernhard Gothic. We scanned in the letters and brought them into Adobe Illustrator, outlining each letter. Illustrator then quickly added the stroke desired, and the drop shadow took a few more seconds. A detailed discussion of *Smart's* design can be found in Chapter 9, "*Smart.*"

Figure 6-7a
Creating the *Smart*
logo's drop shadow

I arranged the necessary letters in a rough

I scanned the rough as black-and-white line art, outlined it with Adobe Illustrator's Autotrace, and accurately spaced the letters and aligned them to the baseline

I copied the logo, filled it with black, and moved it below the face to complete the drop shadow

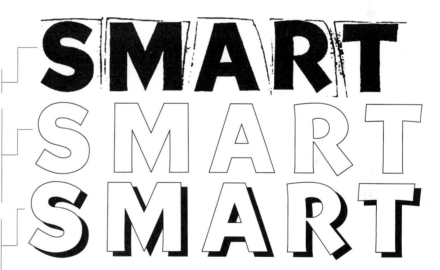

In the old days, getting a sharp outline on type used to be a nightmare, because the process was photographic, and inevitably, the sharp corners were rounded in film duplication. Now, you tell Illustrator how sharp you want those corners to be.

If you want a stroke or outline around type, the face of the letter should always be reversed out. Illustrator and FreeHand automatically build a stroke both ways on an outline—inside and outside. This erodes the letter form, thinning out the thin lines of the type. The solution is to first stroke the type as much as you wish, in whatever color you like. I usually start with black. (If you want a 1-point outline, stroke it 2 points, since only half of the stroke is built up outside the original shape.) Then make a copy of the type, remove the stroke and paint it white or any other contrasting color, and place it directly on top. Thus, your 2-point stroke will become a 1-point stroke and it will be built only on the outside.

Figure 6-7b
Creating the *Smart* logo's customized letter shapes

We felt the logo looked too finished, too perfect, so we added slight curves to the "R" and the "T" to make it look more hand-drawn

Once you have built the outline, then it's easy to make a black version, put it behind, and slip it at a 45-degree angle. (See Figure 6-8.) Normally, the drop shadow is slipped to the right and the bottom. In Adobe Illustrator, lines can be constrained to horizontal, vertical, or 45 degrees, so it is a fairly simply matter to connect the shadow to original type, if you wish.

Using a scanner and the features on the drawing programs allow you to manipulate logos in ways that were previously unheard of. For example, a tabloid newspaper in San José, California created a new section called "Taste," and wanted a new, definitive logo for it. I thought of using their typeface, Schneidler, in the Italic to look like an invitation, but this was too obvious. They wanted something that was less formal.

Figure 6-8
The true drop shadow

When you stroke a letter using any of the desktop stroking tools, it erodes the original form (note serifs).

To avoid this and maintain the integrity of the type, place a copy of the original letter filled in white over the original, and a true drop shadow results

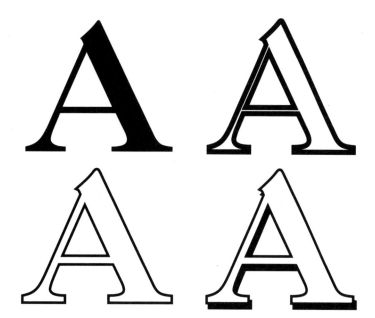

So, I persuaded a calligrapher to quickly write out the word in a style similar to Schneidler, then scanned this in and worked with it on the screen. I used Adobe Illustrator's autotrace tool to take the hand-lettering and bring it into the system. Then it was a simple matter to manipulate the new logo with fades, strokes, outlines, drop shadows, dots, or patterns.

Before DTP, this type of maneuver would have required much more time and effort. In this case, the essential talent of the lettering artist was captured, but we did not have to pay him for all the variations and special effects. (In an even tighter budget, I would have simply traced the type myself in pencil, and then scanned it in.)

As with every other aspect of desktop publishing, the benefits of speed and low cost are only part of the story. Creating logos electronically gives you any number of options very quickly. Your immediate response to these options may lead you to creative solutions you never would have found in any other way.

Bits and Bolts: Desktop Systems

The worst thing about buying a desktop-publishing system is that it seems to be rendered obsolete by the simple act of purchase. As soon as you've got it home and hooked it up, they've brought out a new version, a sexier rival system, or something faster and, sadly, cheaper.

This stalls most of us for weeks or months, as we try to figure out what has the best chance of surviving: PC or Mac, PageMaker or QuarkXPress, and so forth. We all hate to think that today's system is tomorrow's doorstop.

You simply have to make your decisions based on the best information you have available to you today—and plunge right in. The only question to answer is: do you do enough publishing to justify the expense. If the answer is yes, take the plunge. Of course, new options will continue to emerge. Five years down the road, there will be choices that don't even cross our minds now.

If you cannot cost-justify all the hardware and software, think about wading in rather than plunging in. A word-processing solution alone may be more affordable. With a low-cost PC-clone and good text software you can format simple documents. Then when you want to scan in pictures and make a layout, you can go to a local DTP service bureau and rent time on a bigger system. Most of us can't afford to buy into everything at once. But if you do take a smaller step, it is important to plan how your system fits into the full scheme of desktop publishing. For example, if you plan to use a Macintosh for layout down the road, then it may be wise to buy a low-end Mac (an SE, or a used Mac II) to get started.

One note of reassurance: it is hard to make a big mistake if you go with the best-selling, off-the-shelf DTP solutions. Whether you choose Macintosh or IBM for hardware, or PageMaker, Ventura, QuarkXPress, or DesignStudio for page-design software, you will be able to get the job done.

Hardware Platforms: Hard Choices?

The first big question when you're starting from scratch with desktop publishing is which platform—which basic hardware—should you choose. There is an array of "solutions" (as the salespeople would say), ranging from the ubiquitous Macs and IBM-compatibles, to the impressive Amiga and high-end workstations like NeXT or Sun.

Again, it is not a bad idea to take a good look at what everyone else is buying, and it seems that 99 percent of all desktop publishing is done on either IBMs or Macs. There is a kind of black-hole theory in platforms: once the installed base reaches a critical mass, it attracts vastly greater software development. With some 15,000,000 IBM-compatibles in the United States and nearly 2,000,000 Macintoshes, most of the peripherals (scanners, monitors, printers, etc.) used for DTP are made for one of these two platforms.

The question is which one should you choose? If you work for a big company, corporate policy may make up your mind for you. In order to make compatible purchases, most large organizations have a policy on brands and dealers. Not so long ago, the conclusion was invariably IBM. Corporate information systems departments felt comfortable with "Big Blue," and there were many struggles with unruly employees who wanted to bring in something else.

The fast development of desktop publishing has spurred improvements in hardware and in the basic operation systems that make the machines work. The friendly graphic interface of the Mac—the way the screen looks like a desk top, complete with folders and documents that you can move around, plus the rough wysiwyg (what-you-see-is-what-you-get) of the screen—has been enormously successful, and has been adapted by Microsoft Windows and OS/2 to run on IBM-compatibles.

Another essential ingredient of the Macintosh is Apple's effort to get the software developers to follow the same rules in adapting the interface. The little buttons and dialog boxes are all alike, from program to program. The mouse and the menus work the same way, and even the keyboard short cuts (like typing Command-P for print) are the same on the majority of Mac software. This consistency has made it even easier for people to learn new programs on the Mac. And once again, Microsoft is endeavoring, with Windows 3.0 and OS/2, to persuade developers to use similar tools, and create a consistent user environment.

While the IBM world has moved toward the look and feel of Macintosh interface standards, Apple has moved toward IBM in the area of hardware design. Once a cute little table-top unit with a built-in screen, Macintosh now is a simple gray box, in appearance much like an IBM PC. The monitor and other peripherals are added on by sticking their boards into slots inside the computer. The Mac also supports a number of printers—made by companies other than Apple.

The variety and quality of these peripherals, from color monitors to modems, are largely equivalent in either arena, Mac or IBM. And as networks become more sophisticated, it is increasingly practical to use both systems together, getting each to do what it does best. The *New York Daily News*, for example, is planning to use IBM-compatible PCs for text entry and editing, Macintoshes for page layout, and Digital Vax computers to manage the whole thing.

If you are the one making the decision, the common sense approach is to make a list of the things you want to be able to do with the system, then go to dealers and see how much of your requirements each piece of software can meet. Once you've done that, buy the hardware your favorite software runs on.

Macintosh A number of people take credit for the idea of the personal computer, the PC. But it is clear that Steve Jobs and the Apple Macintosh paved the way for desktop publishing. Paul Brainerd of Aldus created the PageMaker program in the first years Macintosh was on the market, creating the ideal application for the machine. (Brainerd usually gets the credit for coining the phrase *desktop publishing.* While perhaps not entirely apt, the phrase stuck.)

The graphic interface of the Mac is a wonderful thing. It is really cute, so cute that Apple marketers have been hard pressed to explain to business people that the Mac is for work, and not a toy. But the toy-like quality of the screen goes a long way toward reassuring people that this computer is not so scary, that it is not going to be so hard to learn—and that it might even be fun. Infuriating as it is to management information systems (MIS) managers, the look is the secret of the Mac. (See Figure 7-1.)

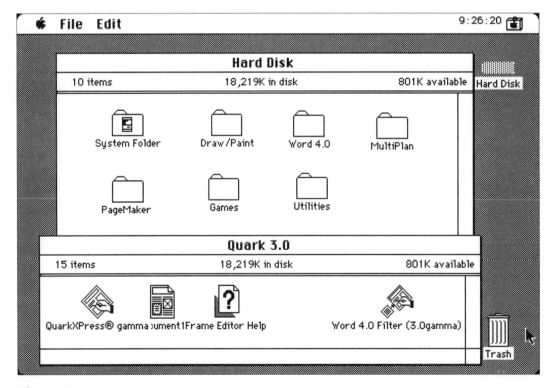

Figure 7-1
The famous Mac screen interface

The design elements of this user interface are surprisingly enduring. The Chicago typeface, used as the main system font on the screen, is sturdy and legible. The icons, while cute, do not get tiresome. The whole interface carried very well into color, and onto larger monitors. Susan Kare and the other creators of the Mac look came up with one of the most important designs in our lifetime. And while it has been copied by other computer designers, not one has yet equalled it, never mind improved on it.

The other enticing feature about working on the Macintosh is that all of the programs look and work in approximately the same way, due to the Apple policy described earlier. This makes it easier to learn, and to train people.

Thus, the user interface is a persuasive argument to go with Macintosh. The same attraction worked for the software engineers, and the result is a full array of programs for word processing, electronic mail, illustration and drawing, photo scanning and retouching, and page layout. Now there is wide enough choice of software, all working on the same platform, to satisfy the demands of professional designers.

But, the Mac is not the only solution, and all this is not to say that you shouldn't bother getting into desktop publishing if you are restricted to a PC, or that you should go out and buy a Macintosh if you already have a PC.

IBM and the Compatibles

The good news about PCs is that they are made by more than one company. IBM licensed their system to all comers, creating competition for performance and price.

And from the beginning, the PCs have been designed as components, like a stereo system. The monitor is separate and the PC is expandable, with extra slots on the mother board to connect a mouse, a monitor, a scanner.

Color is a problem, however. To get a PC to approach the color you find built into a Mac IIci, you need to buy something like the AT&T Targa board, which costs about $2,000. And even then, there's no guarantee that your software will work with that board.

Still, one of the most compelling arguments for the PC is that there are so many of them. Large companies tend to have comprehensive purchasing policies for computers (and everything else). The policy is usually set by the corporate data processing or management information systems department, which traditionally has chosen IBM. With Big Blue behind the concept, there is a large installed base of PCs around the country. It is much more likely that a company will have PCs than Macs.

The clinching argument for many is that PCs are simply cheaper than Macs.

But the cost of hardware is only part of the cost of desktop publishing. The cost of learning how to use it can be more expensive in the long run than anything else. This brings us back to the user interface, which has been the main drawback of PCs. It all has to do with the underlying operating system.

DOS and GEM

For what seems like forever, the IBM PC (and compatibles) has run on a simple character-based, code-driven operating system, DOS. Each software developer cooked up a different user interface to make the program work. For users, this has resulted in a great variety of programs to choose from (as well as cheap clone hardware.) But the price we've paid is less continuity, and a steeper learning curve.

So, on the PC, every program has a different interface. No one is in charge, and you have to learn the vagaries of each piece of software. For example, pressing the Control key and "x" at the same time may give you different results in each of the programs. In one program it may erase whatever is selected on the screen, while in another it may simply repeat the last step. In the Macintosh world, these types of conventions are standardized.

As your office grows and takes on more employees, or takes on more peripherals for the DTP system, there will be more interfaces to learn and more difficulty training new people. The word processor, the scanner, the modem, the illustration software, the font mover, and the page-design program could each have a different interface. DOS is actually not that hard to understand, and it sorts files more effectively than the Mac, but the commands must all be memorized, and that is not what Mac fans call intuitive.

To deal with this problem, a graphic interface, or "shell," for DOS was developed by Digital Research. It was called GEM, for Graphical Environment Manager. A variety of programs could run with this interface—just like on the Macintosh. (In fact, it was so close that Apple's lawyers were able to force some changes in GEM's look and feel.) Taking advantage of this shell, Xerox Ventura Publisher became the first professional desktop-publishing program for the PC.

Microsoft answered GEM with a shell of its own, called Windows. Windows also looked a lot like the Mac interface, prompting a lawsuit from Apple. A number of software manufacturers released programs for Windows. Aldus PageMaker was one of those. However, PageMaker under Windows suffered from slow performance, (the result of Windows running on top of DOS, requiring intensive behind-the-scenes processing by the computer) and relatively complicated procedures for installing and using fonts. Ventura Publisher, the first to arrive on the PC scene, had taken the lead. Because of these factors, PageMaker for the PC, and DTP generally, never really caught on as strongly on PC hardware as it did on the Macintosh.

Windows 3.0

In the summer of 1990, Microsoft brought out a greatly improved Windows version 3.0, which narrowed the gap considerably. (See Figure 7-2.) Its publishing benefits include greater speed, a common user interface for different applications, multitasking among applications, easier font installation and the ability to access up to 16 MB of RAM memory (making it relatively easy to work on large or multiple documents and graphics). A handful of new and upgraded products is already taking advantage of these features (see the software section later in this chapter).

The result is a user interface that is approaching equal functionality with the Mac. Software developers rushed to "port" their product to the new Windows, and such programs as Adobe Illustrator, Page-Maker, Ventura, Microsoft Word and Microsoft Excel are available in roughly the same form on Windows and the Macintosh. (Xerox, meanwhile, has released a Macintosh version of Ventura Publisher.)

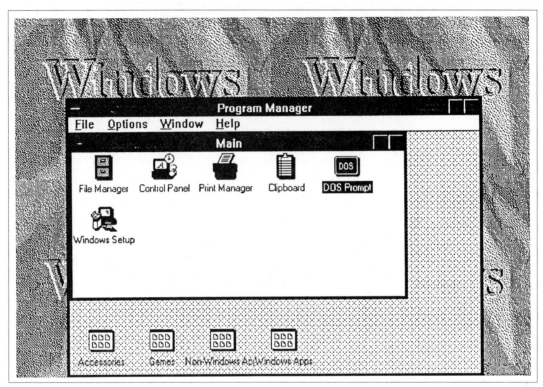

Figure 7-2
Windows 3.0

The advent of Windows 3.0, however, will not cause all developers to move to Windows, nor will it make everyone trash their DOS-based programs (or pay for the upgrade). So, you may find yourself (as I do) using a word-processing program like the original XyWrite, which is mouseless and code-driven, with GEM-based page-layout software and a Windows-based paint program. It's confusing at best.

OS/2
To make matters more complicated, IBM has been promoting a new, powerful operating system, OS/2, also developed by Microsoft and based on new hardware configurations. This operating system has a user interface called Presentation Manager, which is a lot like Windows, and thus, a lot like the Macintosh. As with the Mac,

developers must follow certain conventions to create a consistent user interface.

There has been a certain resistance to changing over to the new system, both from consumers and software developers. This is a chicken and egg problem. OS/2 requires 4 MB of RAM just to run effectively, requiring a major hardware upgrade for the vast majority of users. In lieu of a large ready-made user base, few OS/2 products have been brought to market thus far. Windows 3.0 offers a very similar solution to OS/2, while running on the old PC hardware, so people and software developers are sticking with that for now. With the weight of IBM behind it, helped by more powerful machines, OS/2 will eventually catch on. When it does, the two platforms will be virtually equal. Apple, since the 1987 introduction of the Macintosh II, has developed an expandable machine with the option of different monitors and other peripherals, while IBM has developed a consistent graphic interface.

Multitasking

Multitasking is a big buzzword these days. It refers to the ability of a computer user to run two or more programs simultaneously on a single machine. (For example, while working on a page, you could instantly change to a paint program to retouch a photograph while simultaneously receiving text files from a distant freelance writer over your modem.) Windows 3.0 and the Macintosh operating system called MultiFinder allow a limited form of multitasking, where applications share time on the computer's processor. OS/2 allows true multitasking on a deeper, more sophisticated level.

The granddaddy of multitasking is Unix, the operating system developed by AT&T, and until now used primarily in scientific and engineering workstations. Unix will run on IBM 386 machines, and one version, called A/UX, will run on all of the Mac II family of computers. In 1989 Steve Jobs' company, NeXT, and Sun Microsystems both introduced new Unix workstations, priced under $10,000. Sun has based its computers on the ultrafast and efficient reduced instruction set computer (RISC) chip, and a number of manufacturers, including Toshiba and Phillips, are ready to produce RISC workstations, with technology licensed from Sun—priced at around $7,000. Meanwhile, IBM has licensed the NeXT graphic interface, NeXTStep, as an alternative user interface to its own high-speed Unix platform, the RS2000.

These machines are still aimed at the engineering market, but several developers, including Lightspeed, Interleaf, Quark, and Frame, have announcd or released publishing programs for Unix, running on both Sun and NeXT platforms. (Frame has also released a version of its Unix DTP program, FrameMaker, for the Macintosh.) Their programs are not as rich with features as the leading DTP packages, but NeXT in particular is pushing for more publishing software. What has been a two-way fight may become a real horse race.

PostScript: The Building Block Language

Before making any hardware decisions, it is important to understand the idea of PostScript, which is the glue that holds together desktop publishing. PostScript is a page-description language (PDL) which controls high-end printers of all kinds, from desktop laser printers to high-resolution film imagesetters. Virtually all desktop-publishing software can "write" pages into PostScript. Thus PostScript is a kind of an Esperanto, permitting all the programs to communicate with all the printers.

One Standard for All Machines

PostScript was not the first PDL, or the last, but it is now the standard. The key is that PostScript is *machine-independent*.

In the digital world every output device (monitor or printer) produces a bitmap, a grid of little squares or pixels. An interpreter between your computer and the output device translates your screen images into the little pixels, arranged on a grid. This is called raster image processing, or RIPping.

The interpreter, or raster image processor (RIP), transforms gray-level files from scanned pictures into halftone dots of the appropriate sizes. It also renders outline fonts, whose shapes are described with mathematical formulas, into a bitmap as smoothly as the printer's resolution will allow.

Since the late 1970s at Xerox PARC, engineers had been working on a page-description language that would be machine-independent. That is, the final bitmaps would be interpreted by the screen or the printer at the resolution required. Xerox called this Interpress, but after a series of delays to make a product out of this idea, a number of developers, including John Warnock and Chuck Geske, started a new company and wrote their own PDL. The company was Adobe, and the product, PostScript. PostScript made its debut in 1984 with the announcement of the Apple LaserWriter.

In 1986, the first Linotype PostScript imagesetter was introduced, and suddenly it was possible to make a page on a Macintosh with PageMaker, proof it on the LaserWriter, and when everything was okay send a disk to the Linotronic 100, which would print the exact same file out with everything in place—but in high resolution, as high as 1,270 lines to the inch. Desktop publishing began to merge with professional publishing.

PostScript is what made the DTP jump from in-house publishing to a bigger arena where people who make their livings designing magazines would use it.

Machine independence applies to the computers themselves, as well as the printers. Mac and PC programs both can generate PostScript files, and both systems can be hooked up to a number of PostScript printers.

Moreover, DTP programs on both systems can import PostScript files from other programs. Logotypes and illustrations produced on Adobe Illustrator, for example, can be transferred from Mac to PC and vice versa.

Nearly any page described in PostScript can be printed on any printer with a PostScript interpreter, regardless of its resolution. (Some of the older RIPs have limited memory, and complicated pages can choke them.) Now you can proof a page on a 300-dpi laser printer, and once it is final, send the same file on to a 3000-dpi film printer, which is sharp enough for high-quality reproduction of color photographs.

The NeXT workstation was the first to take PostScript to the screen, called Display PostScript. Once the fonts were rendered with PostScript on the screen, it was a simple matter to send the page to the printer—without a PostScript interpreter. Finally, we got true wysiwyg (what-you-see-is-what-you-get).

Adobe Type Manager and PostScript Level 2

True wysiwyg became available for nearly everybody with the release of Adobe Type Manager (ATM) for the Mac in 1989, and for IBM-compatibles in 1990. ATM allows "on the fly" PostScript font rendering for screen display. It also makes possible smoother bitmapped output on printers like the Apple ImageWriter. Before ATM, you had to keep a set of bitmapped screen fonts for every point size you used. With ATM, all font display on the screen is rendered from the precise, mathematically-described outline fonts installed in your system.

Later in 1990 Adobe released specs for PostScript Level 2, the first major upgrade to the language, for Macs and for PCs running Windows 3.0. Adobe Type Manager has been integrated into the program. Level 2 also features improved color calibration among different display and output devices, better definition of screen angles for moiré-free halftones and better color separations (see the moiré discussion in Chapter 4, "Color Design, Printing, and Proofing"), built-in file compression techniques to help in saving and transporting large graphic files, and improved memory management for imaging and printing.

A level playing field for all software and hardware, PostScript continues to improve. It has to, for now it faces new challenges.

PostScript Challengers: PCL and TrueImage

The biggest contender is Hewlett-Packard, which has been using its own page-description language, PCL, to drive its low-cost LaserJet printers. There are many more LaserJets than PostScript laser printers. The H-P LaserJet III and subsequent models contain a new technique which gives noticeably sharper type at the same 300-dpi resolution. PCL now uses outline fonts, instead of a simple bitmap of a limited number of font sizes. (The format is not PostScript, but Agfa

Compugraphic's Intellifont.) In offices where typesetting quality is not needed, H-P and PCL is a low-budget alternative. (The company also offers a PostScript cartridge, so that ultimately you can move to PostScript and take advantage of its wide variety of publishing solutions.)

A more serious threat to PostScript is a new imaging model owned by Microsoft, called TrueImage. It works the same way as PostScript without quite being a clone. (That is, PostScript files won't run without conversion, as they will with clones such as the Hyphen RIP.)

The Apple Macintosh originally used an imaging model called QuickDraw, which ran the screen and screen-resolution (72-dpi) printer, the ImageWriter. Later Apple brought out the first PostScript laser printer, the LaserWriter, and suddenly there were two imaging models. QuickDraw still controlled the screen, but files were converted to PostScript to print out on the LaserWriter. This created some wysiwyg problems, but people put up with it. PostScript gained in popularity, and the desktop boom was on.

Meanwhile Apple executives began to feel their products were too closely associated with publishing to enter the bigger business market successfully, and they chafed at the royalties they kept paying to Adobe for PostScript. Some time in 1987, Apple quietly began developing a new font format, an extension of QuickDraw, with the code name Royal. At the same time, Microsoft was working on a new imaging model for OS/2.

In 1989 the two companies swapped technology. Microsoft, after much speculation within the industry, adopted the Royal font format—now called TrueType. Apple took TrueImage as its page-description language, and when System 7, the updated Macintosh operating system released in late 1990, is fully implemented, the computer will return to real wysiwyg—screens and printers will once again using the same imaging model. Significantly, the old bitmap fonts, stored in little suitcases, are gone, and typefaces are drawn on the screen using the same outlines as the printers use. (More on fonts, later.)

As this book was being printed, several imagesetter manufacturers were ready to announce high-resolution printers that work with TrueImage.

So now there is a real PostScript alternative, and there are many who feel that the competition can only help the user. However, those who have acquired large and expensive libraries of PostScript fonts and the machines to print them on did not greet the news with much enthusiasm. Adobe itself was dismayed. At an emotional session during the fall 1989 Seybold Conference, the semi-annual tribal gathering of the desktop industry, John Warnock announced that the company would publish its secret font formula, the key to its PostScript monopoly. A book with all the details to the encryption and hinting of the fonts (Adobe's secrets for high-quality font rendering at small point sizes) appeared in March 1990.

Presumably the company would not have made these moves, which really benefited desktop publishers, without the pressure from Apple. And, presumably, Apple would not have gone to the trouble to develop TrueType if Adobe had disclosed its font technology two years before it did.

IBM, after a long company-wide discussion, has endorsed PostScript, but will also support Microsoft's use of TrueImage and TrueType.

Apple and Adobe have since made up, and now Apple is expected to fully support both TrueType/TrueImage *and* ATM/PostScript in System 7 and future hardware releases.

If anything, the current result of this struggle has brought the IBM and Macintosh platforms closer in functionality. So perhaps an alternative to PostScript will help us in the long run. At this point there are very few fonts in TrueType format, and nothing like the array of output devices in black and white or color. It will take a couple of years for the new rival to catch up. If you are buying hardware now, it makes sense to go with the established standard, PostScript.

Monitors, Displays, and Screens

The heart of the DTP system is your computer, and the heart of the computer is the CPU. Hanging on the board are some memory chips which allow the CPU more room to think—basically short-term memory so that it doesn't have to go back to the disk drive with every operation.

In addition to the basic computer unit, a number of peripheral pieces of hardware are necessary for DTP—hard disks for storing data, the keyboard and the mouse for entering data, and the screen for a quick visual display of your work. (See Figure 7-3.)

Figure 7-3

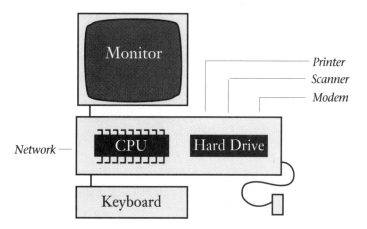

The original PC monitors were separate 13-inch, black-and-white screens, while the Mac had an even smaller 9-inch screen built in. These seem impossibly small to work on now. If you are planning to do a lot of work with desktop publishing you need at least a 16-inch monitor, and a 19-inch is better.

If you are content with black and white then you should consider a high-resolution screen like the Genius monitor for the PC or Sigma Design L-View for the Mac, which can switch to six different levels of resolution. Companies like Radius also manufacture large, monochrome two-page displays that are great for laying out facing pages.

If you are working with color, it is essential to have a color monitor, and buy the biggest you can afford. The current screen resolution (usually 72-lines per inch) is not fine enough to have anything bigger than 19 inches make sense; you have to stand back from the screen to get it into focus! There are no high-resolution color video monitors, short of the $80,000 Sony HDTV screen, used for high-end systems like the Quantel Graphic Paintbox.

The quality of the color is fine for a rough impression of pictures and color tint areas. But there is likely to be wide disparity between various color monitors, printers, and final film output. This is partly because there is yet no standard way to calibrate color monitors to software and output devices. And even if it were possible, room light affects the color noticeably.

Another limitation is the amount of data a standard 8-bit color video board can send to the screen. Although your palette—the colors available for use—is made up of millions of shades, you are restricted to 256 on the screen at any one time. Programs like Studio/8 on the Mac must examine a color picture, and then select from the palette before creating the image on the screen.

With 24-bit video boards, you can get a palette of 16.8 million colors, all displayable at once. This looks startlingly good, but is a lot of information. The screen takes longer to refresh, which can be frustrating if you are trying to do design work in a hurry. But as with everything in the computer business, more power is being thrown at the problem. Radius sells a 24-bit video card with an accelerator that makes the screen refresh almost as fast as the old 8-bit card. SuperMac, Radius, and Raster Ops all make calibrators which keep the monitor tuned to a standard—an important step in creating a uniform color space to work in.

The main problem is that video is always red-green-blue (RGB)—not the cyan-magenta-yellow-black (CMYK) of printing. The high-end color systems like Scitex have ways of simulating printing inks and paper colors. But true color wysiwyg is still a few years away in desktop publishing. A number of companies are addressing the problem of color definition standards. In fact, PostScript Level 2, Tektronix, and others address the issue directly with their adoption of a standard called CIE, which defines color in a three-dimensional space model that closely resembles its perception by the human eye. Eventually, you will be able to tune screens and printers to the same color values.

Scanning

To see all this color (or black and white), you need a scanner—a device that will pass a light over a slide or print, "reading" and digitizing an image so that it can be displayed, manipulated, and output by your computer. To bring a conventional monochrome photograph into your system, the simplest, most useful model is a device with 16 gray levels like the Apple Scanner. With that scanner, the image is interpreted as a bitmapped representation of dots in 16 different tones from white to black—gray levels. With a Microtek 300G scanner, there are 256 gray levels.

Memory is the key issue when it comes to incorporating photos and scanned images. With higher resolution, there is obviously a lot more data. A full page black-and-white picture can take a whole megabyte or more. The Mac has an effective RAM limit of 8 MB, but even if you have less, you may still be able to scan and work on a large graphics file: most high-end graphics programs modify the on-screen image to use less RAM, or use the hard drive for virtual memory.

Color scans, from transparency or print, need even more memory. A little 35-mm transparency slide has so much density of information that, depending upon the resolution of the image, it could take 100 MB to hold it. A publication might have dozens of these pictures, and it is a stretch for desktop technology to handle this much information.

Machines like the Dainippon, Optronics, Scitex, Barneyscan, Howtek, and Nikon scanners can scan 35-mm slides at high resolutions. For larger transparencies or prints, you might use the Sharp or Howtek flat bed scanners, although these generally offer less tonal range at the output stage.

Database software, such as Anaya Photopress, promises a way of finding all these pictures once they're stored. Developers are addressing all of the color issues, and in the next few years we can expect that desktop color will be able to do what can now be accomplished by only high-end systems, costing ten times as much.

Storage Devices

Scanning images requires that you have some place to store them. Since these types of files can be so large, a hefty hard disk drive is an essential part of your system—the bigger the better. If you're working exclusively in monochrome (actually gray scale), you can probably get away with a 40-MB drive. However, if you're working in color, I strongly recommend storage capacity of 80 MB to 300 MB and beyond.

Removable hard disk drives, such as that made by SyQuest and sold under a number of names (including Mass Micro), provide a nice solution. They come with removable cartridges that commonly hold 45 MB of data each. They give you a system with unlimited storage capacity, and they are great for transporting large graphics and document files to service bureaus and other output shops.

Removable, erasable optical drives can take you even further. These use 5.25-inch CD-type disks that commonly store 300 MB of data each. These are produced by a handful of companies, including Pinnacle Micro, Microtech, La Cie, and PLI. The drawbacks: their data access time performance is a bit slower than for some conventional hard drives, and a drive "player" averages about $5000 (40-MB hard drives start at under $1000).

Modems and Networks

Increasingly essential for any desktop publisher is a modem, to link your computer with the telephone, and thus the rest of the world. Nowadays a 2400-baud Hayes-compatible is the minimal norm. (The baud rate measures speed, or band width.) However, if you plan to send DTP files to a local service bureau, you might consider a 9600-baud modem, which can feed out as much as a standard phone line can handle. At this higher level there is no standard, so make sure that you check with the service bureau (or whomever you're planning to communicate with) before you make the purchase.

Another important connection to make is a network, to link the workstations in your office. This is a complicated subject that could fill its own book at this point, but even if you have only two computers, you should consider putting them on a network.

The Macintosh has always had a simple network scheme, Apple-Talk, which at the very least allows a number of machines to use the same printer. With software, you can transfer files from one computer to the other. This is an effective way to back up your files—and is essential if more than one person is going to work on a page. A simple Tops network, or even Claris' Public Folder (which is free!) may do the job.

As your operation gets bigger, you may want to add a central file server. Using Tops, or AppleShare on the Mac, or a number of other alternatives, each computer can be connected to a big hard disk or disks. With sufficient storage, you can keep all files and backup programs and fonts on the file server. Then each of your colleagues can copy files periodically to the server, making a constant backup.

More and more, people are hooking up different kinds of computers. A Tops network card in a PC can join it to a Mac network. You can build a network to chain together different computers—Macs, PCs, Sun workstations, minis, and mainframes.

A more exotic possibility is to connect the network to the modem, allowing everyone to share it. You can even create a remote network so that associates at other offices can log onto your file server and transfer messages and files. The Shiva NetModem will handle both of these jobs.

As networks grow, the simple AppleTalk communications protocol slows down. If you have more than, say, 20 workstations to connect—or if you are planning to move around a lot of big color files, then look into an Ethertalk network. Ethertalk is built into the NeXT workstation. But all IBM-compatibles require a special card for any network. On the Mac, you will need an Ethertalk card for each computer. You get much more speed for this investment. A file moves along the network at about the same rate as copying it from your hard disk to a floppy disk. You can put more users on the network, and the distances between them can be much farther. Putting out a big publication like a monthly magazine really requires a more robust network.

Page-layout Software

If you are going to use DTP seriously, you just have to get used to learning new programs, integrating both hardware and software to form an efficient publishing system (see Figure 7-4). Even if you figure you only need to use two basic programs, in two years there will be substantial changes or better solutions. It's as if you lived in Europe and had to know a number of languages.

Figure 7-4

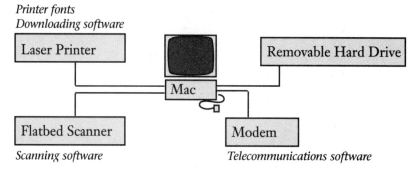

Printer fonts
Downloading software

Laser Printer

Removable Hard Drive

Mac

Flatbed Scanner

Modem

Scanning software

Telecommunications software

Choosing software is similar to buying hardware. You just have to use the best information at a given time, swallow hard, and then make your purchase. The key element is a page-layout software program, the software that assembles and integrates text files and picture files created elsewhere.

As far as I am concerned, there are several page-layout programs on the same functional level—QuarkXPress and Letraset DesignStudio on the Macintosh, as well as Xerox Ventura Publisher and Aldus Page-Maker on either.

There are some expensive alternatives like Lightspeed on the Mac, UNIX-based FrameMaker, or Interleaf, which runs on several platforms. These may be more appropriate for technical documentation, but surprisingly, the mainstream programs offer as many or more features for much less cost. Take a look also at more expensive solutions like BestInfo and Magna which are typesetting front-end systems that have come to look a lot like desktop publishing, but which have some superior typographic controls, and are designed for workgroups and thus have file management capabilities that the page-layout program developers are just beginning to work on. And there are proprietary systems, such as Atex Designer, which is designed to work within a large Atex system—something to consider if your company already has a substantial investment in Atex.

And then there are less powerful programs that may be appropriate if you have very limited needs, like GEM Publisher. Even most of the big-selling word-processor programs do simple layout.

For my money, I stick to competitively priced, off-the-shelf programs. None of them make me totally happy, but by paying market prices, the investment is reduced to the minimum, and when a new product emerges, I am more willing to scrap what I've got and move on.

You should try each of the page-layout programs because each has a slightly different logic, and one may suit you better. Look at how they handle files and how they build pages. Keep flexible; it is easier to adapt to the logic of the programs than to find something that works exactly the way you do.

Ventura Publisher, QuarkXPress, and Ready,Set,Go "think" of pages in terms of rectangles, or frames—a logic reminiscent of the old letterpress days, where all elements are rectilinear. Unlike letterpress, the rectangles can be overlapped. Perhaps a better analogy is pasteup, but where virtually all elements are cut neatly into squares and rect-angles—what the old keyline pros called "square-cut."

Ventura Publisher (PC and Mac)

Ventura builds pages with frames, into which you can put either text or pictures. You can select several frames at a time and move them all together.

After using Ventura on the PC first, I turned to Macs because my colleagues found it easier to learn and because of the wide variety of graphic software. After trying all the DTP packages, I settled on QuarkXPress, because it was the first on the Mac to have the typo-graphical controls of Ventura.

Yet, until Ventura was released for the Mac, I missed some of its fea-tures. I often wonder why the other developers didn't simply make a list of all the features in Ventura Publisher 1.0 and implement them. Some of the rivals, in their third major release, still don't have automatic drop initials or illustration numbering. Since Ventura is the leading PC-compatible DTP system, and there are so many PCs, it may be the most widely used DTP system. Ventura was the first with complete typographical controls of any of the programs—complete control over word spacing, tracking, kerning, and even some rotation. It has always been able to move a letter up and down in small increments.

Ventura also seems to have the most efficient way of dealing with specifying type and creating style sheets (although PageMaker and QuarkXPress also have good style sheet features)—something essential to publication format design, which, of course, is what I spend most of my time doing. You can select and style paragraphs with specifications for font, point size, indents, leading, automatic drop initials, boxes, and rules. You can name and save the styles, and then, using the Paragraph tool, you can quickly select new paragraphs and tag them with the same style.

Words that you've previously styled in bold or italic stay that way when you tag a paragraph. And you can select any number of paragraphs and tag them simultaneously. The tagged paragraphs don't even have to be contiguous—which is impossible with most Mac programs. (I'm told there are a couple of ways to do it in PageMaker.) These tags are permanently attached to the text file and flow out when you save a story so that if you call up that text file in a word processor, you can see the tags and actually change them before they go back into Ventura.

For example, if you set up a style called "Caption," the writer can tag the text as Caption in the word-processing program. Then, when the text is brought into a Ventura chapter that already contains the tags, the caption is styled automatically.

You can build a format for the page and break down the text into all the different styles for headlines, initial caps, captions, and body copy. If you decide you want to change all the headlines, you can do it simply by changing the tag. You don't have to find and select each one. If the paragraph is not tagged, it picks up the default "Body Text" style—which can be changed like any other.

Significantly, only Ventura keeps all of the text and picture files in their original format, so it is possible for writers to work on revisions in their familiar word-processing program. There is a convenient list of these files in Ventura on a menu to the left of the page.

The other programs have style sheets and ways of placing and exporting text files, but none seems to work quite as efficiently as Ventura in workgroup situations common to magazines.

QuarkXPress (Mac—and soon, PC)

In QuarkXPress there are picture frames and text frames, called boxes. You can't put text in a picture box. With the latest version, you can group several boxes and move them together, or you can build them within the same "parent" box. In the first two releases, the user was always grappling with these wretched parent and sibling combinations, and Quark finally listened to feedback, and implemented box grouping.

QuarkXPress tends to have the most robust set of features, allowing color separations and full typographical controls. It was the first with a spelling checker, obviating the need for separate word processing in some cases. The latest version also has a set of menu palettes, which allow quick and precise changes in all the elements on a page. There are now automatic drop initials. Rotation at any angle is possible. And there is a new feature, a library, which lets you store combinations of picture and text boxes which you might want to use repeatedly.

Quark was first to open the way for extensions from independent developers that bring in the functions of the highest-end professional publishing systems. Among extensions are the text-management facility of CopyFlow. And perhaps more interesting, a new entry from Britain, QED, just now beginning to sell in the United States. QED has its own PC-based editing system, but now on the Macintosh, which offers a Quark Xtension which actually takes QuarkXPress pages apart, allowing colleagues to revise different boxes at the same time. When completed, the pages are put back together.

Another early advantage of QuarkXPress was its support for color, including the ability to make last-minute changes in pictures (adjusting brightness and contrast on each color). QuarkXPress supported preseparated color pictures from version 2.0, and now will make its own separations of color TIFF and PICT files.

Perhaps the most important comparison to make while endeavoring to understand these different programs, is how they all treat the master or underlying pages. With QuarkXPress, they are called default pages, and it is now possible to store a variety of default pages and apply them as required. The basic text page is defined on the default, along with any running titles or graphic elements and guidelines. With Ventura, the page itself is the master frame. You can set margins and columns within the frame. Type or graphics can be repeated on all pages by making the frame a repeating frame.

If you like the way a program handles the master page, then chances are you'll like the rest of the program's logic. (See Figure 7-5.)

Figure 7-5
QuarkXPress

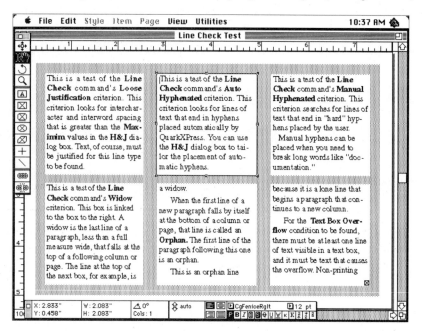

Letraset
DesignStudio
(Mac)

Meanwhile, if you like to work with a grid system, you should try DesignStudio, a descendent of Ready,Set,Go, which is still available. All the programs have a way of organizing pages into vertical columns, but DesignStudio can quickly set up horizontal columns for you. This modernist approach to design can be very effective, and is a great way to explain layout to design newcomers.

DesignStudio is a powerful program, replete with virtually all the features of QuarkXPress, including a library, full type controls and rotation, vertical justification, color specifications and graphics tools, and a recently added pasteboard that, like PageMaker—and now QuarkXPress—lets you store items off the actual page area. Due to the vagaries of marketing, however, it simply hasn't caught on as well with power users. While complicated, there is some evidence that it is easier to learn than Ventura or QuarkXPress, and Letraset offers a compatible product line, including Color Studio and FontStudio. If you are starting from scratch, investigate DesignStudio.

Aldus PageMaker (PC and Mac)

You have to decide if the frame-based method makes intuitive sense, or whether you prefer PageMaker, which works without boxes, and allows a more freeform approach. With PageMaker, the metaphor is pasteup. The objects come onto the desktop and you can place them anywhere. Pictures are not bound to rectangles; they float freely. (See Figure 7-6.)

Figure 7-6
Aldus PageMaker

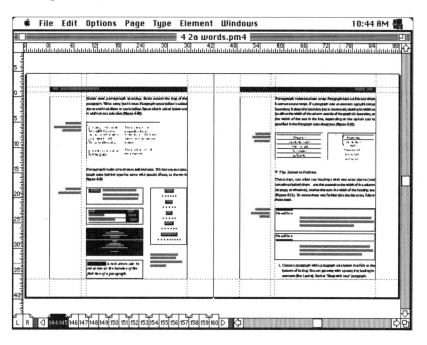

PageMaker was the first full-featured, professional-quality page-layout program. Of course, that status is sometimes a liability because in the resulting battle to add features, it has become more powerful, and much more complicated. Still, it is still the easiest layout program to learn. And, it has until recently been the only one that existed on both the Macintosh and the PC, with the ability to send files back and forth between the two. Ventura can do that now too. (It is rumored that Quark may also be working on a PC/Windows version of QuarkXPress.)

PageMaker 4 offers typographic controls that equal those of QuarkXPress and DesignStudio. It has a built-in word-processing mode, called the Story editor; more powerful text formatting tools; inline graphics that can be anchored to and move with a particular text block; book tools that let you easily create indices, tables of contents, and hook documents together; color separation abilities (with Aldus PrePrint); and a Links feature for keeping track of files in a workgroup-publishing situation.

Word Processors

The essential piece of software is your page-layout program, but there are a number of other programs needed to work with it. First, you need a way to deal with text—a word-processor.

Now all the major layout packages have word-processing tools, and it is possible to write and edit text in the same program as you do layout. At *El Sol*, a new daily newspaper in Madrid, all the reporters and editors actually write and edit in QuarkXPress, which allows them to quickly check the lengths of stories, and avoid the need to "pour" text into a layout.

Some writers prefer to work in a word-processing program, and take advantage of more extensive spelling checkers, thesauruses, and search-and-replace functions. Used to typescript pages, they like to see a familiar 8.5-by-11-inch page format, with wide double-spaced lines—and leave the typesetting to someone else.

It seems that Mac writers favor Microsoft Word, which is also available on the PC, while PC writers by and large prefer WordPerfect. Both are excellent.

A powerful alternative on the PC is XyWrite, which was based on Atex, the code-oriented program used by many newspapers and magazines. XyWrite is difficult at first, but it is so fast that it is worth the effort. It has an unsurpassed ability to move around the typical mass of copy every editor must deal with.

File Conversion and Transfer Solutions

One problem everyone doing desktop publishing eventually encounters is converting files from one word-processing format to the desktop layout program. Fortunately the DTP programs now have filters that translate all the popular word-processing formats. These allow you to save text in nearly any other format—which is useful if you want to send copy back to the writer or the editor for revision. (The Ventura paragraph tags go with the file, and the text will flow back into your chapter without being restyled.)

More complicated is the problem of bringing files from an IBM-compatible PC to a Macintosh. The best solution is to have both machines on the same network, such as TOPS. With the Mac IIx, Apple introduced a 3.5-inch disk drive that can read IBM-format disks, and a file conversion utility that converts the data into Mac format. It works both ways, and most characters, including foreign accents, are converted without a hitch.

Another solution is to convert the file to ASCII (the universal computer code for letters, numbers, punctuation, and math signs), and then send it from one computer's modem to the other computer's modem. You can do this directly, using communication software on both ends, such as Microphone for the Mac or Crosstalk and Smartcom for the PC.

Or, go through an electronic mail service, such as MCI Mail. This course is sometimes the easiest, since often the reason you are converting files is that the machines are in two different offices. With E-Mail you don't have to wait for the other person to get the computer ready.

MCI Mail, which works with all computer communications software interactively, connects with other E-Mail systems, telex, and fax. The fax service actually turns any fax machine into a printer, which is great if you are on the road with your laptop. The service will also print out documents for you, put them in the mail, or send them via overnight courier, around the world.

On the Mac, you can get software called Desktop Express, an easy front-end interface, which allows you to send a Macintosh file to any mailbox—slowly, but effectively. More cumbersome is the PC equivalent, Lotus Express, but there are people who swear by it.

When sending files over the phone lines, it is worthwhile to compress them—temporarily shorten their size—for faster (and less expensive) transmission. This can be accomplished with one of several compression utilities, like StuffIt for the Mac or ZIP for the PC.

Graphics Software

The most vaunted tool of desktop technology is the ability to create graphics—which can include anything from halftone photographs to diagrams to complicated financial charts worthy of the most lavish annual report. In the newspaper world, a graphic usually means an information graphic—a bar chart, pie chart, fever line graph, or diagram—the kind of thing that *USA Today* made famous. In computer parlance, a graphic is any kind of pictorial element, anything that is not text.

Creating Illustrations: Draw Programs

The programs that make up graphics software fall into two categories: those that "draw" and those that "paint." Drawing software works with outlines, either straight-line vectors or curves that are filled with tones or colors. Painting software deals more amorphously with bitmapped images, which include photographs. The first group is generally preferred for creating art—the newer programs are PostScript-based, are very precise, and can produce art that can be output independent of printer resolution (see the discussion of PostScript earlier in this chapter).

Claris MacDraw (Mac)

In the Macintosh world, MacDraw was the first graphic drawing program. It is based on vector (straight line) outlines. It's become the standard for newspaper graphics. Associated Press wire graphics, for example, are sent in MacDraw format. The current version, MacDraw II, handles color. However, its typographical tools are somewhat limited, and its files tend to get quite big and are slow to print. Resolution is only as good as originally created. If you have made the decision to use the PostScript standard, you want software that works in PostScript, so that the resolution is determined by the final output.

Adobe Illustrator (PC and Mac)

Illustrator stands as the most important graphics program of the micro era—but not because it is easy to understand. Many artists have a hard time learning Illustrator, and laymen are initially confounded. It really demands that you accept its own logic, the logic of the Bézier curve and PostScript. Creative people tend to resist expressing their work in algorithms of any kind. Artists who will admit to using logic of any kind may find it difficult to change to an entirely different kind of thinking.

This, of course, is the problem with all software. Writers, designers, artists all have their own way of doing things—all slightly different. The software developers seldom can make a program work the way people worked before computers. (For one thing, the tools are different: a mouse is not a pencil; a video screen is not a pad of paper.) But even if the software captured the work habits of one artist, the next one to come along might have entirely different work habits.

The designers of Adobe Illustrator did not endeavor to simulate the easel or drawing pad. There is no palette, no brush, no little paint roller like the bitmap painting programs such as MacPaint or PC Paintbrush. There is a pen, but it doesn't draw. It plots points on a curve. You get to love the precision of control points. The points contain information about the direction and intensity of the curve.

Once a "path" has been completed, the tone or color fill and the outline "stroke" (the weight of the line that builds upon the stroke) can be set.

This does not sound like fun, but Adobe included a way to bring in scanned images (your rough sketches or photos, to crib from) to use as templates to build the artwork. Once you have mastered the program's logic and interface (which can literally take months), Illustrator makes it possible for nonartists to draw perfectly smooth curves.

In successive versions, Adobe added a blend tool, that allows airbrush-style fades and the ability to actually merge two different shapes in any number of intermediate steps. (See Figure 7-7.) There is a freehand tool, added in response to the rival program FreeHand, which allows the mouse-adept user to trace a path directly, letting the program place the control points, but experts don't find it exact enough. An autotrace tool can make copying the original art even easier.

Figure 7-7
Using the blend tool

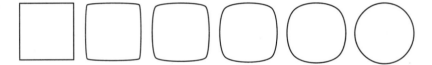

However, once you get the hang of Illustrator you start editing these autotraced outlines with the original pen tool, placing the control points on the curves precisely and making the corners sharp.

The real benefit of the program is not as a replacement for water-color illustrations or airbrush artwork, although some artists have done beautiful work with it, particularly at daily newspapers where Illustrator has become a workhorse. What Illustrator does best is graphics—technical drawings, logotypes, symbols, and ornaments. It also provides an array of special effects for typography—outlines, shadows, and distortions.

Of course, other programs can do these things, but the bitmap paint programs, which may be more intuitive to use, create fixed low-reso-lution results—fine when the ultimate product is to be printed on a

300-line laser printer, but too coarse for anything but spot illustrations in a magazine.

Illustrator files are straight PostScript, and like all PostScript, the resolution depends on the final output device. Like PostScript fonts, artwork created in Illustrator can be scaled to new sizes without changing the quality of the final.

Adobe is reported to be bringing out a new version of Illustrator by the end of 1990, which will have desktop-publishing-like tools for specifying typography.

Once you are willing to embrace its logic, Illustrator becomes an indispensable route to the real design power of a computer.

Aldus FreeHand

Some artists prefer FreeHand, which notably has better controls for type, including kerning and tracking, and a sophisticated way of using layers to create graphics.

The main difference between this and Illustrator is the interface—how the points are shown on the screen, and how you use the various tools. Which you like better, you must decide for yourself.

Corel Draw (PC)

Corel Draw was the first big PC product for high-end graphic illustration, and has become very popular for people doing DTP with Windows 3.0. It started out as a PostScript-based utility for creating customized display fonts with elaborate shapes, background patterns, and other effects. Now it has full drawing capabilities and some of the most powerful type manipulation tools in the business.

The Corel drawing screen does not allow you to directly edit finished images. You draw the object outline directly, and can only see the finished image, with all textures and fills in place, by pulling down a preview screen. Unfortunately, you can't actually work on the preview screen.

Corel Draw has good features for editing font outlines, autotracing bitmapped images that you have brought into the program, and general drawing. The package comes with several collections of finished clip-art files, which may be individually loaded and edited.

Micrografx
Designer (PC)

More Mac-like than Corel, Designer is a full-featured, Windows-based drawing package with an extensive library of clip-art files available at extra cost. Its drawing screen and tools are excellent and, unlike Corel, you can work with finished images, complete with fills and textures. It works well autotracing bitmapped images, and can be used with a companion product, called Graph, which allows you to create charts and graphs.

Arts & Letters
Graphics Editor
(PC)

Arts & Letters, published by Computer Support Corporation, is the easiest and most Mac-like of all the Windows-based PC illustration programs. It takes a different approach to art than either Corel Draw or Micrografx Designer: it begins with the assumption that the user is not an experienced artist and needs a library of basic graphic forms to *compose* art rather than have to draw it. It's based on a system of 15,000 ready-made, interchangeable graphic symbols, which may be combined in the same drawing on the screen. Once they're on the screen, they can be rotated, slanted, given any number of attributes, stretched, and edited into thousands of variations.

Even for professional artists it's a great tool. It has excellent freeform drawing tools, and allows work on a finished, filed image, or on an outline (as with Corel) to save screen redraw time.

Arts & Letters has excellent support for color output, and works with many high-end output devices, including Linotronic imagesetters.

Manipulating Graphics: Paint Programs

The word *paint* in desktop jargon refers to bitmapped images. Scanned pictures are recorded as bitmaps, and paint programs are generally used for retouching as well as for creating artwork.

These programs have grown from the premise that artists would use them to create pictures to the notion that designers would use them to retouch pictures. Most of them can do both pretty well as creation tools, but the majority of artists still work the old-fashioned way, on paper. They then take the illustrations and scan them into the system.

Scanners come with software to run them, including some simple paint and bitmap editing tools. But you will also need some kind of painting program to manipulate the pictures more thoroughly.

Right now, desktop technology has reached the level where you can make photo layouts as easily on a machine as by hand. The paint-retouching software can handle silhouetting and retouching. This is great for design, presentation, and black-and-white printing—but the next step is to combine DTP with high-quality, four-color separation systems. The developers are working on this from different angles.

Claris MacPaint and Silicon Beach SuperPaint (Mac)

The granddaddy of paint programs is MacPaint, which a four-year old can figure out in about three minutes. (Somewhat longer for adults.) MacPaint allows you to go in, select "fat bits" and then turn off or on one pixel at a time. This is bitmap editing. The program is a great way to learn the Macintosh interface, but as a tool it now seems rather limited. (The size of an image, for example, is no bigger than the original 9-inch Mac screen.) Even the more powerful and recently updated SuperPaint, which combines both paint and draw features in one simple interface, seems a bit old hat nowadays.

Letraset ColorStudio and Adobe Photoshop (Mac)

Both of these high-end color manipulation programs are really state-of-the-art. They are best used not for *creating* art, but for manipulating and retouching scanned images. With them, much of the technology recently seen only in the high-end Scitex or Crosfield systems comes to the desktop.

Both have "acquire" menus, so that you can run scanners from within the program. Both import and export files in a number of standard formats. Both have anti-aliased typefaces, abstruse ways of adjusting color levels and values, color separation capabilities, and a deep selection of image-processing features. To use them you need 2 to 8 megabytes of RAM and 2 to 10 megabytes on your hard disk.

With these programs you can use masking, which allows you to silhouette, semi-automatically, areas of a picture, and then locally adjust the color (or in black and white, the contrast and brightness). Once an object is masked, you can combine it with other images, or masked areas, in surprising ways. You can even paint through a mask, allowing pictures to merge in delightfully subtle ways. These programs also let you adjust different tonal ranges of image—for example, you can lighten the highlights without changing the shadows.

They both boast a virtual 24-bit working environment. This means that everything you do in Photoshop or ColorStudio is calculated in 24-bit "space," the highest color capability available in the Macintosh environment, even if you are running the program on a machine with only 8-bit color graphics. Therefore, your final output will have maximum resolution and tonal range, given the data of the scanned image, regardless of the limitations of your Mac.

Photoshop goes even further in this regard than does ColorStudio. It can work in virtual 24-bit mode even if you have 4-bit graphics, or even a monochrome machine like the Mac SE.

The sad thing is that one quickly learns how much one does not know about color. I would say the learning curve for these doesn't level off until after the first year. But the power is worth the effort, for ultimately you will be able to produce excellent quality four-color separations on the desktop.

Digital Darkroom

If you don't work in color, but work instead with gray-scale images such as scanned, black-and-white photos and other bitmapped graphics, you'll want to check out Digital Darkroom, published by Silicon Beach Software. It is one of the better applications for composing, retouching, and enhancing these types of images.

Pixel Paint Professional

Pixel Paint Professional, published by SuperMac Technologies, is another capable color painting and image-manipulation program. It features brush and painting tools that work like the real thing, making the program more intuitive and easier to learn. You can actually mix colors on screen, just as you would with an artist's paint palette. At the same time, it boasts plenty of high-end desktop power for importing and exporting images, special effects, image processing, and color separation.

PC Paintbrush IV Plus and Publisher's Paintbrush (PC)

Published by ZSoft Corporation, PC Paintbrush was the first paint program available for the PC. It was originally a rather low-end application used mostly as a scanning utility and was bundled for free with the Microsoft mouse. PC Paintbrush has grown, however, and is now a capable color manipulation program in its own right (now bundled with Windows). Its sister product, Publisher's Paintbrush, is even more powerful, offering a complement of sophisticated painting and retouching tools for the PC/Windows environment, including access to expanded memory. The PC Paintbrush family saves graphics in a format called .PCX, which has become a standard among major DTP and business applications, including Ventura Publisher.

Moving Upstream

These advanced color paint programs are striving to do on the desktop what it took years to develop in the high-end color systems like Scitex. For example, you can rotate color photographs, and silhouette figures while keeping the edges soft ("unsharp masking"). And you can clone areas and apply them elsewhere to extend backgrounds. You can universally change a particular range of colors to another range, thus turning blue products to red.

The power now available is astonishing, but there is still some question about how to print these pictures that you have manipulated so beautifully.

As mentioned earlier, there are inherent problems with PostScript color that must be solved before desktop publishing color will be as good as the expensive digital systems that are used for magazines and print advertising.

Another problem, already mentioned, is memory. A big picture will choke a PC, if loaded into RAM. Some programs handle this by using the hard disk as virtual memory. But even then, the amount of storage needed to hold enough pictures to fill a magazine seems enormous to those of us who have just gotten used to 100-MB hard disks. We're talking about gigabytes (thousands of megabytes) here.

But people are working on it. Already there are digital darkroom systems running on PCs at daily newspapers. They bring in color pictures from the Associated Press in compressed form. Picture editors can view them on the screen, select the ones they want immediately, and file the rest.

There are a few desktop solutions that have had reasonable success achieving what is kindly called "pleasing color," if not art book reproduction quality. Cybergraphics and Prepress Technologies offer comprehensive color separation software which can be brought into standard DTP systems, using off-the-shelf scanners. Howtek sells a complete system running on 386 PCs, with hardware and software, for around $100,000. The Howtek system is not PostScript, but PostScript files can now be RIPped and incorporated.

Crosfield, Scitex, and Hell all have color prepress links to popular DTP packages. These systems let you strip low-resolution "samples" of color graphics into pages on the desktop, then send your final page files and high-resolution graphics to the prepress shop for final color correction and output. (See "Linking to High-end Color Systems," below.)

A new separation system expected soon from the Spanish firm Anaya Systems, promises excellent four-color PostScript using a new imaging technique that creatively deals with the vexing screen angle problem. This is a very interesting development, because it fits in with the off-the-shelf software, standard hardware approach to desktop publishing. For example, you can use QuarkXPress, Adobe Photoshop, and a Linotronic L-330 with the Anaya screening technology.

On-the-Shelf Or Off-the-Shelf?

Linotype and Agfa have announced PostScript color systems that address the issue of color space—wherein you can get similar results on the screen, the color proof, and ultimately on the press.

And Scitex has jumped over the high-end fence and now offers a scanner, Smart Scanner II, and a PostScript color film plotter, called Dolev. Both can be used as peripherals to a desktop-publishing system. The Dolev printer is controlled by a PC-based workstation that uses Scitex technology to do color correction.

These may be the most advanced desktop solutions available today, but they are not cheap. (Systems start at around $200,000.)

This is more than off-the-shelf shrink-wrapped software, and before considering it you should take a look at what is available in your local computer store.

Linking to High-End Color Systems

There are several ways for desktop systems to link with the high-end color systems, like Scitex, Hell, and Crosfield. Scitex Visionary, an extension of QuarkXPress, with several useful improvements, was one of the first to be proven.

With these links, layout is done on the Mac, using low-resolution files either scanned on site, or converted from the high-res files from the color system. Text is poured in, everything proofed, and then the page files are sent to the big system, where heavy-duty color correction and top-quality film output can be controlled. Technicians at the color separation service bureau can change the geometry of the layouts, and even the type if corrections are ordered at the last minute.

As part of Visionary, Scitex has included a PostScript interpreter called VIP, which can bring any PostScript file into a Scitex system. Crosfield countered with StudioLink and Hell with ColorScript.

These are very practical solutions for quality desktop publishing. The problem with Visionary (beside the $5,000 per workstation list price) is that many color pages do not really require that pictures be assembled or stripped together on any system. Color separation houses themselves will routinely strip by hand any pages with single color pictures, so as not to tie up the Scitex system, for which they can charge as much as $1,000 per hour for elaborate retouching jobs.

At *Smart* magazine, we approach color with a combination of these tools. We bring elaborate graphics into Scitex via VIP. Then we scan single pictures, for the final prepress version, on a Scitex scanner at the color house. Then they are stripped by hand. But a publication that uses a multitude of pictures on a page (a catalogue, for example), may find that Visionary is the cheapest route.

The goal is to find a way to keep all the color—and everything—in one continuous desktop system. Work that is done on the desktop, such as silhouetting and retouching, should be saved for the final high-resolution system. In the next few months (or years, perhaps), the color quality of PostScript, along with the speed of processing will inevitably move color publishing from the expensive priesthood of color separation houses into your own hands. The technology will do for color what it has done for type. Get ready!

The Font Problem

Fonts are at the heart of desktop design, since the first benefit has been the saving in time and expense of outside typesetting. But fonts seem to have caused more problems than anything else.

It all started with the operating systems of PCs. The folks who developed DOS for the IBM-compatible PC—and Finder for the Mac—came from the computer world, where fonts meant bitmaps, either for the screen or for the printers. (Later it got more complicated, because the squares could be turned into shades of gray or different colors.)

With the Macintosh, the same font was used both on the screen and on the dot-matrix printer, the ImageWriter. This got people familiar with the concept of wysiwyg. There was something very pleasant about getting the same results on the screen and the printer, for a writer, or for a secretary who was just trying to get out a letter that was centered on the page. It was less pleasant when you wanted to use a size of type that was not stored in the font suitcase. For example, the Mac would scale down a 24-point font to make 20-point type. The results could be funky.

EL SOL

Edición Madrid   Sábado, 7 de julio de 1990   Nº 47 / 75 pesetas (con Bolsa Fin de Semana, 150 Ptas.)

La Otan certifica el fin de las dos Europas

La Alianza Atlántica se adapta al espíritu de los cambios en los países del Este

La Alianza Atlántica ha firmado la defunción de la *guerra fría*. La Declaración de Londres es el documento más importante de los últimos años. La principal organización militar de Occidente acepta adaptar sus objetivos fundacionales a la nueva realidad de Europa.

Para Felipe González, es indicativo que, "dentro de un documento que, "dentro de un documento de seis folios, dos estén dedicadas a la Conferencia para la Seguridad y Cooperación en Europa". Aunque este foro no va a sustituir a la OTAN en sus funciones defensivas, la Declaración de Londres asegura que la

CSCE "debe tener un papel más activo en el futuro de Europa". El documento aprobado ayer por la Alianza supone el final de la división de Europa: "La unificación de Alemania significa que la división de Europa ha sido superada". E insiste en la necesidad de una Alemania dentro de la OTAN y de la CE.

La OTAN se reconoce como "la asociación militar con mayor éxito de la Historia". Ha ganado la guerra sin necesidad de celebrarla. La Alianza ofrece al Pacto de Varsovia la firma de una declaración conjunta "en la que se afirme que ya no somos adversarios y que nos comprometemos a no utlizar la fuerza".

Los 16 jefes de Estado y primeros ministros presentes en la cumbre de Londres han ratificado la propuesta del presidente Bush, y han cursado una invitación oficial a Gorbachov y a los otros líderes del Pacto para que asistan al Consejo Atlántico de diciembre en la sede de la OTAN en Bruselas, "no como una mera visita, sino como un primer paso para el establecimiento de lazos diplomáticos regulares".

La OTAN se compromete también a no ser la primera en lanzar un ataque, y ha encargado a sus expertos la elaboración de una nueva estrategia militar, alejada del actual concepto de *respuesta flexible*.

> **Declaración histórica de la cumbre Atlántica de Londres**
> *Página 19*

George Bush, ayer, durante la cumbre de Jefes de Estado de la Alianza Atlántica. *REUTER*

La Audiencia libera al 'gal' Mendaille ante la pasividad del Gobierno

La Audiencia Nacional ha decidido que ya ha transcurrido un tiempo "razonable" de tiempo para seguir manteniendo en prisión al *gal* Georges Mendaille, y le puso ayer en libertad condicional bajo fianza de 500.000 pesetas.

Mendaille permaneció en prisión desde su detención en Gerona en febrero de 1989, a raíz de una reclamación de la justicia francesa que le acusa de asesinato y de pertenecer a la banda armada GAL (Grupos Antiterroristas de Liberación).

El tribunal decidió que Mendaille se presente diariamente ante la comisaría de policía o puesto de la Guardia Civil cercano a su residencia, le retiene el pasaporte, y da orden a las fuerzas de seguridad para que "procedan a la vigilancia del reclamado" para evitar que abandone España. En octubre de 1989, los tribunales españoles resolvieron a favor de la extradición de Mendaille, tiempo que la Audiencia considera más que razonable para que el Gobierno tomara una determinación.   *Página 3*

Alberto Muñiz, con Amparo Pavón, la joven que se desdijo en sus acusaciones contra él.   *EL SOL/ Ramón Cotelo*

El honorable 'Tío Alberto'

Los jueces le declaran inocente de abusos deshonestos

ALBERTO MUÑIZ, *Tío Alberto*, no pasará los próximos 50 años en la cárcel. La Audiencia Provincial de Madrid no ha encontrado pruebas de los delitos de abusos deshonestos y de corrupción de menores de los que se le acusaba, y le ha declarado inocente.

La Ciudad Escuela de los Muchachos de Leganés (Madrid) estaba desierta ayer por la mañana. Una nutrida comitiva de niños acudió a la Audiencia para enterarse de un veredicto que celebraron con alborozo. Alberto Muñiz se mostraba tranquilo y a la vez cansado por los días de incertidumbre transcurridos desde que en 1988 fuera denunciado por sus propios pupilos de abusar sexualmente de ellos.

Tío Alberto pasó toda la mañana en su despacho, donde recibió las felicitaciones de los vecinos de Leganés, que prácticamente invadieron la Ciudad Escuela de los Muchachos, y de los simpatizantes.

La acusación popular puede aguarle la fiesta, porque estudia la posibilidad de presentar recurso ante el Supremo.   *Pasa a página 13*

La policía reprime a miles de manifestantes en Albania

BERNA G. HARBOUR
Enviada especial-Belgrado

La policía dispersó ayer violentamente una manifestación de más de 10.000 personas que se habían congregado en el centro de la capital, Tirana, para exigir al Gobierno comunista la adopción de reformas políticas.

Los incidentes tuvieron lugar en las cercanías del barrio diplomático. Allí, más de 2.500 albaneses se han refugiado en las embajadas extranjeras para abandonar el país.

La situación en las legaciones extranjeras es crítica. Tan sólo la embajada de la RFA concentra a 2.000 asilados. Los países afectados por esta oleada continúan esforzándose por buscar una solución a la crisis ante las dificultades para atender adecuadamente a tan elevado número de personas.

El Gobierno de Albania ha asegurado a los refugiados que, si abandonan las embajadas, podrán pedir pasaportes sin ser objeto de persecución.   *Pasa a página 21*

Pensiones mínimas

	Con cónyuge	Sin cónyuge
Jubilación		
Más de 65 años	47.010	39.950
Menos de 65 años	41.130	34.850
Invalidez permanente absoluta		
	47.010	39.950
Viudedad		
65 años o más	38.880	
Entre 60 - 64 años	29.010	
Menos de 60 años	26.290	
Pensiones del S.O.V.I.		
Vejez e invalidez	28.560	
Viudedad	26.290	

Las pensiones suben un 9,2% de media
Página 25

Las gasolineras podrán fijar libremente los precios a partir del martes
Página 23

HB pide un informe psiquiátrico del etarra Rubenach
Página 6

La Bolsa de El Sol

Revista, Pasatiempos, Cómic de Superhéroe, Curso de Inglés y Fichas de Cocina de Temporada

---

El Sol

Launched in 1990, *El Sol* is a Madrid daily newspaper that is completely produced with desktop technology. More than 100 Macintoshes are networked. Reporters write directly in QuarkXPress. Color photos are scanned in and separated on the desktop, and the finished PostScript pages are beamed through fiberoptic fax lines to the printer, 35 miles away.

MOTHER EARTH

NEWS
THE ORIGINAL.

MARCH-APRIL 1990 : $3.00.
No. 122 : CANADA $3.95

GREETINGS. THIS IS THE PLANET EARTH

ON the night of April 22, Earth Day, the contents of this issue will be broadcast into deep space from Mt. Everest. They will travel through the universe forever.

INSIDE: MESSAGES FROM JIMMY BUFFET, RAY BRADBURY, GAYLORD NELSON, KURT VONNEGUT, PETE SEEGER, ANN LANDERS, JAMES DICKEY, JEREMY RIFKIN, DR. HUNTER S. THOMPSON, POPE JOHN PAUL II, AND OTHERS

0 70989 37964 0   04

Mother Earth News Anniversary Issue
This cover was created for the 20th anniversary of *Mother Earth News* and Earth Day. The illustration was drawn by Jonathan Hoeffler in Illustrator and separated on the desktop. The file was so large that it took almost 24 hours to print it at 2,540-lines-per-inch resolution, a record for the service bureau.

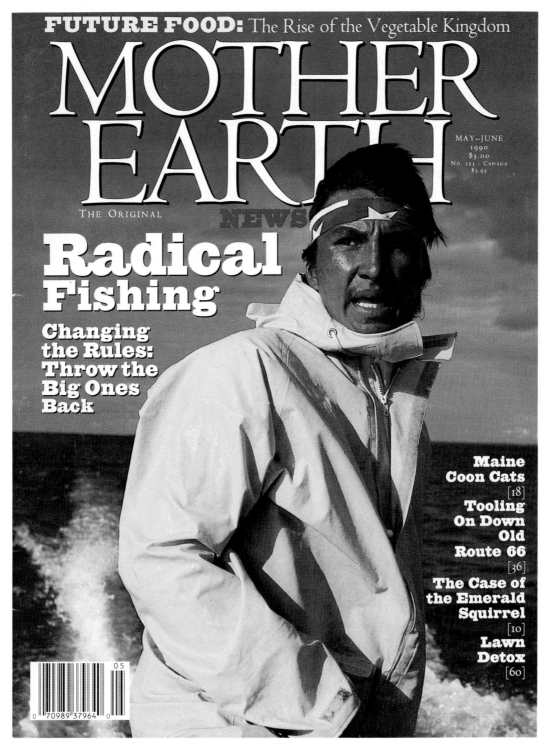

FUTURE FOOD: The Rise of the Vegetable Kingdom

MOTHER EARTH

THE ORIGINAL

NEWS

MAY–JUNE
1990
$3.00
NO. 123 : CANADA
$3.95

Radical Fishing

**Changing
the Rules:
Throw the
Big Ones
Back**

**Maine
Coon Cats**
[18]
**Tooling
On Down
Old
Route 66**
[36]
**The Case of
the Emerald
Squirrel**
[10]
**Lawn
Detox**
[60]

0 70989 37964 0   05

Mother Earth News

So far, color expertise has not been built into desktop software, and unless you have the training in
color, it is better to leave separations of photographs to others. At "Mom," we designed the type
(logos, titles, coverline) on the desktop and scanned the photo in for position only. For the final
printing the photograph is stripped in conventionally.

Color Separations
In printing four-color photos, the art is separated into four different color plates, Cyan, Magenta, Yellow, and Black (CMYK). The initial "K" is used for black so that it is not confused with blue.

Four-color Composite
When the four different plates are angled at standard (and exact) screen angles and light is shined through, the final four-color image results.

Duotone

Duotones are made by printing a photograph with two colors instead of four, so instead of being black and white, the photo comes out black and blue, or black and red, or black and yellow. These are cheaper to do than black and white, and if used carefully, can add a lot to your design.

Color Label

This label for a fashion section of *Smart* magazine was created in Illustrator and separated in QuarkXPress. To do this kind of work traditionally would require obscene numbers of overlays, and diligent and tedious pasteup work.

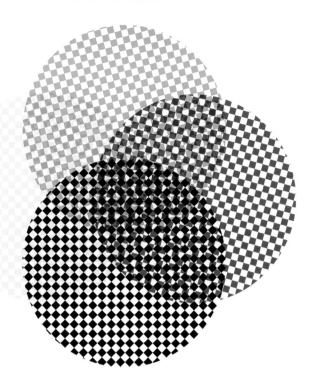

Black 45°

Magenta 75°

Yellow 90°

Cyan 105° *

Screen Angles

In order to get the correct color and alignment when light is shined through the four separated screens, the angles must be absolutely perfect and the light source direct.

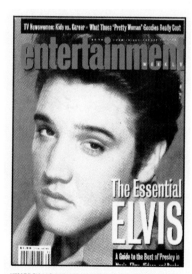

"THERE'S NO WAY THIS MAGAZINE COULD HAVE BEEN PUT OUT WITHOUT MACINTOSHES," SAYS

Moirés

Moirés result when the screen angles conflict (are not correct), and create a "beating pattern."

Type 90

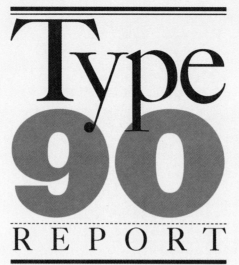

An occasional review of events leading up to the international conference on type and design in Oxford, England, from August 31 to September 4. Sponsored by Association Typographique Internationale (ATypI).

REPORT

N⁰ 1 : APRIL 1990

Type90 is a world-class meeting of designers and graphic artists concerned with the future of type. During four days at the end of the summer in one of the most beautiful university towns in the world there will be:

500 Conferees
20 Speakers
50 Workshop Leaders
2 Typographic Playrooms
12 Type Design Exhibits
20 Exhibits of New Type Technology
And a Blizzard of Parties

O*xford, England, is a delightful site for a design conference. Type90 conferees can lodge at the historic college, Christ Church, a short walk to most events. Nearby is the Bodleian library and a wealth of bookstores and other attractions of a college town. To the west are the Cotswold hills. Oxford is less than an hour from London's Heathrow airport, and easily reached by train from Paddington station.* [*More on travel, accommodation– page 6*]

Late this summer Oxford will attract the world's leaders in typographic design

Traditionally the domain of publishers, type is rapidly becoming a tool used by everyone. We are at an important juncture. Type is leaping the old boundaries of the printing world and is coming into everyday life. A world conference, Type90 has been called this summer in Oxford to look at the issues from every possible angle–aesthetic to technical, legal to lighthearted.

[*Continued next page*]

Using Color
The first color that I reach for after black is inevitably red. It is striking, and some say there is an instinctive reaction to it as a sign of danger, but I use red because I like it. The red and black combination is pleasant on a cream stock, like the one used for this newsletter.

In commercial typesetting bitmaps were also used, but at much higher resolution, imaged by cathode ray tubes onto photo paper. By the 1970s newspapers and typesetting shops were using computer terminals, but the letters on the screen were only generic characters. The paradigm was the typewriter, and there was no felt need to make typewriter type look like typeset type.

The first laser printers used bitmaps as well, but printing typefaces started making their way into the office. Fonts were held in memory, in bitmaps, or, if Times Roman and Helvetica were not enough there were cartridges that you would stick into the H-P LaserJet holding a few other fonts.

As people started using personal computers to do the work previously done by typesetting machines, fonts quickly became an issue. One consideration was that if you wanted a variety of typefaces and larger point sizes, a good deal of disk space would be needed. And then there was the matter of resolution. Economical laser printers produced only 300 dots to the inch, about a third of the fineness needed for quality typesetting.

What was needed was a better imaging model than bitmaps. That was solved with the introduction of PostScript in the mid-1980s. (See the PostScript discussion earlier in the chapter.)

PostScript fonts are stored as outlines, mathematical descriptions of each character. There is a scaling mechanism that sizes the outline to the desired size. The trick is that at small sizes the outlines can overlap the raster, or grid, awkwardly, creating letters that are lumpy and uneven at low resolution. To deal with this, Adobe added "hints" to the outlines, that indicated, for example, that the vertical stems of a lowercase "m" were the same width. (See Figure 7-8.)

It was only a matter of time before the desktop computers became big and fast enough to handle font scaling for the screen. The NeXT workstation was first to introduce Display PostScript, both for fonts and pictures. Sun Microsystems made their own version of Display PostScript called News, which brought font scaling to the monitors of their Unix workstations in a format called F3.

On the desktop level, QuarkXPress was the first to include a font "rendering" feature. If Bitstream and other nonencrypted PostScript printer fonts (called Type 3 or user-defined fonts) were kept in the Mac's system folder they could be used to "paint" the type on the screen.

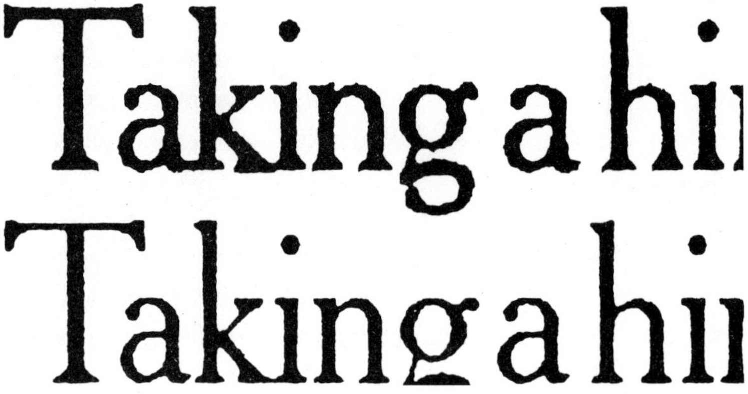

Figure 7-8
Enlarged 400 percent from a 300-line LaserWriter proof, the first line of type here is unhinted Cheltenham. The second line is a Type 1 hinted version of the same font

Taking a hi

Taking a hi

This intervention was made obsolete by Adobe's release of Adobe Type Manager (ATM) and specs for encrypted (Type 1) fonts. Now, all the font developers are producing Type 1 fonts, either with tools licensed by Adobe or built themselves from the specifications the company has published. Also, Bitstream has released its own software-based font rasterizer, called Facelift, which works with the company's Speedo font format.

ATM scales Type 1 fonts (but not nonencrypted Type 3 fonts) "on the fly" for the Macintosh. Although not a full implementation of display PostScript—picture files still must be shown in DTP by their encapsulated bitmaps—ATM brings wysiwyg back to the Mac.

Working with Fonts

Before Macintosh System 7 and OS/2 Presentation Manager, you had to sort out two different kinds of files to get fonts to work on both the Mac and the PC: screen fonts and printer fonts. With the Mac, the screen fonts contained the metric information of the space around each letter. On the PC this was usually another file, a width table.

The problems involved with everyday font handling are not the enjoyable part of desktop publishing and tended to lead a designer away from the PC platform and toward the Mac, which has always had a standard way of handling fonts in all software. All other things being equal, Ventura (running on GEM) and PageMaker (Windows-based) have a hard time with fonts.

The problem is that the original system developers had no idea that people would start collecting fonts in great numbers. Just having Helvetica a few years ago seemed pretty good. But now a designer will want dozens, or more likely hundreds, of fonts on his computer. (The last time I counted, I was up to 850.)

After some years of complaints about font ID conflicts that created havoc with DTP files sent to service bureaus for output, Apple brought out a new screen font format (NFNT) with more font numbers, and specific ranges of numbers assigned to particular manufacturers. This has helped, but it is a temporary solution.

But even if you can live with the current implementation of screen fonts, font downloading is another matter. With GEM or Windows on the PC, sending fonts to the printer and getting a page out can take up to five minutes, as opposed to less than a minute from the Mac. In addition, most new PostScript fonts (except for Adobe's) are created for the Macintosh system and are not all available for the PC.

On the PC, if you want to use fonts not built into the printer—and who doesn't?—it's easier to download the fonts "manually" before you start printing than to wait for the "automatic" downloading. On the Mac, it doesn't make much difference. One solution is to put all the additional printer fonts on a hard disk connected on the printer, which is possible with the Apple LaserWriter NTX or the Varityper VT600, which, like all imagesetting RIPs, comes with one. But now that you need printer fonts in your CPU system to render type on the screen, we're back to where we started.

Font Wars

When first introduced there was no guarantee that PostScript would catch on, but sooner than its developers could dare hope, it was the desktop imaging standard. For a short reign it appeared that the incompatibility of software and hardware would be solved forever by PostScript. No such luck.

Like any success story, PostScript attracted competition. Fonts became understood to be at the heart of a computer operating system, and the manufacturers wanted control over the imaging model.

As we've discussed, in Apple's Macintosh System 7, there's an entirely new font format called TrueType, an extension of the Mac's original QuickDraw screen display scheme. As with ATM, TrueType screen fonts are derived from the same master outline as used for the printer.

What is a poor desktop publisher to do? There are some inherent advantages to the TrueType technology. The difference has to do with the hints. TrueType has all the information in the outlines needed to optimize the font at any resolution. With PostScript, the hints are minimal, because much of the optimizing is done in the printer's PostScript interpreter, the RIP. (With ATM, this is done in the computer, using some interpreting code, which explains the slightly slower screen refresh rate.) Each PostScript printer must have its own computer, which explains the $2,000 price difference between the PostScript LaserWriter and the LaserWriter SC, which has no interpreter.

Depending on the interpreter in the printer, TrueType will download whatever sofware and data structures are required to get the best quality.

In other words, if a QuickDraw printer is being used TrueType will rasterize the outlines on the CPU and download a stream of bits (fully rasterized type). If it is a PostScript printer that has enough memory, it will download the TrueType rasterizer ahead of the fonts and rasterize at the printer. If all else fails, it will download an unhinted PS font.

TrueType outlines can be hinted in more sophisticated ways than PostScript type. For example, the weight of a font can be adjusted, so that it is more legible at small sizes, but as the type gets larger, the shapes can become thinner, more elegant. In the trade, this is called optical scaling. Efforts have been made to do this with PostScript fonts, post facto, but there is no way to control these mutations (or interpolations) in a PostScript outline.

Of course, putting these adjustments into a font takes considerably more design time. The first fonts to be released with System 7 do not contain this extra layer of information. But the opportunity is there, and it is a challenge to Adobe to bring similar refinements to PostScript fonts.

In the meantime, there is likely to be the same delay waiting for TrueType fonts as there was in the early days of PostScript. (Designers remember getting very tired of Palatino, the most elegant font included in the LaserWriter Plus, or even ITC Galliard, which was an early favorite among PostScript downloadable fonts.)

Since Microsoft has adopted TrueType for its OS/2 operating system, there is little danger of TrueType going away. And, as mentioned previously, TrueType will run on PostScript printers, and there will be ways to convert PostScript fonts to TrueType fonts, and perhaps vice versa. Foundries like Linotype and Bitstream are expected to issue their entire libraries in TrueType eventually. And high-resolution TrueType/TrueImage printers will be sold side-by-side with PostScript imagesetters, and will probably be compatible.

While things always seem to be becoming more complicated, there are also more ways to convert from one standard to another. And one thing is clear, PostScript is likely to remain the one standard that will cross all platforms and bridge the gap between desktop and professional publishing.

Production Management

One of the great beauties of using desktop publishing is that the process is actually the same as traditional publishing. Text editing comes first, then layout, then pasteup. The stages are the same. So, the production management problems are the same, and it's important to remember that no matter how powerful the machine you're using is, it cannot keep track of what you need to do without a well-conceived system.

Traditional publications keep track of all the little page elements either in file folders or flat file drawers. On the desktop, it is equally important to have a strict file management system. It doesn't have to be complicated, just rigid enough so that if everyone follows it, nothing falls between the cracks.

Basically, the larger a publication is, the more you need specialized stages in the production flow. On the smallest publications, one person may do everything, and people may wear many hats. On the largest, people only do parts of tasks. For example, contrast a newsletter put out by one editor/art director/layout person, to a Condé Nast publication, where someone's job can consist entirely of cutting out captions. The bottom line, however, is that both of these publications have to go through the same steps to come up with a finished product.

A successful file management system allows you to quickly find the status of each element in your publication. Has a headline been written yet? Has a story been laid out yet? Does it need to be cut? So much time can be saved later on if you think about your organization before you dive in. Arrange tasks so that the evolution of a file in your system works intuitively with the order of the tasks. Then, assign responsibilities in your office according to the overall structure of your production system.

Surprisingly, it is often more important for a smaller publication to maintain a strict copy flow so that fewer errors are missed. On larger publications, there are more people to catch them.

When people get computers, there is a tendency to rely on them too much. Machines can't check everything yet, and it won't be happening soon. Production management is just a less tenuous way of describing crisis management, and there is no software yet that can identify the difference between a problem and an intentional omission. A computer can easily tell you if something is present in the system. It's another matter to find what's missing or wrong.

Some file management software on the market claims to be able to handle your production. In fact, more errors will be made trying to adapt your particular situation to these complicated systems than if you try to do everything in your head. The worst way to run production is using someone else's system, which may not follow your logic and may not fill your needs. An easy way to think about these programs is that they are like the spell checkers that come with many word processors. They recognize if a word is not in their dictionaries, but they cannot tell if it is a typo or just an unknown word.

Of course, some of the more adventurous desktop publishers, like *MacUser* magazine, have written their own database management programs using software like 4th Dimension.

Eventually, file management software may get to the point that the machine can tell you, "Page 3 would be done if you would write the caption, dummy." But, what if you didn't want a caption there at all? There is no way to communicate intent to the machine. You still have to look over its shoulder.

In this chapter, I will present a simple production management system that should basically relate to the needs of any publication. Start from this to create your own tailored, simple system. The primary goal is to guard against losing anything, and to create a series of stages where someone will look at the material and decide what is missing and where the file has to go next.

I have identified six stages between the time that copy comes in to the point that pages are ready to go out. Naturally, there are other tasks before and after, but these are the ones related to desktop publishing—text entry, text edit, copy edit, page layout, page revision, and then output, as shown in Figure 8-1. At any stage, you can make the decision to go back to the previous one and start all over again. The writer can be instructed to rewrite, the editor can be asked to cut the length, the designer could be asked to rework the layout. You may have more or fewer stages depending on your production needs, but this is a good model to start from.

Figure 8-1
Six stages of copy flow from when it comes in to when pages go out

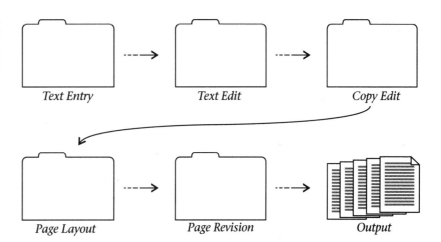

| Text Entry | Text Edit | Copy Edit |

| Page Layout | Page Revision | Output |

Naming Files—The Flow

I can't say it enough: the watchword is simplicity. Set up a series of stage folders (read *folders* as *directories* if you are working on the PC) for each step in the copy flow system. Then, each story or page has a story subfolder (subdirectory on the PC) which moves from stage to stage. The story subfolders hold the elements of the page—headlines, sidebars, captions, illustrations. As a page gets closer to the end of the process, subfolders are copied into successive stage folders for further work. There is work added at each step.

The position of a story in the process is determined by the folder in which it is found. Within the subfolders, it is important to clearly identify each of the elements. I like using the PC-style name extensions to indicate the kind of file you are working with. Change the extensions only when the kind of file is changed, not when the file enters another stage in the process. Figure 8-2 provides an example.

Figure 8-2
In copy flow, the file name extensions change only when the type of file changes, not when the file enters another stage in the process

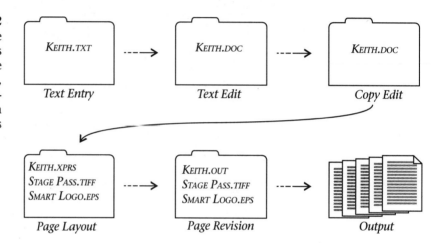

In the example we used a .TXT extension for ASCII files, .DOC when they were in a word-processor format, .EPS for encapsulated PostScript files, .PAG for page-layout files, and .OUT for finished pages. By looking at a list of titles in a folder, you can identify not only the story name, but also its stage in the copy flow system.

On some publications, I have seen extensions used to indicate a story's stage in the hierarchy. It turned out to be a mess, because there wasn't a certain place, a stage folder, where you could find all the stories at the same stage.

In the system I propose, the location of the file determines its place in the hierarchy. This location system is particularly useful when it comes time to compose pages. Not only are all the elements for a page in one subfolder, but the page-layout program can be instructed to look in the page-layout stage folder.

Say your cover story on Keith Richards comes in initially as a raw ASCII text file, call the story KEITH.TXT (as we did with a recent *Smart* magazine cover). When the file is put into a word processor in the next stage, the new version could be called KEITH.DOC (document).

The KEITH.TXT file travels in the KEITH subfolder up the food chain. Every piece you need, every computer file, that is associated with that page, goes in that folder including headlines, pictures, notes, messages, loose scans, and working files. Editors and art people have to be good about not cluttering up the folders with all kinds of junk which will confuse the next person. But, remember it is always safer to pass the garbage around than to recklessly delete files.

The idea of slugging each story with a simple name of five letters or less comes from the newspaper world. Everyday at *The New York Times,* The White House correspondent files a President's day report called PREXY, which may or may not make it into the paper. Everyone on the nation desk knows that the story PREXY is filed by the guy in The White House who writes about the President's day. Nobody even has to open it up. Sometimes it is used as the top story; sometimes it's not. But everybody knows what it is and where it can be found when it's needed.

This may all seem incredibly basic, but for many people, it is logical to name stories with numbers or the author's name. Names should be descriptive of the story, and recognizable. Everyone in the office can't know author's names, especially if stories haven't reached his or her stage yet. Also, author's names tend to be longer than five characters.

Take, for example, the cover story about Keith Richards in *Smart* magazine (see Chapter 9, "*Smart*"). Call it COVER so it has a generic place label or call it KEITH. Call the sidebars, KEITHA and KEITHB. Call the second complete rewrite of the Keith story KEITH2, and the complete rewrite of the Keith sidebar KEITH2A. Of course, each of these story labels needs a three letter extension to identify the kind of file, as shown in the callouts of Figure 8-3.

Pictures also need names when you bring them into the system. Often many more photos are scanned in than are used in the end. It

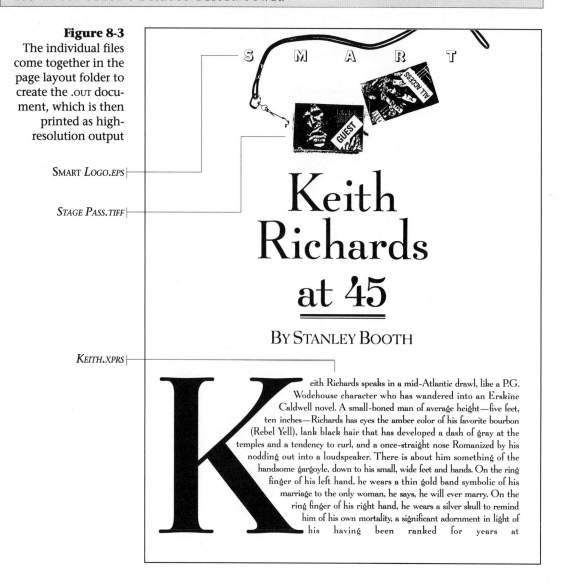

Figure 8-3
The individual files come together in the page layout folder to create the .OUT document, which is then printed as high-resolution output

SMART *LOGO.EPS*

STAGE *PASS.TIFF*

KEITH.XPRS

SMART

Keith
Richards
at 45

BY STANLEY BOOTH

Keith Richards speaks in a mid-Atlantic drawl, like a P.G. Wodehouse character who has wandered into an Erskine Caldwell novel. A small-boned man of average height—five feet, ten inches—Richards has eyes the amber color of his favorite bourbon (Rebel Yell), lank black hair that has developed a dash of gray at the temples and a tendency to curl, and a once-straight nose Romanized by his nodding out into a loudspeaker. There is about him something of the handsome gargoyle, down to his small, wide feet and hands. On the ring finger of his left hand, he wears a thin gold band symbolic of his marriage to the only woman, he says, he will ever marry. On the ring finger of his right hand, he wears a silver skull to remind him of his own mortality, a significant adornment in light of his having been ranked for years at

gets confusing if you can't identify them from the file names. (If you number them you will lose track and have to keep opening picture files to find the one you want.)

Name photos when you first see them. It's easy when you work closely with other editors and art directors. If a subject is smiling, that photo becomes SMILEY. The shot of a press pass becomes PRESS. With a mnemonic file name, it's more likely that you will remember the picture. If someone asks you where the picture of the press pass for the KEITH story is, for example, you know it's called PASS.EPS and it will be in the KEITH subfolder.

Create a Date Chart

Your copy flow system is not complete without an up-to-date chart chronicling each story's progression in the hierarchy. List the stories down the left and across the top, list all the stages—from entry to output, as Figure 8-4 shows. Then, put dates in the appropriate grid squares when a story goes to a new station. The chart should be kept in a readily accessible place for everyone—on the file server if you work on a network of computers. Then everyone can consult and update it easily. With this one central record, each person can tell what is coming up, what is expected from them, and how long they have

Figure 8-4
The copy flow chart should be kept in a central location or on the network so that everyone can refer to it and update his or her work

STORY	IN SYSTEM	COPY EDITED	PROOF-READ	FACT CHECKED	CORREX IN	TO PAGE	PAGES	
							TO FINAL PAGES	TO REPRO/ FILM
TABLE OF CONTENTS	✓	✓	✓		✓	✓		
LETTERS PAGE	✓		✓	✓				
COVER STORY (KEITH)	✓	✓						
ENTERTAINMENT COLUMN	✓		✓	✓	✓	✓		
FOOD COLUMN	✓							
MEDIA COLUMN	✓							
FASHION STORY	✓	✓	✓	✓	✓	✓	✓	

been holding onto particular projects. The chart also helps prevent using old versions by mistake—especially in a multi-user set up.

All of this may seem a bit pedantic and unnecessary, especially if you work with a small staff. However, when you are juggling a number of stories, scans, and headlines for each issue, you'll quickly find that a little organization goes a long way. When you lose something or print the wrong version of a story, it is too late to organize a system.

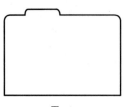

Text

Start with the Raw Text—Stages 1, 2, and 3

Unless you use photos exclusively, text should be the backbone of your production structure. (Though photo books have been done on the desktop, at this stage it doesn't make much sense.)

Type can be brought into your system in two different ways—from outside computers through modem or disk, or from manually input hard copy. If it is coming from a different word-processing program, it must be converted to bare-bones ASCII files (.TXT). If your writers use the same word processor as you, it can come in as a styled (.DOC) file.

ASCII is the most basic text level you can work with. It's a standard that was agreed on in the computer community so that everyone can read each others' files. None of a word processors' styling instructions are translated when ASCII files are translated over electronic mail or through a conversion program. All of the text is simply converted to basic ASCII characters. The ASCII character set contains the alphabet, the numbers, and a few other random symbols, including the international monetary sign. (The set has a pound sign, a dollar sign, and a yen sign. The international monetary sign—a circle with a cross—is for everyone else.) PostScript uses only ASCII characters.

The next, more complex level, is to manipulate or edit your text in a word-processing program. I suggest using the simplest one possible. Anything too complicated overpowers this stage in the system. Some of the most advanced word processors are actually rudimentary desktop-publishing systems and can confuse your page-layout software. Most of your styling should be done in the page software, in Page-Maker, QuarkXPress, or Ventura Publisher. On the Macintosh, a basic word processor like MacWrite is probably good enough. Many people use Microsoft Word because of its good dictionary. If that's why you want Word, then use it. But don't spend a lot of time styling type and formatting copy in Microsoft Word—unless the styles can be read by your page program.

When it first hits your system, text sits in the text entry folder until editors are ready to edit it in the document file. Of course, the editor may take one look at a story and send it straight back to the writer to start all over again. When it comes back, the story starts out at the bottom of the chart again. When there is a clean edit, the editor sends the story subfolder to the copy editing phase. Of course, as backup, a copy of each story subfolder should be left at each stage.

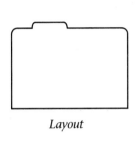

Layout

To Page Layout (.PAG)—Stages 4 and 5

Once you have converted stories into pages in QuarkXPress, you don't need the text files any more. With Ventura you do, because it feeds the information in and out as needed, and with PageMaker you have the option of linking to text files. With all of them, you need to keep the photo files. Photo scans use so much memory that it would be unwieldy to copy them all into the pages.

With QuarkXPress, text files are copied into the page file and are edited right on the desktop. It is possible to export them (send them back to the ASCII formats) with or without style tags if you need to do extensive work on the text. But, for the most part, it is easier and safer to edit right in the page program.

With Ventura Publisher you import and export text regularly because the styling tags go back and forth when corrections are made. Formatting and pasteup positions are preserved through the editing process.

What this all means is that if you are using PageMaker or QuarkXPress, your editors should learn to edit on the page program. Then there is no way they will work on the wrong version of a story, and the story won't have to be restyled every time there is a minor editorial change. Of course, a story should not go to pages until the copy is pretty clean so that editing changes don't radically change the length. You might want to do early trials when the story first comes in, to spec photo, layout, and headline needs, but this should be done with the idea that it could change drastically with the edit.

Though they're scared at first, it's not too hard to teach editors to use the page-makeup software for editing and even a little layout. It's actually a good thing because they find out how hard and time-consuming it is, and they respect the designers more. Also, some editors have a very good eye and should be able to get the job done. Everything moves faster if you have an editor who can say, "Well, it's just a column. Let me throw it into a column template to see if it fits." They won't have to wait for an art person to fit the story, only to find that they have to cut the story further. The more people on your staff who can do basic desktop publishing, the more time and money you can save, which is probably one of the reasons you turned to desktop publishing in the first place.

One final hint is to use a printout to proofread or to copy edit. (It's easier to spot mistakes.) Then enter your changes on the screen.

In the page process (.PAG) you may have two steps (two sets of proofs) to allow for revisions, especially if there is a lot of processing to be done. If you are a little more rough and ready, you can go directly from Page Revision to Output.

Output

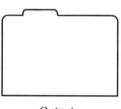

Output

When a page hits the Output stage, everything is assembled to be sent out to a Linotronic or Compugraphic high-resolution output machine. You can leave behind any extraneous text files and previous versions. The only file left should be the page-makeup file and any files associated with it (picture files in QuarkXPress and PageMaker).

In addition, you need to include any data files which specify fonts and preferences. On the Mac, you will have a package of screen fonts, and with Ventura Publisher you will include a width file. The font package will be the same, unless of course, you change fonts between issues. These are just the screen versions, because you have to assume that your service bureau has the final fonts. Be sure to check in advance because ethically you are not allowed to lend your printer fonts unless you have a multiple-printer license. Good service bureaus get all the fonts or will special order them if requested. If you have a custom font (in which case, you own the license and can hand them out to anyone you want) be sure to include the printer fonts in your data files.

The safest thing to do from either platform is to print PostScript to disk. The service bureau simply takes the file and downloads it to their imagesetter. If they don't have the fonts, you can include the fonts in the PostScript file automatically, thus avoiding the licensing issue.

Don't Send FPO Photos as Part of Your Printer File

Another thing to beware of is sending your "For Placement Only" (FPO) photos to final output. These scanned-in photos, which are used in the system for layout only, will take a lot of time and money to print, only to be cut out for the real photos. Pictures take longer to print than text pages, so even if you have your own machine, the printout can take 10 or 15 minutes per page. The solution is to save a photocopy or laser printout of the picture and paste that down on the board to give the printer your positioning.

Film Negative or Film Positive?

As with all the other stages in the process, your final output may not actually be final. Often it will take a number of tries to get all of the little problems worked out. An interesting question is what is the final output. With current desktop publishing technology, you have the choice of printing directly to a film negative or a film positive. A PostScript printer can handle any of these from the same page instructions. You just have to tell it what you want.

If there is anything that the printer needs to strip in, like ads and photos, you don't want to print your final output in film negative. Even when your pages are complete, you may not want to print your final output as a negative, because that makes it almost impossible to fix last minute errors with a knife. In addition, printers expect facing pages to be stripped together. PostScript originally could not handle this because it is a single page-description language, but PageMaker 4 and QuarkXPress 3.0 can now handle spreads. You can't really print a spread unless it is made up as a bastardized double page.

More importantly, most printers are still more used to getting the mechanicals from their customers on a board, and they may have trouble handling your film if you print it out yourself. If you give them a mechanical, printers make the negatives in their own systems and may have an easier time printing them in the end. They may be able to register negatives with pin registration and hang them on a big plate maker. It is important to always remember this interface with the printer for best results.

I like to have a mechanical, particularly if halftones are for position only. You may not notice two serifs overlapping on laser outputs, but in the final output you can just fix it with a knife. Similarly, if there is a hyphen that falls off, or a minor spelling or spacing problem which doesn't warrant the time and money of another output, you can fix it. The key is to make sure that you don't start to say, "We'll fix that in pasteup," too early in the game. The best way to work is to imagine that you are going to get the whole page done perfectly, and then glue it down to a board in one piece. When this does happen (usually only on simple pages), I love it.

On complicated pages with a lot of intricate elements, you may not like the scans as they come out of the final output, so you just do a new scan without resending the whole page. The pasteup stage gives you a reflective check and seems a little safer than going directly to high-resolution printing. If you do decide to go directly to negative, be sure that you get a blueline proof from your printer.

Whatever form you choose for your final print, it is critical that you inspect the pages when you get them back from the service bureau to make sure that they are reproduceable. Be sure that the service bureau is producing solid blacks. If their chemistry is used up or worn out, it will create a gray that may not appear to the naked eye. Put the page on a light table. If you can see light coming through the "black" areas, it is not good enough. You can also check it with a densitometer.

If it's going to be your final output, make sure that it's good enough to be your final output. In addition to checking the density, check that your type is not thinned out. You can start to lose hairlines with poor output. PostScript type is so razor sharp and thin anyway that if it gets any thinner, you don't want it.

Of course, between editorial and art considerations (and errors), it often seems like you keep making final output with no end. You have to stop going back and forth with the service bureau when the marginal results aren't worth it. Do the final changes conventionally. If you are putting together a big magazine with a lot of ads or four-color, it is unlikely that those ads and pictures are even scanned into the system. So, in the end, the printer is going to have to strip all of these in anyway.

Networks—Backing Up and Storage

A key issue for any file management system is security, making sure that there is no chance that all of your work is destroyed or unretrievable.

When files are obsolete, they should be moved to an organized archive. On the Macintosh, this consists of a buried set of hierarchical folders which parallel the active ones. The archive should be somewhere everyone can get to so that if a tragedy happens, anyone can find the files.

Some people keep their archives on floppy, but that becomes an entirely new nightmare. If you are on a network (and if there is more than one of you, you should be on a network), there is no need to use floppies for backup. On a network, the easiest backup system is to have each peripheral machine attached to a 40 MB disk, and then have a file server with a memory of about 100 MB or 1000 MB (a gigabyte). (See Figure 8-5.)

Figure 8-5
Example of an economical and secure publishing network

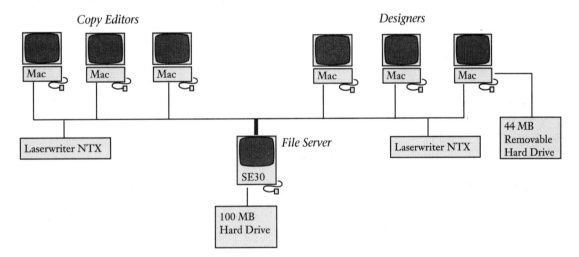

Then the simple rule is that everyone who is working on a file at the end of the day copies it to the file server and to his or her own disk. So, if the file server disk ever goes down, people should be able to replenish it from their own disks, and if an individual's disk goes down, the file server should be able to replenish it. The file server should also have copies of any programs and data files you use. Even personal letter files can be backed up and locked on the file server.

If you are not part of a network, consider getting a second hard disk to keep as a twin. I have never known anyone to be sufficiently backed up at the time of a disk crash if they were using a floppy backup system. Nobody wants to spend the time pushing floppies in and out of the dumb slot. When you are busiest, you are least likely to do it, and that is when the disk is going to go down.

Disks do go down. This is an important thing to remember; no hard disk lasts forever. Every machine that I have ever used has had a disk crash at some point. Usually the problem is a damaged boot block on the disk, so it can't reboot and it doesn't have enough room left to repair itself.

There are a bunch of ways that disks can get hurt. You can wipe out a disk by just putting an audio loudspeaker too close. A power impulse in the middle of a program will zap your PRAMs. I cannot emphasize enough how essential it is to back up your files.

Using any of the backup methods means that your hard disk will include a library of everything you ever use. Every once in a while, you have to make previous versions obsolete or you will run out of room, particularly if you have any pictures.

Forty megabytes seemed like a lot of disk space until we started using more photos on the desktop. Now it seems like nothing. One hundred megabytes is more typical. Soon, we will have better storage media like CD-ROM where we can write onto compact disks. WORMS are the next phase (Write Once, Read Many times). Once you save something, you won't be able to erase it.

A portable hard disk is an interesting option for backing up your files, especially if you are a lone operator. You can just pick it up and carry it to the office or home or wherever you are going. Then all you have to do is boot any Macintosh from your portable disk, and you are home. You just have to be sure that you have all of the possible screen drivers for each machine you use. Also, when you get home, you have to remember to back up any work you did on the road.

In this vein, the next step on the portability front is increased modem speed so they become "gateways" operating like networked machines in the same room. Then you will be able to access your home environment without carrying anything. Computers with these high-speed modems will essentially become networked across the phone lines.

The big computer companies like Apple and IBM are already completely networked worldwide. If you work at IBM and you go to any workstation in the world (they have something like 185,000), you can log on and get your work or electronic mail. In this communication area, the computer CPU will be a lot like the telephone. Though the handset hasn't changed much, the telephone system is continually changing. The way we access things is the same. What we are accessing is different.

Smart *Magazine*

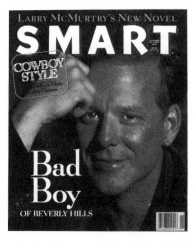

The number one reason to get into desktop publishing (as opposed to some other kind of publishing) is to save money. Everything else is gravy. At *Smart* magazine we found out just how much gravy there is. In fact, it never would have gotten off the ground without this technology.

Smart is a consumer magazine, in the same general vein as *Esquire* or *Vanity Fair*, but with a special emphasis on good writing. In that respect, it's really an old-fashioned magazine, one directed at readers rather than "scanners" or "flippers."

It costs a lot of money to start a big magazine. The launch of *Vanity Fair,* some say, took $25 million. A lot of that money is wasted. At big publishing groups, much time is spent arguing between various vice presidents and their staffs. So many people are involved, that more people are needed just to provide communications between them. In the process, the idea for the magazine can get lost, hacked to death by corporate functionaries whose main interest is their own careers. This can lead to failure. Time, Inc. dropped many millions on aborted projects like *TV-Cable Week* and *Picture Week*. Realizing that its own bigness was smothering the infant magazines, the group gave up trying for a while. It let others do the entrepreneurial work and then bought in when the risk was reduced (as in the case of *Parenting*). The conventional wisdom for the big players has become: don't plant seeds, buy seedlings, or full-grown trees.

The essential ingredient in starting a new magazine is zeal. You need a nearly mono-maniacal entrepreneur, one who will not stop until the magazine is standing on its own. With *Smart*, that zealot was Terry McDonell, a seasoned editor who had lead both successful (*Outside*) and not-so-successful (*Rocky Mountain*) launches. McDonell was not averse to starting with lots of money or the backing of a huge corporation, and he worked months lining up a deal with Lorimar. Circulation tests gave a green light, and millions of dollars were assured, but at the last minute in the increasingly familiar corporate merger, Lorimar was absorbed by Warner and sold off the publishing group, among other divisions, to help finance the deal. (Ironically, a year later Warner got into publishing in a much bigger way, by merging with Time.)

With months of effort wasted, most would have given up. But McDonell had the eye-blazing determination of a true magazine entrepreneur. He figured that at the least, he could get out a single issue. If it sold well on the newsstand, he was sure he could raise the money to go quarterly, then bimonthly, and ultimately monthly.

Don Welsh, who had headed the Lorimar Publishing Group was game—but his cash had been used in the leveraged buyout. The new Welsh Publishing Group was ready to sell ads, and handle circulation and manufacturing. My own design firm came in to do the design. And McDonell raised money for editorial and prepress production. Small amounts came from friends, many of them in the movie or music business. Writing and some other services were traded for equity in *Smart*.

How much did it cost? "Well," McDonell likes to say, "under a million dollars." Just how much under a million, he won't say.

Less Is More

The biggest cost in editing and designing magazines is people. *Smart* had to reduce the staff to a smaller group—to the minimum needed to come up with the ideas that really make a magazine.

The way to keep the staff down is to maximize the amount of work each person can do. You have to give you staff the right tools, and nowadays that means personal computers.

McDonell had a Macintosh Plus, and I brought one from home (hooked up, hilariously to a Xerox single-page monitor). And that was it at the beginning.

But we quickly found that fewer people actually get more done. There is an analogy from the computer world—the chip. As chips have gotten smaller, information travels faster, and computers have become more powerful. Magazines traditionally have big staffs because of the amount of unavoidable, labor-intensive work. There is an enormous amount of paper: manuscripts in various versions, typesetting galley proofs, layouts, page proofs. It becomes a loop: the more paper there is, the more people you need, the more paper is produced.

Before desktop publishing, technologies had been advanced to cut through this cycle. In big newspapers and magazines, editorial front-end systems (like Atex) automated word processing and eliminated the need to rekey text for typesetting. But staff structures remained about the same. There wasn't much you could do about the size of the staff if you didn't want to reduce the number and quality of words and pictures. Only when the page-layout function was glued to word processing (by PageMaker and subsequent programs) did the real potential emerge. Curiously, it was the low-end personal computer industry that brought the solutions that publishers needed. Not only did the hardware cost a fraction of the mini-based systems (like Atex), the software was available in shrink-wrapped packages at the neighborhood software store.

Desktop programs put the production tools in the hands of the people who actually do the thinking and make the decisions. A top editor or art director no longer has to wait for an assistant to finish the job. The computer does it instead. Desktop publishing for big-time publications in effect cuts out the "middle man." Assistant editors, assistant designers, and pasteup people are increasingly unnecessary. This represents an enormous savings in time and money.

But it goes beyond this. Cutting out the middle men not only saves money, but the people actually doing the work come closer together, for efficiency. Without the delays and dilutions of paper-shuffling intermediaries, everybody gets more turned on by the process. It's like instant gratification. You see results so fast that you are empowered to do more work. As there is more inspiration, quality improves. Hence, the apparent paradox: fewer people make better magazines.

Collaborative Desktops

This is what is so exciting about desktop publishing. It's more than just new technology; it's not a video game. It is a release of creative energy. And there is more. So far, we've been talking about increased efficiency in terms of one editor or designer sitting at a workstation and get much more done. But magazines are collaborative products, and desktop publishing is being adapted as "groupware." Networks are linking the workstations; large monitors are allowing interactive presentations.

We see more editors and designers sitting down to actually work together—not just talk. This is so different from the way things used to be done. The simplest example is when an editor will sit at the keyboard revising text in a layout with the art director just watching. Immediately, they can see the result; they can incorporate and go on—or try again. In the past, there would have been a delay while new type was set and "comped" in. Sometimes it wasn't worth waiting, and they would go with the unimproved version. This is where the quality issue comes in.

Another workgroup situation seen frequently at *Smart* is when the designer is running the mouse, with the editor sitting along side, making suggestions, calling out copy changes, suggesting alternatives, which are put up on the screen for comparison.

Smart's covers work this way. After initial discussions on the subject,

Terry McDonell and I edit the pictures (also together) and scan in the choices. Then, we sit down and look at it on the screen together. Each picture is brought into the cover template—with the logo and some dummy heads already in position. We both make comments, and adjustments are made immediately—changing the headline style, rewriting the headline, making pictures bigger or smaller, or even replacing pictures. The revised version is then immediately available; it can easily be printed out to take home overnight, or to show to others for their reactions. The iterations of the Duvall cover appear in Figure 9-1a–9-1f. The development of the cover which opened this chapter is shown in Figures 9-1g–9-1i.

The design process for *Smart* covers is now compressed into an hour (for the first pass)—instead of a day or more at conventional magazines. In the bad old days, when the pages came back to the editor from the art department, they invariably weren't what he had envisioned and the whole process started over. With desktop publishing you immediately see the ideas on the screen, for better or for worse. Even the mistakes happen faster.

The point is that design cannot be described; it must speak for itself—that is, it must be seen. Magazines must always struggle to combine the verbal (the editorial side) with the visual (the design side). Sadly, many designers are not very articulate; and many editors have a hard time with imagery. Traditional publishing took so long that layouts could only emerge as series of iterations—proofs. Desktop publishing cuts out the constant ricocheting back and forth until no one is happy. The new tools allow editors and designers to truly collaborate.

At least, they're working that way at *Smart*. Two designers can work together, or a designer and an editor can sit down and start pushing things around on the screen until they're happy. Sometimes, against all precedent, you will see the chief editor sitting at the keyboard adjusting a layout with the startled designer looking on. This is actually more in the spirit of the magazine form than the rigidly defined job descriptions of the past. Magazines are a team endeavor—there is no room for inflexible, individual artists. A good editor is able to sublimate his or her own ideas to the larger idea of the magazine. The designer must blend his or her own ideas to the larger personality of the

Figure 9-1a
We selected the final photograph of Robert Duvall, positioned it on the cover, and filled the *Smart* logo with white so it would contrast against the neutral background

Figure 9-1b
We roughed the position of text and gave the dummy to the editor so he could write final copy

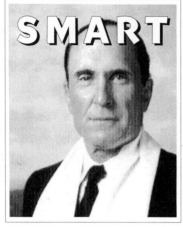

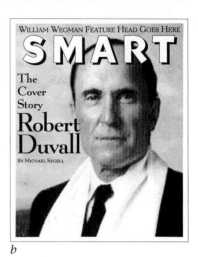

a

b

Figure 9-1c
To highlight a fashion feature, we drew a dingbat in Adobe Illustrator and incorporated it into a sticker, which was later tilted and placed in the lower-right corner of the cover

c

d

Figure 9-1d
We included a small picture (separated from the logo by being framed in a shadow box) to call attention to a feature on photographer William Wegman

Figure 9-1e
Trial positioning of some of the cover elements

Figure 9-1f
The final cover layout, including all elements and the final text correctly positioned

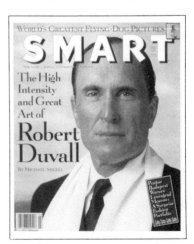

e

f

Figure 9-1g
An early comp of a cover featuring Mickey Rourke

Figure 9-1h
Experimenting with the cover elements

Figure 9-1i
The printed Rourke cover

g

h

i

magazine. But no one editor or designer has a personality big enough for a great magazine.

Of course, as a magazine grows it may be hard to keep the staff small. If *Smart* becomes a big success—it has already become a monthly—I don't know how much we will be able to maintain the close contact. That is the challenge. Right now we are working at the outward limits of desktop publishing. If the software developers can keep up with us (and they have so far), we should be able to keep a good deal of the intimacy and no-nonsense quality of the *Smart* office as the magazine grows and prospers. And since the work habits developed around DTP, *Smart* should be in an excellent position to show how these tools perform at a bigger scale.

Smart Machinery

Each person on the editorial staff has a Mac. This is axiomatic. The system won't work with some people on and some people off the network, because a magazine is like a convoy. Everyone must travel at the speed of the slowest.

For example, if a copy editor is working on paper proofs only, and not entering the changes directly on the screen, then someone else must do that work. This means there you are turning a designer into a typesetting operator, or adding another production hand—which defeats the purpose.

It is a mistake to use DTP to simply replicate the old system. Instead, desktop publishing makes the typesetting function completely invisible, allowing everyone to concentrate on editorial quality instead of production.

The first issue of *Smart* was done with a very small staff and very slim resources. We actually had only four Macintoshes, the two Pluses we brought from home and two rented SEs, as well as one rental LaserWriter NT. With only four full-time people at that time, each had a machine, and the system worked. The art director's workstation had a large vertical screen, (a full-page Xerox page monitor), and each station had at least a 40-MB hard disk. Since all the Macs were connected to the printer with inexpensive PhoneNet cable, it was a simple matter to buy Tops network software to connect the machines. Tops will run without a separate Macintosh used as a file server. You simply "publish" files on your hard disk so that others on the network can "mount" them.

Even the barest system can produce incredible results (with all due modesty). When some people from Apple came to see our set up, they were astonished that we didn't even have any Mac IIs. We would have liked them, but just couldn't afford the cost. Figure 9-2 shows our system.

The first issue was in essence a test, although this was never pointed out. If there had not been a good response on the newsstand, that would have been it. We would have returned the rental machines and gone on to other endeavors. The first issue was also a test of the practicality of using this low-end system to put out an upscale publication.

On the basis of the first issue, however, we raised enough money to skip the quarterly plan and go bimonthly. Our budget was tight, but we had proved that the new tools worked. On reflection we found that we couldn't have done it without them.

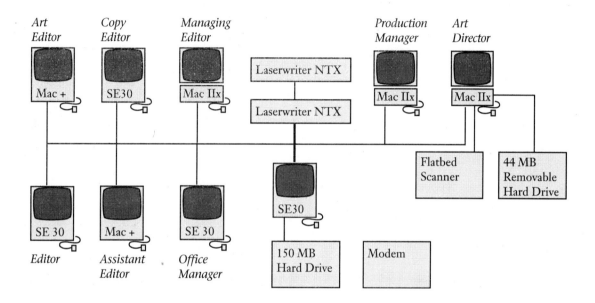

Figure 9-2
The *Smart* network

With moderate funding, *Smart* moved up to a system that looks more like those in the advertisements—Mac IIx machines with big screens. But, there are still some small Macintoshes, including the ones we started with. At the beginning of 1990, just before the magazine went monthly, the system was as shown in Table 9-1.

There are just eight workstations. And despite the axiom, ("One person, one Mac"), *Smart* still hasn't been able to buy computers for the two fashion editors, the regular freelance researchers, or the receptionist/secretary. All in time.

A file server links all the stations using a very simple AppleShare network. We found this easier to use than Tops. The production manager serves as "network administrator," assigning passwords and setting up zones in the network to restrict access to certain files.

Everyone saves his or her files on the network so colleagues have

Table 9-1   The *Smart* System

User	Equipment
Editor	Mac SE with 80-MB hard disk
Art editor	Mac Plus with two floppy drives only
Copy editor	Mac SE with 80-MB hard disk
Assistant editor	Mac Plus with two floppy drives only
Managing editor	Mac IIx with 80-MB hard disk and Radius full-page monochrome monitor
Art director	Mac IIx with 80-MB hard disk and E-machines 16-inch color monitor
Production manager	Mac IIx with 80-MB hard disk and Radius full-page monochrome monitor
Office manager	Mac SE with 80-MB hard disk
All	2 Apple LaserWriters IINTX with 20-MB hard disks
All	Mac SE 30 as file server with 150-MB hard disk
All	300-dpi, 16-gray scale, b&w Apple Scanner
All	Hayes-compatible 1200-baud modem
All	Mass Micro 45-MB removable hard disk
All	Continuous, battery backup power supply

access as needed. The files are pushed along from folder to folder, as pages are developed.

At *Smart*, we don't simply use this technology as a typographical and layout tool. It is also a visual layout tool. Over the last three years, as the machinery has gotten better and I have worked with it more intensely, I have realized this more and more.

Generally we've found that the bigger the monitors the better. As the magazine produces more and more color pages on the desktop, it seems that everyone needs color monitors. (There is some dispute whether 19-inch monitors justify the cost over 16-inch monitors.

There are no more pixels on large monitors. They're just bigger.)

The power supply protection (connected to the file server and its disks) was added when we suspected that surges in the electrical line were crashing the server. We use removable hard disks when we want to move a lot of big color files around, or to archive files at the end of the issue.

To make sure all files are backed up, everyone has to remember to keep a copy of every story underway on a personal hard disk as well as on the file server.

Designing on the Screen

It seems that we are doing more and more on the screen. And so the pictures are essential. After a rough edit of the photos for a story, we scan in each image—even though we know we won't use every one of them.

At first this seemed cumbersome, and we would just photocopy the pictures and paste the images on proofs. But, bit by bit, with the easy-to-use Apple Scanner, we stopped using the Mac simply as a pagination machine. We start the design from ground zero. The art director of *Smart*, Rhonda Rubinstein, will sit down with everything in her mind—not even a pencil sketch, and within minutes have a first rough of a layout.

Color is the next step. We've put off buying a color scanner because of the cost, but there is another issue. While the black-and-white scanner takes no more time than walking over a few times to the Canon and sizing the pictures, the color scanner isn't nearly as fast. For the time being, we send out for color scans (which can be costly) for the cover and special layouts. But soon the color scanners will be faster and cheaper, or *Smart* will be richer (or all three).

All the software we use is off-the-shelf. Not only is it the cheapest option, but it may become obsolete next week when something new and better is released. We don't want to be tied to an expensive custom-designed system. The main software is QuarkXPress 3.0 for basic page design and production. Adobe Illustrator handles special type treatments, ornaments, and small graphics, though some of us prefer Aldus FreeHand. We also have Letraset ImageStudio for manipulating photos and Studio/8 for color photos. For text manipulation, the editors tend to use Microsoft Word, but we actually do some of the text processing right in QuarkXPress—after the text has been flowed into layouts.

Some **Smart** *Design Background*

Smart got its name from the early twentieth-century magazine *Smart Set,* edited in its heyday by H.L. Mencken. Thus the design of the magazine should evoke the same literary tradition as *The New Yorker* or the old *Vanity Fair.* This great magazine tradition was almost forgotten in the 1980s. *Smart* is an antidote to the choppy yuppie-style magazines of the last few years, with their focus on getting and spending. *Smart* is a writing-oriented magazine and in so far as it is visual, it uses photographs only—not illustrations. We decided to get away from the rut of commercial illustration, which seems to have been stuck on the same repetitive forms for the past few years. (And, realistically, at the rates we could pay, we could not expect to attract the best illustrators). Undoubtedly the time will come for *Smart* to commission art, but we hope to stick to the principle that the meaning, the content, always comes first.

Frankly, we wanted *Smart* to be solid and a bit traditional; we wanted it to look like it might have been around since the good old days.

Magazines have come to have front-of-the-book sections—partly as a way to get a lot of advertising up front. Readers have come to expect them, and reader habits should always be taken into account.

Smart's front section is called "Smart Set," after the magazine's namesake. It contains a few spreads with short items, but none of the usual catalogue extolling the virtues of a new espresso machine, or whatever. Then come the columns, with a lot of text on the page, which tells the reader that this is a serious, writerly magazine in which the text doesn't need a lot of design elements.

The practical benefit of the conservative design is that these pages help the ads stand apart (a distinction appreciated by the advertising department, which puts the best customers in the front). But the readers also like it. In some magazines it is hard to tell what is an ad and what is editorial. The fact that economic pressures have, for the most part, caused publishers to abandon feature wells (uninterrupted editorial sections), makes it imperative to design around the ads. Of course, the solution varies with the kind of advertising in a magazine.

One of my favorite spreads in *Smart* was in the second issue where there is a full text page opposite a full ad page. It's reproduced in Figure 9-3. It happens to be the kind of ad we want to get in the magazine, from big national advertisers. In a situation like this we're telling people, "You're not idiots. You're like us. You like to read, and your attention span is a little greater than the average watcher of MTV."

Figure 9-3
A spread targeted at those who like to read

But this does not mean you should abandon efforts to get people started reading. Smart's text type is plenty big. It's generally 9 point (on 11-point leading), and there are healthy old-style margins around the text. So, we let it stand for itself. There are always devices to attract readers to the top of an article. In the columns, for example, the lead is set large, with a big initial and special wide measure.

One reason you don't see many full pages of text in most magazines is because of the number of people working on each story. Each article and page has an editorial or art person saying, "We can't make my article look dull." In fact, plain, readable pages don't look dull. If you design the introduction well enough to get people to start reading it, and it is well written, who cares how much graphic junk is in it? The main point is: make it easy to read.

Typography

Typography is an important design element in *Smart*. Since we have opted for a spare traditional style, the type is not overshadowed by other design elements and therefore must be strong enough to stand on its own. The text type is ITC Stone Serif, and *Smart* was one of the first to use it.

Designed by Sumner Stone of Adobe Systems, it was the first type to be designed for PostScript. (And much of the design work was done on the Mac, using Adobe Illustrator.)

In the effort to conjure up the feeling of the grand magazine of the 1920s, we looked for a 1920s typeface—one that was not generally in use. We found Lucian, designed by Lucian Bernhard in 1930 (see Figure 9-4). It is a more handsome relative of Bernhard Modern, which has become extremely popular since *Smart* began. (Perhaps there is a connection; perhaps not.)

Lucian has a nice blend of classicism and the roaring twenties, with just a bit of Marlene Dietrich. Of course, others weren't using it, at least in part, because it had never been digitized for PostScript. (Linotype had made Lucian available for its non-PostScript equipment about the time *Smart* was being formatted.)

We went to The Font Bureau to make a PostScript font. David Berlow undertook the project personally, and produced Lucian Demi Bold in time for the first issue.

More weights have been added since then. The Italic took more

Lucian Book

ABCDEFGHIJKLMN
OPQRSTUVWXYZ
abcdefghijklmn
opqrstuvwxyz
1234567890

Lucian Demi

ABCDEFGHIJKLMN
OPQRSTUVWXYZ
abcdefghijklmn
opqrstuvwxyz
1234567890

Lucian Ultra

ABCDEFGHIJKLMN
OPQRSTUVWXYZ
abcdefghijklmn
opqrstuvwxyz
1234567890

work, since the original Italic was simply a sloped roman, and Berlow thought it lacked the elegance the magazine wanted.

So far, there are three styles: Book, Demi Bold, and Ultra. A Bold is planned, as are Italics for each.

In one clever design solution, Berlow made the weight of the Demi Bold work as small caps for the Book. This avoids the usual phototype problem of small caps that look too light.

The format, however, still relies on the demi weight for most headlines. Others are used for accent, or for an exceptional headline. The feature section of *Smart* is an eclectic affair, but the default headline face is Lucian Demi Bold. This is to give the editorial pages a more cohesive identity—both to make them stand out from the ads inside the magazine, and to make them stand apart from other magazines.

Smart is divided into three parts: a front-of-the-book section, a feature section, and what we call the "Special."

"Smart Set"

The front section takes the name of Mencken's magazine which inspired the publication from the beginning, *Smart Set.* It starts with a fast-paced collection of short news items, set in a four-column grid, but with much latitude allowed for boxes and pictures. The headlines call on all the different styles of Lucian, and the text type is varied, in part to create a feeling of liveliness, and in part simply to make the items fit.

The section continues with a series of spreads, usually with just one column of text and a big picture. Finally, come the columns, where the famous writers' names are big attraction for *Smart* readers. Here we have opted for a fairly old-fashioned approach, with text-heavy layouts. The columns are designed to work best as left-hand pages, to give the advertisers their favorite far-forward, right-hand positions. All the "Smart Set" pages are bordered with a gray Oxford (thick-thin) rule. These are there to signal that these are editorial pages, but there is something else at work, too. The Oxford border was a trademark of *Rolling Stone* magazine, the alma mater of many of *Smart's* editors and contributors. We were subtly suggesting that *Smart* comes out of the tradition of that magazine's quality in the 1960s and

1970s. Interestingly enough, *Rolling Stone* revived elements of its old format, including Oxford borders, soon after *Smart* appeared.

The Feature Well

With the feature section, we label and departmentalize each story, to provide regular signposts. They help the editor avoid writing headlines that are actually labels. By putting little wavy lines under the labels, we signal this is the beginning of another story.

We have also experimented with repeating other visual effects to hold the sections together. The palm trees in the first issue were used as a leitmotif to hold together three different stories. Figure 9-5 shows how we created them.

Figure 9-5
Creating the palm trees

We scanned a sketch of a palm tree into the machine and then autotraced it with Adobe Illustrator

We reworked the rough edges…

…until the finished icon was filled with black

Some of the articles used the icon reversed inside a black box

A typical feature was the one on Keith Richards. In designing the story opener we put the spaced-out *Smart* logo at the top to indicate that the magazine is officially beginning—a convention followed by many magazines.

Since in this issue the magazine was starting on a single page (opposite an ad), I wanted bold, classical typography for the opener, but when I saw the "K" had so much power, I saw the potential for a big drop cap. Figures 9-6a–9-6g show the progression of this feature design. I just couldn't resist blowing it up all the way. Usually with a

Figure 9-6a
Using Adobe Illustrator we loosely spaced the *Smart* logo to appear at the opening of the feature section

Figure 9-6b
We flowed the story into the provisional page and set the headline space

Figure 9-6c
We selected, styled, and shot a photograph of a stage pass from the Keith Richards' tour, and then we scanned it for positioning at 300 dpi

eith Richards speaks in a mid-Atlantic drawl, like a P.G. Wodehouse character who has wandered into an Erskine Caldwell novel. A small-boned man of average height—five feet, ten inches—Richards has eyes the amber color of his favorite bourbon (Rebel Yell), lank black hair that has developed a dash of gray at the temples and a tendency to curl, and a once-straight nose Romanized by his nodding out into a loudspeaker. There is about him something of the handsome gargoyle, down to his small, wide feet and hands. On the ring finger of his left hand, he wears a thin gold band symbolic of his marriage to the only woman, he says, he will ever marry. On the ring finger of his right hand, he wears a silver skull to remind him of his own mortality, a significant adornment in light of his having been ranked for years at number one on every list of rock stars next in line to die.

eith Richards speaks in a mid-Atlantic drawl, like a P.G. Wodehouse character who has wandered into an Erskine Caldwell novel. A small-boned man of average height—five feet, ten inches—Richards has eyes the amber color of his favorite bourbon (Rebel Yell), lank black hair that has developed a dash of gray at the temples and a tendency to curl, and a once-straight nose Romanized by his nodding out into a loudspeaker. There is about him something of the handsome gargoyle, down to his small, wide feet and hands. On the ring finger of his left hand, he wears a thin gold band symbolic of his marriage to the only woman, he says, he will ever marry. On the ring finger of his right hand, he wears a silver skull to remind him of his own mortality, a significant adornment in light of his having been ranked for years at number one on every list of rock stars next in line to die.

Figure 9-6d
Then we turned to the text, looking for a good way to start the story

Figure 9-6e
I drew two lines that repelled text in the shape of the letter "K"

K eith Richards speaks in a mid-Atlantic drawl, like a P.G. Wodehouse character who has wandered into an Erskine Caldwell novel. A small-boned man of average height—five feet, ten inches—Richards has eyes the amber color of his favorite bourbon (Rebel Yell), lank black hair that has developed a dash of gray at the temples and a tendency to curl, and a once-straight nose Romanized by his nodding out into a loudspeaker. There is about him something of the handsome gargoyle, down to his small, wide feet and hands. On the ring finger of his left hand, he wears a thin gold band symbolic of his marriage to the only woman, he says, he will ever marry. On the ring finger of his right hand, he wears a silver skull to remind him of his own mortality, a significant adornment in light of his having been ranked for years at number one on every list of rock stars next in line to die.

Figure 9-6f
I colored the rule lines white (so they wouldn't show up) and then dropped in the letter "K"

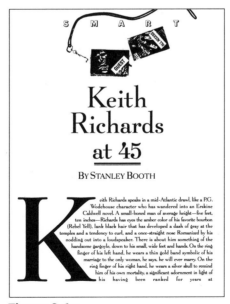

Figure 9-6g
The final page, opening the feature section

drop initial, the text is inset to fit the capital letter. Sometimes, the first line is indented less, to better fit the initial.

Contouring text around the initial is tricky (sometimes too tricky), but can work beautifully with a really big letter. You can draw rules in QuarkXPress, and they can repel text. After drawing the rules parallel to the two arms of the "K," I extended them to push back the text on the right. Then, I selected the rules and changed their color to white—so they wouldn't print. It only took two or three tries to get it right. The big trick is then trying to find the rules later if you need to move them!

The text of this introduction was selected and resized (with 4 points automatically added) until it fit exactly. Check out the QuarkXPress manual for the short-cut key commands that handle size, leading, and tracking for text. With them you can quickly make a text block expand or contract to fit or fill the required space.

The little skull dingbats were used for breaks in the story—a Keith motif. They came straight off a poison label. We scanned them in, and using Adobe Streamline, we turned them into PostScript files in a hurry—no editing involved.

The Special

The book section is my favorite part of *Smart*. It is a 16-page piece of writing, usually fiction. The design is simple. It's all text with a little ornamentation, much like a similar section in *Trips* (see Chapter 10, "*Trips,* A User-Friendly Magazine"). It is another acknowledgement on our part that readers are grown up and that they can and want to read. *Smart* is not aimed at semi-literates. By giving a decent amount of space to good writers, we attract the attention of good writers and of readers who appreciate good writing. People should turn to it and think, "Well, I've got this. I can read this." *Smart* is not just to flip through. Like the clean design, solid content is kind of a novel idea at this point in the evolution of magazines. With *Trips* we had a similar notion; you would have peaks and valleys—text pages and then some picture pages—but all would contain a lot of real content.

With desktop publishing, it's easy to make the book section fill 16 pages exactly. In the second issue, we enlarged the type to make a 10,000-word story fill. In the third issue, we had a 24,000-word story (see Figure 9-7), and we really wanted to get it all in, so we reduced the point size and leading until it fit.

Figure 9-7

The book section, where we trust our readers want to read

There were some misgivings that we had reduced the type too much. Reduced type is something to be used only as a last resort. We ended up with 8-point Stone Serif, which is about equal to 9-point Times Roman, which is about as small as can be comfortably read.

Trips:
A User-Friendly
Magazine

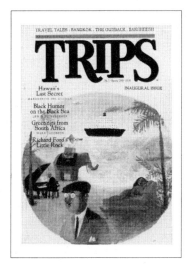

Trips was the first magazine in which I used desktop publishing for real. No more predictions, no more experimentation. It was a question of loading up the boat and pushing off to sea.

The magazine was started by the Banana Republic clothing chain, part of The Gap, so there was the financial backing of a major corporation behind the experiment. The company's two founders, Mel and Patricia Ziegler, had both worked as journalists before starting their now famous clothing company, and were firmly committed to the project. Just as they had broken all the rules in the retail business, they wanted to try something new with their magazine.

Sadly, they didn't get much of a chance, since after the first issue Banana Republic was reorganized. The Zieglers were out of the company, and the magazine was out of business. It was a pity, since it was truly an original publication. But, few ever got to see it.

Trips was one of the first, noncomputer magazines to use off-the-shelf hardware and software to produce a major magazine. The results were amazing to us—even more so because no one on the outside could really spot it as desktop-produced. Though we had the late nights and last minute changes common to all startups, the entire 160-page première issue was produced in four weeks by a relatively small startup staff using a combination of PC computer technology and traditional methods.

When we could save time or improve results, we used desktop publishing. However, we still did some of the more creative features traditionally. Many people feel they have to make everything work on the machine immediately. At *Trips* our philosophy was that just because we had the system didn't mean we had to make everything work on it all at once. We used the time saved with computers to concentrate on quality illustration, to research typefaces for headlines and drop caps, and to play around with innovative borders and graphic elements. As we got more and more proficient on the system, we did more and more with it.

I must admit that the desktop technology didn't seem to save any time at all in the beginning. I think it is a law of publishing that however many people you have, they still work too hard and too late every night. At *Newsweek* (my previous employer), there were nearly 100 people in the art and photo departments, yet every deadline seemed to turn into an all-nighter.

We had kept the *Trips* staff small—partly because the magazine was intended to start as a quarterly, and partly because we assumed the desktop-publishing equipment would mean a cut in work, but the first issue took time because the equipment was new to most of the staff.

Those of us who were comfortable with the technology had to get involved with functions usually handled by typesetters, or typographers. As desktop publishing was new to the world, and we were new to desktop publishing, we tried to learn to walk before running. This was appropriate for *Trips* and for anyone starting out with desktop publishing.

Our familiarity with the technology and the state of the technology in 1987 were both on the rough side. Most people considered that the tools were not yet meant for professionals. But there were already many things that could be done, one step at a time.

We went into the project assuming that we could handle word processing on the PCs and composition typesetting on paper. It was up to us to discover how many of the missing links we could do in desktop publishing: layout, design, color, and film stripping.

Of course, it is easier to move into desktop publishing with a new publication. With an existing publication, it is much more complicated. First, there is the issue of existing equipment (front-end systems like Atex or typesetting equipment) that was expensive, and which, in the absence of desktop-publishing technology, would still have some years of productive use. The people who manage these systems are usually the last to want to go into desktop publishing—if only because of the fear, sometimes justified, that it will put them out of a job. But even after everyone agrees to go to desktop publishing, there is a big lurch while the people are being trained and production methods are being converted. Some staffers have just figured out the old system, and they are reluctant to learn new software, a new way of doing things.

Production Specs

In 1987 (eons ago) the IBM-compatible PC was neck and neck with the Macintosh in terms of suitability for professional publishing. The PC had the most popular word-processing programs; the Mac had the easy user interface and the friendly mouse instead of all those codes. Aldus PageMaker was the first DTP program, and still the easiest to learn, but the Mac screen (until the advent of the Mac II later in the year) was still tiny. And when push came to shove, the PCs were cheaper.

Since money is the reason anyone decided to go to desktop publishing, it was almost a foregone conclusion that *Trips* would buy PCs. For the actual hardware we chose IBM clones, with inexpensive 13-inch monitors and dot-matrix printers for the editors. The two art workstations consisted of AT-clones, and 19-inch gray-scale monitors, and a mouse. We bought an Apple LaserWriter Plus for the PostScript, a Microtek 300C scanner, a modem—and a Macintosh to round out the design system, which is shown in Figure 10-1.

Figure 10-1
The lack of a network in the *Trips* production setup meant we played a lot of floppy frisbee

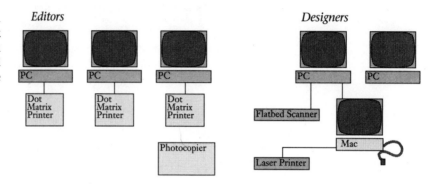

Writers and editors at *Trips* used XyWrite, which has become the standard professional word-processing software, based originally on Atex. It is fast and powerful, and writers who have worked at newspapers with Atex are happy with its command codes. (As am I—this book was written with XyWrite.)

Because of its ability to flow text in and out of pages, thus keeping the files compatible with the original word-processing software, we chose Xerox Ventura Publisher on the PC for page composition. It was particularly well adapted to text-driven magazines, and feature for feature had better typography controls than anything on the Mac.

The text came in by disk, by modem, or it was simply typed in at the office. Before the story was edited, a floppy disk copy of the story (in XyWrite) went to the art department so they could start to work on layouts. In hindsight, I see that we should have networked all of the workstations from the beginning, but without experience I was reluctant to jump into networking. Under deadline pressures, playing floppy frisbee complicated the process. But one editor kept track of all the stories by keeping a master floppy and backing up everything on a hard disk. Ultimately, this is the way it is done even with sophisticated systems with complete file management features—one person still has to take responsibility for the flow of copy.

Production Flow

When a story was accepted, the editors would give a floppy with a rough text file to associate art director Margery Canter and me, so that we could read it and assign freelance photographers, illustrators—even calligraphers.

Page layout might have started as a sketch on a napkin or the back of an envelope, but we would then quickly start roughing the pages out in Ventura Publisher. We found that by flowing text into Ventura, we could quickly get an idea of how long the story was. We could budget an approximate space and leave windows for the art work. We quickly found that comping up type on Ventura was much faster than the old method of photocopying dummy type and pasting it together —never mind the older method of carefully sketching and tracing it out by hand.

The photos were for the most part copied on a Canon laser copier and pasted into the layouts by hand. But bit by bit we started using the scanner (which could connect to either the Mac or the PC) to introduce pictures electronically. Eventually we realized that the goal is to get everything into the system. With each step that we incorporated, we saved time and money.

We would get an idea and use Ventura to set the type, paste it on a layout board, and then put the photocopies of the pictures in place. We would then adjust the size of the pictures and redo the layout to fit the new space. We could check copy length long before editors were finished with pieces by flowing rough text into rough layouts at any stage in the process. There was no waiting around for type and galleys. Typefaces could be chosen and headlines put in for placement. A major cost savings here resulted from not having to reset type to fit copy.

When the final text was poured in, we could see immediately if the story was long or short, and could either adjust the layout or alert the editorial department to make changes.

In order to keep track of the progression of the screen, we reduced all working layouts to one-third size and put them on a wall. We could see both the overall feel of the magazine, and an overview of what was left to do. People walking by would offer random comments—much like readers.

The hardest thing in designing a magazine is figuring out how the reader will react to a layout. It's the right instinct for this that separates the pros from the amateurs.

Of course, in the early stages we were often working with a number of alternative layouts for the same story, so the proofs on the wall were continually changing. Knowing we could generate new layouts and boards quickly with desktop publishing actually let us be more critical of our work. We were never afraid to get rid of a less-than-perfect layout because the time and resources necessary to produce a new one were little.

To move the process along, it is important to let the editors see proofs as early as possible. Traditionally, page proofs have been done near the end of the production cycle, and some nightmare situations have come up when editors finally saw pages. With desktop publishing, editors and designers can work together earlier, either on the screen or on hard proofs, to fit copy and mold the final look of a story.

Ventura Publisher easily produces the typesetting, with the right typefaces, point sizes, and hyphenation of the final pages, so editors can head off many pasteup difficulties right on the screen. One screw up can ruin a lot of careful typographical work on a page. One of the nicest features of Ventura is the loose-line feature which highlights lines with too much word spacing. An editor or art person can go in and fix the problems with discretionary hyphens, missed by the hyphenation and justification algorithm in the program. This allows better typography, and fits more text into a column—making everyone happy.

The tendency of editors used to traditional production flow is to leave many copy checks until the end ("We'll catch it in the proofs.") At *Trips* it fell to the art department to educate the editorial side about their role—or else the designers (all two of us) would have been quickly reduced to typesetting operators. Some publication designers get nervous when they see the editorial types wading into pages. But my observation is that it is only a positive process. It can't hurt a magazine to have editors who understand layout (or a designer who can write). After all, in most cases it is an editor who has the final say over layouts (and everything else). A good editor knows when a story is good, even if he wrote it himself. The same should go for a layout.

Soon the editors at *Trips* learned the software and got involved with molding page layouts. The artificial split between "word people" and "picture people" was closed, if only a little.

Finishing the Pages

When copy was finally complete, and the layouts agreed on, we would take the text files (with the embedded Ventura paragraph tags and other style codes) and bring them back into the page layout.

Then we made the final layout manipulations to get the text to fit, such as enlarging or reducing pullquotes and photos. At this point, all copy changes were made directly on the Ventura Publisher files. (Thus, it was an advantage to have editors using the same kind of computers as the designers—they could run both their word-processing programs and the DTP software.)

Some quick negotiations would ensue over cuts or widows, and a final proof (we hoped) would be printed out on the LaserWriter. There was a final approval process for the art director and editor-in-chief, so there were no surprises when the printout came back from the service bureau.

We sent the disks to the service bureau for reproduction on a high-resolution PostScript film printer—in this case a Linotronic L-300. (A large monthly might justify the cost of buying an imagesetter like this, but service bureaus are much more cost effective for everyone else.) You can be fairly certain of getting back an identical, but higher-resolution representation of the laser-printed proof.

All the same, you still have to proofread the linoed pages when they come back, because you always miss something—and it is possible that there could be some kind of file error. Or, sometimes you make a last-minute mistake in the rush to get the disk out. As an extra check, we used the final print from the service bureau as another stage for comprehensive proofreading.

Then we went ahead and pasted up the pages in the traditional technique for offset printing. In some cases the pages were totally clean, but other times we would correct spacing by knife rather than send a page back to the service bureau. Again, the rule of thumb was to do everything the easiest way. Photocopies of the pictures ("for position only") were pasted into position. Type from outside the system—hand-lettering or lines set in typefaces we couldn't get in PostScript—was glued down.

Magazine Concept and Design

The concept for *Trips* (see Figure 10-2) was an alternative travel magazine. This focus had a lot to do with Mel and Patricia Ziegler, who always said there was a magazine trapped inside their catalogue. It was a folksy, chatty, journalistic catalogue they originally had put together themselves. It was like an underground newspaper, compared to other retail efforts, and it helped make the stores immensely popular. The 1960s consciousness of this alternative effort was very much part of their approach. They had wanted clothes that were made of natural fibers that went against the slick polyester that was popular at the time, and they wanted a "natural-fiber" magazine as well.

The Zieglers wanted a travel journal unlike the slick magazines interested mainly in tennis and golf resorts with fancy restaurants. They wanted something which included elements of adventure travel. Their sense was that exploratory travel had more to do with *National Geographic* than with *Travel and Leisure*. They wanted their publication to have some hip, youthful elements so the result would be something like a peripatetic *Rolling Stone*.

A Ziegler slogan was "break the mold." In order to distinguish the magazine from every other magazine on the market, we decided to change the size. This goes against conventional wisdom—as does any move that takes a publication outside conventional manufacturing and distribution channels. But going to book size (7 by 10 inches) clearly stamped the magazine as something different. It gave the feel of old-time magazines, like *Scribner's*. Oddly, very few people made the connection that 7 by 10 was also the size of *National Geographic*.

Figure 10-2
Trips cover

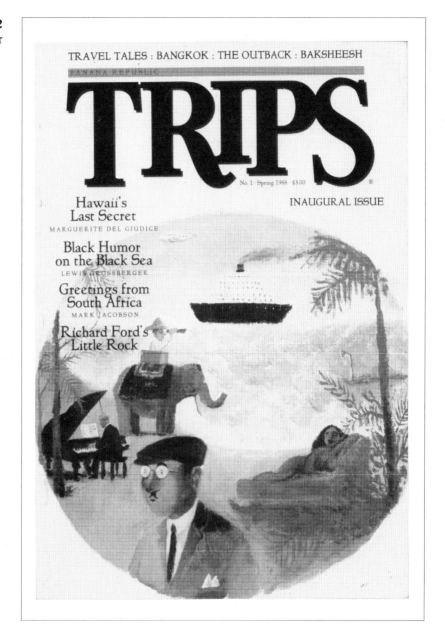

There were risks in an odd size. There would be fewer printers who could bid competitively. Distributors would complain about odd-size boxes; the magazine would fall short in newsstand racks. We felt that whatever we lost would be worth it. Magazines were getting too much alike. To stand apart would be worth the cost. From the beginning, we knew this was not going to be a big newsstand magazine—it was sold by subscription and in Banana Republic stores. So, the commercial practice of putting a big celebrity on the cover didn't really apply either.

Another attempt to distinguish the magazine was to choose a different kind of paper stock inside. We wanted to be economical, and somehow ecological, but we didn't want to look cheap. We settled on an economical coated paper that had a matte finish, called Panagra Suede. In terms of advertising, this was not such a great idea because the ads and all our pictures looked more muted than with glossy paper. The combination of an odd size and the matte paper also complicated the selling of ads. But there was a price to pay to get that natural-fiber feeling.

Cover

Not using a celebrity wasn't the only nontraditional element of the cover. We cropped the picture into a circle. Our idea was to alternate photography and illustration in this space.

A circle is a powerful shape, and it is found in nature more often than a square, but designers usually shy away from it because they are so much a part of the rectilinear world, and circles don't fit. Photographers hate circles because their work is framed as a rectangle in the viewfinders and that is the basis of their entire aesthetic. Illustrators tend to resist the circle as well; it is hard to think of any paintings by the great masters that are circles.

But once I tried it on the *Trips* cover, I had to have a circle. Somehow the circle made the page look a little bigger, and there was automatically a center and a focus.

Another guiding concept for the cover was that the illustration was to represent the contents of the entire magazine. Magazine people have gotten into the habit of restricting the cover picture to the "cover" story—only one story in the magazine. As a quarterly, we felt this might be a bit limiting, and we wanted to have something a bit more old-fashioned, a *New Yorker* cover rather than a *People* magazine cover.

The Format: Inside Pages

When planning the grid for the inside pages, I worked with the same associations used in choosing the size and paper. Since I wanted a bookish feeling, I used traditional, classical margins—the inside margin is the smallest, the top is wider, the outside wider still, and finally the bottom is the widest. We used a three-column layout in the front of the book, and then two columns for the feature section. We had to figure out how to fit traditional advertising designed for traditional "junior" size to our smaller page.

We had to have margins of some width, so the ads definitely had to be reduced. I came up with the idea of splitting the difference between a full bleed to the edge of the page and the nice wide margins of the editorial pages. By not reducing the ads all the way to our text size, we kept them as big as possible. Figure 10-3 shows the result.

This was nice because it also set off the ads as distinctly different from the editorial matter. They had different margins, and made the editorial sections stand out.

Once the margins and columns were set, we had to come up with the type and type size. Before desktop publishing, designers would spend a lot of time figuring out a rational pica size for the columns and gutters.

With galley type, you probably could have .5-pica widths, but it wasn't easy to get Linotype operators to set a lot of odd measures like 13 picas and 1 point wide. You had to come up with a magic formula. For example, if your text width was 41 picas wide, you could have 13-pica columns for a three-column measure, and 20-pica columns for a two-column measure—both with 1-pica gutters. With desktop publishing, you don't have to worry about these formulas. You work much more intuitively, and let the machine figure out the numbers.

If you decide to change from four-column width to three-column width, the DTP program easily handles the weird measure. You get so that you don't even know what the pica measurements are.

Finally, we had to come up with the specific typefaces. In the 1960s when I started designing magazines, the most common body type was 9 on 10 (9 points on a 10-point body, to use the Linotype expression)

first class, worry deeply when the beluga caviar runs out and has to be replaced with ossetra, and who maintain that there's no point in eating *risotto nero* if you have it anywhere but downstairs repeat downstairs at Harry's Bar in Venice.

The people who travel in either of these ways have one thing in common: they rely on a lot of other people—tour guides, travel agents, *majordomos*, bus drivers, chauffeurs, head waiters—to see that they have a good time. The people we like to think will be our readers don't fit into these two broad categories. They might have just enough cash to share a room for four at the YWCA in Bangkok, or they might be able to fly their private jet to Rio before setting up base camp in the Grande Hotel. What they will have in common is a curiosity about how a foreign country or city works and a desire to see for themselves, without a lot of third-party help, what is actually going on. In other words, they won't just fly to a hotel, go to the monuments, museums, and restaurants recommended by Fodor's or Michelin, send off fifty boastful postcards, and spend their last two days at the hotel pool so they can flaunt their tans to the folks back home.

THEY'LL want to know why there seem to be so many policemen on every block, and why the newspapers didn't report the explosion down the road last night. And they'll want to know why the monks are beating the gong in the temple in Mandalay, and the reason some Sikhs wear brilliant blue turbans.

Although we would like ev-

eryone to enjoy TRIPS, there are some, let us call them holiday-makers, who we believe won't find much to comfort them in our pages. They're the sort of people who say in a restaurant in Florence or Hong Kong that the spaghetti or roast duck they get in the Italian and Chinese restaurants back home tastes far better than what's in front of them. They're the men who wear replicas of their national flags in their lapels and the women who awkwardly drape their bodies in the sarongs, saris, and *áo-dài* in which the women of Indonesia, India, and Vietnam look so elegant and graceful. They're the sort of people who believe if you speak English VERY LOUDLY to a Spanish-speaking waiter in Buenos Aires

Lapel diplomacy. Asking for it

he will understand you. They're the tourists who go into local restaurants in Mexico and Thailand and say they just love native food, but please don't make it spicy. These last might be the greatest menace of all, because they're the ones who convince local restaurateurs to water things down for all foreigners.

Blandness, it's the curse of the modern world. Bland food, bland politicians, bland music, bland prose, bland mags, bland travel. That's what gives us the only qualms we've had about starting this magazine—do we publish the names and locations of those secret places, the cantinas, the inns, the bistros, the churches and pagodas, the quiet valleys and lonely lakes that we find out about? Well, yes, we will, because we know that if you're reading this, you haven't got a national flag stuck in your lapel. ●

Barbados in Action

It's not just a castle, it's a kingdom.
For reservations, call your travel agent or 1-800-228-9290 and **ask for the exclusive TRIPS' rate.**

No. 1 : Spring 1988

Figure 10-3
Note the different margins for the ad and editorial elements

Times Roman by 13 picas wide. Every designer has a default body type specification that he starts with when determining a text style. When we were working on the *Trips* format, there wasn't a huge selection of types in PostScript. We wanted a classical book type for *Trips*, but very few were available.

One was Palatino—which was beginning to be overused because it was included in every LaserWriter. The only real classic in the early releases was New Baskerville (see Figure 10-4), so we used it. Now, there are hundreds of families to choose from.

The next step was to test the typeface. The actual number of lines you get on a page may change with the typeface chosen. Each design needs special attention to achieve the desired effect—different leading, different tracking, different point sizes. People often ask what is the best point size for a magazine. But each type is different; 8-point Times

Figure 10-4
New Baskerville

ITC New Baskerville

A B C D E F G H I J K L M N
O P Q R S T U V W X Y Z
a b c d e f g h i j k l m n
o p q r s t u v w x y z
1 2 3 4 5 6 7 8 9 0

ITC New Baskerville Bold

**A B C D E F G H I J K L M N
O P Q R S T U V W X Y Z
a b c d e f g h i j k l m n
o p q r s t u v w x y z
1 2 3 4 5 6 7 8 9 0**

ITC New Baskerville Italic

*A B C D E F G H I J K L M N
O P Q R S T U V W X Y Z
a b c d e f g h i j k l m n
o p q r s t u v w x y z
1 2 3 4 5 6 7 8 9 0*

looks about the same size as 9-point Baskerville. It is important to try it out, not just on the LaserWriter, which thickens body type appreciably, or even only on high-resolution output. It is best to test it all the way through, and print up some pages.

In an existing magazine you can sometimes sneak in a test of a new typeface in a special article. With a new magazine there are undoubtedly some advertising sales materials that could use some sample pages with the experimental type.

Show the test around. It is much better to hear bad reactions (such as "I can't read that," or "That is too fussy.") before going to press. After all it is the readers you are trying to please, and the type above all should be easy to read. Our final decision at *Trips* was to use New Baskerville—with 10-point type on 12, or 10 with 2 points of space between the lines.

"The Thorn Tree"

"The Thorn Tree" section was frankly modeled on *The New Yorker* "Talk of the Town" and was a series of short notes, anecdotes, and little tips about travel (see Figures 10-5a and 10-5b). We needed a section that could soak up a lot of the partial page advertising in the front of the book. Though this is prime space and the advertising department wants to take care of the most impressive full-page advertisers, a lot of regular customers might just take a half page in each issue, and positions need to be opened up for them.

All magazines tend to have regular front-of-the-book sections for this reason. Our treatment of "The Thorn Tree" along with the partial ads combined to make it a slightly newsier, funkier part of the magazine. We wanted it to feel like an informal bulletin board. The name, "The Thorn Tree," came from the old custom of travelers in Nairobi, Kenya tacking messages to a thorn tree at the New Stanley Hotel. This was a kind of early form of communication among travelers in the bush. We made a mild reference to it by overlapping the items in the section.

The main text ran journal style; that is, one item following the other. We varied the typographical style of each item to add more of

Figure 10-5a
"The Thorn Tree"

THE

THORN 🌳 TREE

THERE'S an old thorn tree in the courtyard of the New Stanley Hotel in Nairobi where travelers used to pin their urgent, cryptic messages. It was, effectively, Kenya's first postal system. We borrowed the name for this column. Items will be culled from letters, news clippings, documents, anything concise and interesting that crosses our desk. Travelers' tales, tips, observations, complaints, and cultural artifacts are welcome. Send menus, photographs, labels, headlines. You might have important ideas on how to live cheaply in Tokyo, or how to cross the border from Afghanistan to Iran without leaving any major parts of your anatomy behind. Or you might have what seems a trivial idea of no great import, but which will save us all a lot of misery.

NEW STANLEY HOTEL

Telephone: N° 2532.

Telegrams: "SNUGGERY."

NAIROBI. Kenya Colony.

MUSEUM OF TRAVEL ART

No. 1 : Spring 1988

17

An Ace in the Hole

AN example of the latter is a suggestion that appeals to us because of the number of times we've had to ball up our underpants and stuff them in the drain because there are no plugs in ninety-three percent of the world's hotels. It came from Inez Campo of West Hartford, Connecticut. She tells us that she carries a golf ball that fits most drains. Now you probably won't find that sort of advice in the glossier travel magazines because the Plaza Athénée in Paris and the Hassler in Rome always have bath plugs. But we expect our readers to be spending lots of time in far less grand establishments.

• • •

Rules of the Road

ANOTHER friend, Tony Clifton, the much-traveled war correspondent who is now the *Newsweek* bureau chief in San Francisco, gave us some of his rules for staying happy on the road. Among them: Always carry a spare roll of toilet paper in your bag because you often can't get it outside the First World. You can use it for the traditional purpose (a great relief after handfuls of dry straw), you can use it for barter, to insulate your boots, wrap wounds and fragile antiques, stuff it damp in your ears to muffle noise . . . Never trust an airport x-ray machine

---

a bulletin-board look. Short, boxed items punctuated the running text. The Ventura Publisher paragraph tag tool made it quite easy to change the styles as needed to fit the section. We could easily change a box back to running text with an automatic drop initial. The little bullets between the items were actually made with another paragraph tag.

When we finished the layout, it was not as "New Stanley Hotel" as we wanted, so manually we changed all the headlines to different typefaces randomly. We called Dan Solo of Solotype in Oakland, who has a fantastic collection of old typefaces. I just made a list of the typefaces I liked and he used one for each headline. (This sort of display type is still scarce in PostScript.)

BY PLANE
BY BOAT
BY JEEP
BY HORSEBACK
BY FOOT

Brazilian Adventures

Explore a world few adventurers have yet to see. VARIG's Brazilian Adventure Programs bring you to Brazil's western border and the Pantanal, an area of 230,000 square kilometers and home to some 600 species of birds; to the fabled Amazon and Marajo, the largest alluvial island in the world. You'll photograph wildlife on Safari, trek the Amazon rain forest or fish for any one of 174 species of sport fish.

And the best part of these programs are their structural flexibility which allows you to create your own Brazilian adventure experience.

To find out more, send in the coupon below or call your travel agent today.

Name:
Address:
City:
State: Zip:

VARIG Brazilian Airlines
P.O. Box 10019
Long Island City, NY 1101

We're very interested. Please send us your Brazilian Adventures brochure.

anywhere that says: THIS MACHINE DOES NOT AFFECT FILM. Almost all will at least dull your film. Carry lead-lined insulator bags, or hand-carry your film . . . When you're in a foreign country, never do silly, funny, or insulting things with the national flag . . . Fill up the bathtub in your hotel room at the first sound of gunfire. One of the first things that happens in insurrections and civil wars is that the water supply gets cut off.

• • •

The coolster's Thai beach of the early eighties, Koh Samui, has been discovered by tourists. Jen Bleakley of Santa Fe warns that they have packed the beaches, have insisted on videos in guesthouses, and get noisily drunk at night. Those who want empty beaches, low prices, and home cooking have moved further south, to Krabi Beach. We hope none of the Samui bores reads this.

• • •

Everybody Must Get Stones

TACKY it may be, but cheap it ain't, and to some people, it's, like, holy. Jon King of Palo Alto, California, reports that the Jewelry Factory in South Lake Tahoe has for years supplied gemstones to the likes of Sammy Davis Jr. and the late, great Liberace. Good customers like these have, well, shrines dedicated to them. The Factory houses some of Liberace's stage outfits and a facsimile of his candelabra. It glitters with enough lights, sequins, and other shiny stuff to half-blind you. You gotta go, King says, it's the Chartres of South Lake Tahoe.

• • •

Factory original: ivory and ice for Liberace

BAYOU DINNER?

THE grand and famous restaurants of New Orleans are suffering badly from touristitis these days. This disease leads to an inability to change a menu, a tendency to equate quantity with quality, and a lack of attention to detail caused by the need to process large numbers of diners. We'll take a closer look at this in future issues. But if you're going to New Orleans, and want a few suggestions, we hear that . . . Uglesich's at 1238 Baronne Street is a great lunch place. It has been run by the same family since 1924 and serves the food that made the city famous: jambalaya, crawfish bisque,

étouffée, gumbo, and soft-shell crab. *Habitués* recommend that you eat late, around two or so, when the crowd has gone and owner Anthony Uglesich has time to talk . . . The best place to get oysters right off the bar is Felix's, at 739 Iberville Street . . .The music scene (and we don't mean middle-aged white men in straw-boaters playing Dixieland) is still very much alive in New Orleans (think of the Neville and Marsalis families). Tipitina's at 501 Napoleon Street is well-known, but if you haven't been before, go for the mix of jazz, rock and roll, blues, and Cajun music they serve up night after night.

• • •

T R I P S

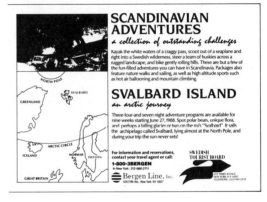

Takashimaya's O2 Bar: A breath of fresh air KOGURE KURITA/GAMMA

Airheads

ANYONE who has ever been to Tokyo knows that the air there is so polluted it makes Los Angeles smog taste like champagne. This probably explains the latest rage in the Japanese capital—oxygen bars. Our friend Alan Brown, who has spent the last few months there, says that one of the hottest bars is called, not surprisingly, O2. It's a high-tech spot housed in the Takashimaya department store in the Nihonbashi district of Tokyo. A single shot of oxygen costs 100 *yen*, which is getting close to a dollar these days (there was a time when you could hear near filled a Zeppelin for a buck). You can even get six-packs to take home at places like the Seibu department store. Think what a boon a snort would be on a New York subway at five o'clock on a Friday, or first thing Sunday for that hangover.

SCANDINAVIAN ADVENTURES
a collection of outstanding challenges

Kayak the white waters of a craggy pass, scoot out of a seaplane and right into a Swedish wilderness, steer a team of huskies across a rugged landscape, and bike gently rolling hills. These are but a few of the fun-filled adventures you can have in Scandinavia. Packages also feature nature walks and sailing, as well as high altitude sports such as hot air ballooning and mountain climbing.

SVALBARD ISLAND
an arctic journey

Three-four and seven night adventure programs are available for nine weeks starting June 27, 1988. Spot polar bears, unique flora, and perhaps a falling glacier or two on the m/s "Svalbard." It sails the archipelago called Svalbard, lying almost at the North Pole, and during your trip the sun never sets!

For information and reservations, contact your travel agent or call:
1-800-3BERGEN
In New York: 212-986-2711

SWEDISH TOURIST BOARD

Bergen Line, Inc.
505 Fifth Ave., New York, NY 10017

NORTH POLE
SVALBARD
GREENLAND
ICELAND
NORWAY SWEDEN
ARCTIC CIRCLE
GREAT BRITAIN

No. 1 : Spring 1988

Figure 10-5b
"The Thorn Tree"
continued

The Features

New magazines typically have a generous proportion of editorial to advertising pages, and *Trips* had the luxury of having really two feature wells, one of which included a long, 16-page text piece. Thus we did not have to keep to a strict typographical style to make sure that readers would always know that they were looking at stories and not ads.

Within the feature well we could vary the style, both in images and type. (The text type and the two-column configuration remained the standard for features, however.)

A typical story was on Tonga, as shown in Figure 10-6. In my effort

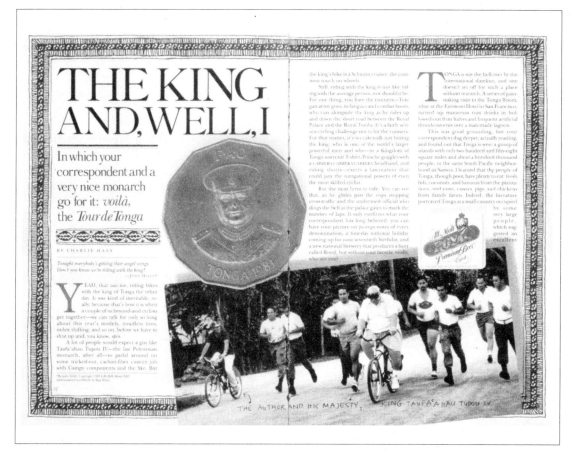

Figure 10-6
Tonga feature story

to get to the roots of the Banana Republic psyche, this story was the most successful. I had wanted to evoke old-fashioned magazines, but also the touchy-feely, hippie, ethnic, and old-line British Empire elements which defined the catalogue.

In describing the magazine the editor-in-chief often used the word *authentic*. He wanted writers who were real travelers, not simply paid journalists going to some fancy hotel in Laguna Niguel because the hotel paid for the trip.

Charlie Haas, the writer, was going off to Tonga because he persuaded the editor that he should take his mountain bike and ride it with the 400-pound King of Tonga for a little exercise. He asked me which photographer I was going to send. I didn't have the budget to send one, so I just told him to pick up some stuff—some old beer cans, coins, souvenirs, litter. I asked him to get tourists to take a picture of him with the King. He couldn't believe it, but it worked perfectly.

The idea of the layout was easy, but working with Ventura Publisher on it was pretty funky at that point—mainly because of the desire to tilt the pictures and slant the edge of the text columns.

The tilted pictures were handled by scanning them at an angle. The text skew was harder. We had to build a tiny little frame one line tall for each line indented.

To finish out the layout, we had an airbrush artist paint some shadows on the items. The borders were taken from an encyclopedia story on Tonga and the Pacific Islands, so they were authentic as well—though they did not come back with the writer. I wrote the captions onto the layout with my own handwriting—a first for me—but somehow about right for the postcard-to-home look.

Bits

To break up the feature stories, we included a number of fillers, much the way newspapers used to fill out columns with short news items off the wire. Figure 10-7 shows an example. You don't see them much anymore, since with electronic composition, pictures can quickly be resized to take up the slack. But in the old days, the most entertaining parts of a paper were the little stories at the bottom of the page—usually, for some reason, odd stuff from England.

For *Trips*, we made a special effort to find these fillers and fit them into the spreads. They created a relief from the longer stories. We figured these anecdotal items sprinkled throughout would provide easy access for readers who were just flipping through, as magazine readers frequently tend to do.

The problem was that we had to overcome the tendency for people to assume that these items were related to the surrounding story. The "bits," as we called them, had grown longer and bigger than fillers, and started looking like sidebars.

In magazines and newspapers, sidebars are secondary items associated with a story, and often fenced off with a box or some rules. This is a convention that readers are now quite used to.

Figure 10-7
In an effort to set off the "bits," we put a fancy border around them, used a different body type, tinted the box, and changed the column width

An an effort to set them off, we put a fancy border around them and used a different body type—changing from Baskerville to the new Stone Informal. We also tinted the box and changed the column width. But the convention of sidebars is so entrenched that most people still got mixed up at first. It was the kind of device that readers could only be sure to understand after seeing them in a few issues.

Book Section

My favorite section of *Trips* was the special book selection. The notion was we would have a piece of writing separate from the rest of the magazine, one that was longer than the rest. In the first issue it was about an island in Hawaii, the one place tourists can't generally get to. The piece was called "The Forbidden Island." Some of the spreads appear in Figures 10-8a and 10-8b.

A sight like this would drive The Owl crazy: Ni'ihauans of old happily carting friends of the Robinsons ashore as if they were royalty. 'Do not make a proud race bow,' he told me.

H. VON HOLT

72   No. 1 : Spring 1988 No. 1 : Spring 1988   73

Figure 10-8a
Some detractors said
this text-heavy section
looks like *Reader's
Digest,* but I didn't take
this too hard—there is
a reason why it is the
best-selling magazine
in the world

By doing a little photo research we found old pictures of the island which an airbrush artist tinted for an antique look. Perhaps the most effective decision was to run the whole 16-page section on uncoated ivory book paper. Some detractors said this text-heavy section looked like *Reader's Digest,* but I didn't take this too hard—there is a reason that it is the largest magazine in the world. And the *Reader's Digest* is small, and its design is based on book design as well.

The little frames around the illustrations were simple to construct in Ventura. They are a combination of a frame with two frames inside. One holds the picture, and one holds the caption. A separate hairline divides the two inner frames, and we added the little shadows with other rules. In conventional predesktop-publishing design, you had to draw these kinds of rules with a Rapidograph or a ruling pen, but you

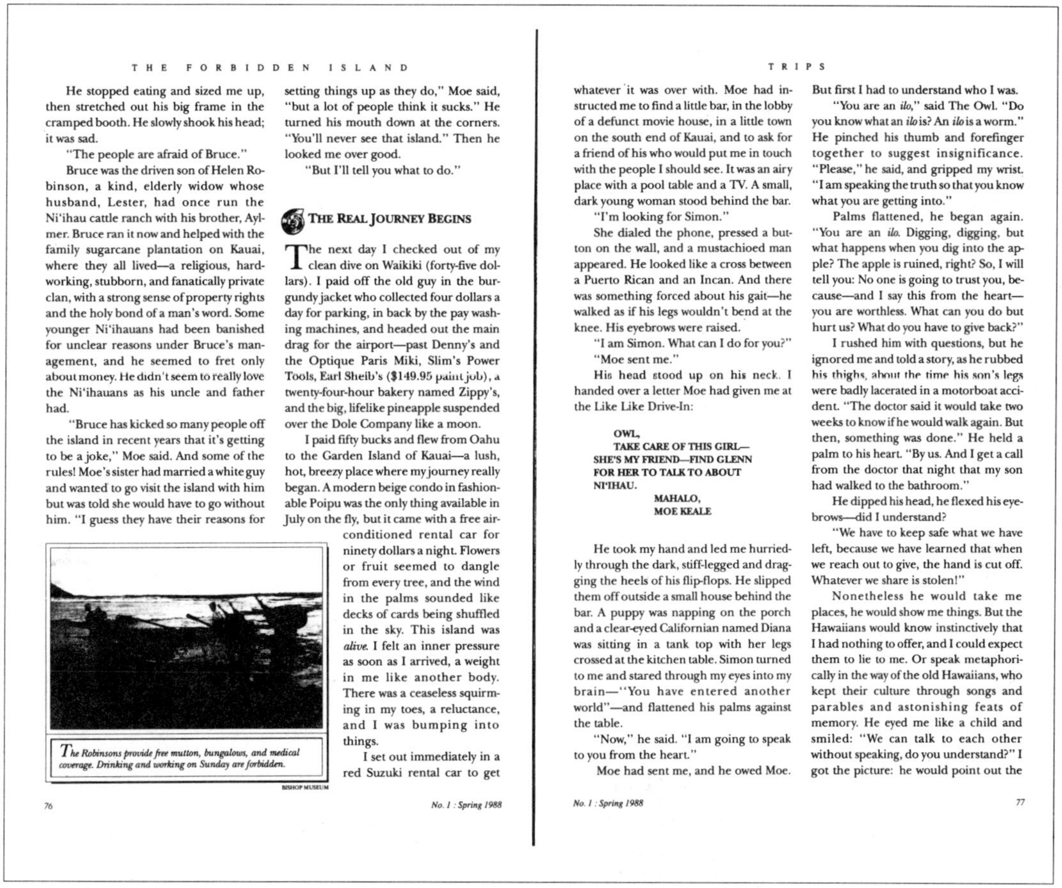

THE FORBIDDEN ISLAND

He stopped eating and sized me up, then stretched out his big frame in the cramped booth. He slowly shook his head; it was sad.

"The people are afraid of Bruce."

Bruce was the driven son of Helen Robinson, a kind, elderly widow whose husband, Lester, had once run the Ni'ihau cattle ranch with his brother, Aylmer. Bruce ran it now and helped with the family sugarcane plantation on Kauai, where they all lived—a religious, hard-working, stubborn, and fanatically private clan, with a strong sense of property rights and the holy bond of a man's word. Some younger Ni'ihauans had been banished for unclear reasons under Bruce's management, and he seemed to fret only about money. He didn't seem to really love the Ni'ihauas as his uncle and father had.

"Bruce has kicked so many people off the island in recent years that it's getting to be a joke," Moe said. And some of the rules! Moe's sister had married a white guy and wanted to go visit the island with him but was told she would have to go without him. "I guess they have their reasons for

The Robinsons provide free mutton, bungalows, and medical coverage. Drinking and working on Sunday are forbidden.

BISHOP MUSEUM

76

setting things up as they do," Moe said, "but a lot of people think it sucks." He turned his mouth down at the corners. "You'll never see that island." Then he looked me over good.

"But I'll tell you what to do."

THE REAL JOURNEY BEGINS

The next day I checked out of my clean dive on Waikiki (forty-five dollars). I paid off the old guy in the burgundy jacket who collected four dollars a day for parking, in back by the pay washing machines, and headed out the main drag for the airport—past Denny's and the Optique Paris Miki, Slim's Power Tools, Earl Sheib's ($149.95 paint job), a twenty-four-hour bakery named Zippy's, and the big, lifelike pineapple suspended over the Dole Company like a moon.

I paid fifty bucks and flew from Oahu to the Garden Island of Kauai—a lush, hot, breezy place where my journey really began. A modern beige condo in fashionable Poipu was the only thing available in July on the fly, but it came with a free air-conditioned rental car for ninety dollars a night. Flowers or fruit seemed to dangle from every tree, and the wind in the palms sounded like decks of cards being shuffled in the sky. This island was *alive.* I felt an inner pressure as soon as I arrived, a weight in me like another body. There was a ceaseless squirming in my toes, a reluctance, and I was bumping into things.

I set out immediately in a red Suzuki rental car to get

No. 1 : Spring 1988

TRIPS

whatever it was over with. Moe had instructed me to find a little bar, in the lobby of a defunct movie house, in a little town on the south end of Kauai, and to ask for a friend of his who would put me in touch with the people I should see. It was an airy place with a pool table and a TV. A small, dark young woman stood behind the bar.

"I'm looking for Simon."

She dialed the phone, pressed a button on the wall, and a mustachioed man appeared. He looked like a cross between a Puerto Rican and an Incan. And there was something forced about his gait—he walked as if his legs wouldn't bend at the knee. His eyebrows were raised.

"I am Simon. What can I do for you?"

"Moe sent me."

His head stood up on his neck. I handed over a letter Moe had given me at the Like Like Drive-In:

> OWL,
> TAKE CARE OF THIS GIRL—
> SHE'S MY FRIEND—FIND GLENN
> FOR HER TO TALK TO ABOUT
> NI'IHAU.
>
> MAHALO,
> MOE KEALE

He took my hand and led me hurriedly through the dark, stiff-legged and dragging the heels of his flip-flops. He slipped them off outside a small house behind the bar. A puppy was napping on the porch and a clear-eyed Californian named Diana was sitting in a tank top with her legs crossed at the kitchen table. Simon turned to me and stared through my eyes into my brain—"You have entered another world"—and flattened his palms against the table.

"Now," he said. "I am going to speak to you from the heart."

Moe had sent me, and he owed Moe.

But first I had to understand who I was.

"You are an *ilo,*" said The Owl. "Do you know what an *ilo* is? An *ilo* is a worm." He pinched his thumb and forefinger together to suggest insignificance. "Please," he said, and gripped my wrist. "I am speaking the truth so that you know what you are getting into."

Palms flattened, he began again. "You are an *ilo.* Digging, digging, but what happens when you dig into the apple? The apple is ruined, right? So, I will tell you: No one is going to trust you, because—and I say this from the heart—you are worthless. What can you do but hurt us? What do you have to give back?"

I rushed him with questions, but he ignored me and told a story, as he rubbed his thighs, about the time his son's legs were badly lacerated in a motorboat accident. "The doctor said it would take two weeks to know if he would walk again. But then, something was done." He held a palm to his heart. "By us. And I get a call from the doctor that night that my son had walked to the bathroom."

He dipped his head, he flexed his eyebrows—did I understand?

"We have to keep safe what we have left, because we have learned that when we reach out to give, the hand is cut off. Whatever we share is stolen!"

Nonetheless he would take me places, he would show me things. But the Hawaiians would know instinctively that I had nothing to offer, and I could expect them to lie to me. Or speak metaphorically in the way of the old Hawaiians, who kept their culture through songs and parables and astonishing feats of memory. He eyed me like a child and smiled: "We can talk to each other without speaking, do you understand?" I got the picture: he would point out the

No. 1 : Spring 1988

77

Figure 10-8b

could never hope to make them as clean or as precise as you can with DTP. The cheaper technology can actually be more perfect than what it is replacing. (For example, the little picture credits, the only component which had to be pasted on later because they were vertical, are the only crooked elements in the final layout.)

Working within the 16-page constraint was very easy because the type could be expanded and the leading increased or decreased to make the story fit the space exactly. Once you flow the text, you can make it work quickly through trial and error. Goodbye type specking!

Picture Stories

To balance the long text pieces, we included a number of longer visual stories, photos, or illustrations. Figure 10-9 shows the opening of one.

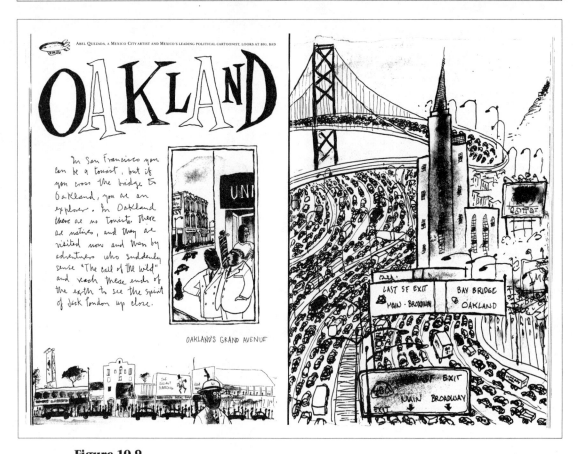

Figure 10-9

Art features, like this sketchbook piece on Oakland by Abel Quezada, must have content and balance some of the text-heavy pieces

The idea was to have a magazine that wasn't relentlessly visual or text-oriented. We wanted peaks and valleys so the reader could have a chance to really get into a story and then find some relief with a few pages of visuals.

In looking for these art features, we felt it was important that there was content inherent in each of them. We didn't want to simply present some pretty pictures. For the first issue we settled on a fantastic photo piece on Australian cowboys by Hokan Ludwigsson, a Swedish photographer (see Figure 5-3), and a sketchbook piece on Oakland, California by Mexican artist Abel Quezada. Both told stories with a firm sense of place. They took the reader away in the same way that the narrative book section took them to the Forbidden Island.

In the second issue, we designed a 19-page photo-essay (taken on assignment by Ludwigsson). The subject was Peshawar, Pakistan—the Khyber Pass crossroads then filled with intrigue and journalists covering the Soviet-Afghani war. It is rare for consumer magazines to give this kind of space to photography, and that is a pity.

Sadly, these pictures, and the rest of issue two, were never printed.

Image *Magazine*

Even if all other magazines went out of business, there would be enough work redesigning the Sunday magazines in newspapers to keep thousands of designers employed.

These "supplements" (editors hate that word) are always trying to come up with a new formula to attract more revenue. Publishers keep wanting to make these weeklies self-supporting—separate profit centers within the Sunday paper. This may be unrealistic. The trend is not healthy; there are fewer independent Sunday supplements every year. Perhaps only one is a big money maker: *The New York Times Magazine.* But this is enough to create expectations of profit everywhere else. Instead of thinking of their Sunday magazines as a lure for readers, like the comics, publishers put pressure on magazine staffs for better performance.

The case in point is the magazine in the Sunday *San Francisco Examiner.* A few years ago the publisher, William Randolph Hearst III, decided the pleasant, traditional supplement, *California Living,* was not doing well enough, and the editors called in a new team. They created *Image,* essentially a Northern California regional magazine, like *Texas Monthly* or *California* magazine. A distinguished design firm did the design, and Hearst hired a veteran magazine editor.

It was an ambitious and expensive undertaking. But after only two years, management decided it wasn't bringing in the ads they predicted, and called for another overhaul. Hearst persuaded the columnist and longtime-magazine editor Warren Hinckle to take on the project. And since I was working on consolidating the design for the whole newspaper, I inevitably got involved.

To curtail costs, we decided to produce the magazine largely with staff talent—staff photographers and staff writers from the newspaper—replacing an army of freelancers. While this was not popular among Bay Area photographers and writers, it was quite a good thing for the staff. News photographers again had access to the quality, four-color reproduction of *Image;* reporters could write for the larger Sunday audience. After a short period of upheaval, we established a new format and decided to use desktop-publishing technology to design *Image* every week.

Macintoshes were already in use in the *Examiner's* art department, and it was a natural step to bring them into the magazine. We purchased Mac IIx systems with 19-inch color monitors for the two art directors and the managing editor. The DTP program we chose was QuarkXPress.

At first, we output pages at a local service bureau, Krishna Copy, but as the magazine got up and running with desktop-publishing equipment, we bought a Linotronic L-300 to output final film for all the type and rules. (The prepress house still scanned and stripped in the halftones.)

The design itself was quite simple; the reasons for implementing it were not. But unavoidably the business direction of a publication had more to do with the new look than anything else. The budget is always a constraint on the design. It's only when the bottom line issues are addressed that you can really create the right format for a publication.

The Editorial Thrust

The editors decided to focus on the city of San Francisco. This acknowledged the fact that the circulation of the *Examiner* is basically limited to the Bay Area. Within the Bay Area, San Francisco clearly provides identity for residents. They may live in Walnut Creek, but they tell relatives back east that they live in San Francisco.

Also, "The City," as the paper styles it, is the cultural center for the whole area—music, ballet, and so on. There is also an indigenous San Francisco pop culture, which was missing from the previous incarnation of the magazine. The Summer of Love—"Are You Going to San Francisco? Be Sure to Wear Some Flowers in Your Hair"—will never really be forgotten.

The trick in this case was to do it all with mirrors, or, actually, with inhouse talent. Some of the staff had to be persuaded to work for the magazine in addition to their regular news assignments. To get them interested, we had to let them know that the new *Image* was going to be a showcase for their own favorite projects. It turned out that many photographers had been working on "pet projects" over the past weeks and sometimes months, and so had many reporters. This is the best kind of journalism anyway. Warren Hinckle wanted to get away from the predictable suburban desk mentality of most Sunday supplements, and to inject elements of surprise seldom found anymore in the city magazine formula that had been tried during the previous incarnation of *Image*.

The Style Spin

In working on the design for the magazine, two things became clear. We had to capture the San Francisco feel, and we had to keep the format simple and flexible so one or two people on the staff could produce it every week with Macintoshes.

Furthermore, the new design had to complement the rest of the newspaper as well. The typefaces we were putting into the

Examiner format were Cheltenham and Franklin Gothic Condensed, so naturally, these typefaces were used in the magazine.

For art we naturally turned to photography because more staff photographers than illustrators were available. The novel idea was to make the pictures big. It is cheaper to have one big picture than ten tiny ones. And of course, one big picture is usually more effective. This does not seem particularly brilliant, since many Sunday supplements started out as the picture sections—"The Rotogravure." They were a bonus for the readers, really a life raft in the rest of a paper's sea of text.

For subjects, we decided to go to pictures of people, San Francisco people, whether they were celebrities or not. This sounds like another obvious move, since "people journalism" has been a successful formula for 20 years now.

But the fact that it has become a cliché, that people are interested in people, doesn't make it wrong. When I was working on *The New York Times Magazine,* I was constantly pushing the editors not to assign a general story about, say, the rain forest, but rather to profile someone involved with saving the rain forest. On Sunday morning people can handle only one sermon. Now we figured, let the rest of the *Examiner* deal with the sociology, tax boards, and press releases from all over. *Image* would approach things through a personal point of view.

In order to find a style spin, I turned to some of the famous San Francisco publications from the 1960s, namely *Rolling Stone* and *Ramparts.* The first design of *Rolling Stone* was inspired by the *Sunday Ramparts,* a weekly newspaper published in San Francisco during a bitter newspaper strike. In fact, the boards of the old *Sunday Ramparts* were used to paste down the first issues of *Rolling Stone.* The *Rolling Stone* designers used the same Oxford border (a thick and thin rule) around every page.

Warren Hinckle was the editor of *Ramparts* and is now a columnist for the *Examiner.* He volunteered to overhaul *Image.* (Ironically, Dugald Stermer, the art director of *Ramparts,* had designed the predecessor Sunday magazine, *California Living.* The style was still right.) Hinckle and I were given fairly broad editorial powers to try to make the magazine visually stronger and to bring it in on budget.

We didn't want to copy the 1960s, but to recall a vivid period in San Francisco journalism.

Designing the Cover

Another reference (or association) for the new format was the colorful history of the *Examiner,* and the Hearst press in general. The year before, the paper had celebrated the hundredth year since William Randolph acquired the newspaper and started publishing. His grandson, Hearst, brought together the old *Ramparts* team of Dugald Stermer, and Warren Hinckle produced these issues. They mined the old issues of the *Examiner* and reprinted Mark Twain and others. They designed the centennial issues with the flavor of old Hearst papers of the 1910s and 1920s, when Hearst was the Murdoch of American papers. The *Baltimore American,* the *Los Angeles Herald,* and a dozen others shared a style of typography then. Often, Cheltenham Old Style was mixed with a skinny face called American (or Herald) Gothic for the headlines. This Gothic was ideal for fitting into the narrow columns, and was really characteristic of the classic style of American newspapers in the 1920s. *The New York Times* still uses Latin Elongated, which performs the same function.

However, for most papers these supercondensed types had long been abandoned, and American Gothic was not available for the Autologic typesetting machines in use at the *Examiner.* So Will, something of a Macintosh wizard, realized that the typeface had no curves—those had all been chamfered off—and figured he could make a font with the program Fontographer.

He is probably the first publisher in 300 years to cut his own font, but it turned out quite well. They used it for the centennial editions, and it was natural to include it in the redesign project—and the first section to be undertaken was *Image.*

The Logo

The logo for *Image* was a very simple thing to construct using Adobe Illustrator and the American Gothic font. We made a number of variations and chose the one shown in Figure 11-1 in the end. The solid type in the middle is the typeface. The outline—the white and black parts of the logo—were produced by evenly stroking the typeface in Illustrator. The original typeface is stroked black, for 12 points. Then a

Figure 11-1
Creating the
Image logo

We stroked the
basic logo with a
3-point line

On top we placed
a copy of the logo
filled with black
and stroked with a
1-point rule

Then, we created a
drop shadow filled
with 50% black

white version, stroked 1 point less, is placed on top of that. Then the original type is placed on top of that. Underneath all of these elements, we slipped a gray drop shadow at a 45-degree angle to lift the logo off the page slightly. This shadow overprints the photograph or background behind it.

One important comment about using this stroking capability is to remember that with Illustrator (and all PostScript-based type manipulation programs) you are not just making an outline, you are making an inline at the same time. Thus, the face of the letter is being cut away. This distorts the design badly, and thins out the thin strokes and serifs very quickly as the stroking is made thicker. To avoid ruining the design of the type, paste the same words or letters filled with a contrasting color "in front" without stroking them.

Other Cover Images

As a variant on the Oxford rules, we included a Scotch (thin-thick-thin) border around the cover, with a division at the top for the logo. This left room on either side of the logo to billboard some of the stories inside and include a secondary picture. We figured with the extra billings we could eliminate the contents page—a luxury in a 20-page magazine—and use the space for actual content.

The main headline is usually in Franklin Gothic Condensed, but it moves around according to the picture.

For the photo itself—and staff resources indicated that it usually was not to be an illustration—we decided we wanted portraits. The talent of the staff photographers made this the right choice, and a great formula to work with every week.

A Sunday newspaper magazine should be a relief and complement to the rest of the newspaper. Hard news does not really belong in this magazine. It should be the bonus for reading the rest of the sections—fun, nonthreatening, and accessible.

Inside: The Front-of-the-Book

By making the cover serve much of the function of the table of contents, *Image* could get off to a faster start. The first inside editorial page (with the masthead crammed onto the bottom) is, really, the whole front-of-the-book section, composed of short, gossipy items about people. Each item is only about 50 words, a length readers like and editors abhor.

Hinckle called this page "Seeing the Elephant" (see Figure 11-2), which had some old-time San Francisco significance. In the first years of the twentieth century, if you had done all the bars and caught up on all the gossip, you were said to have "seen the elephant." Finding great items for this page was a little difficult because the long lead time made it impossible to get live gossipy stuff that would keep. Occasionally, we got a juicy item when we had a line on something that no one else was likely to get, but in general, *Image* gets around the problem by treating fairly innocuous items in a more arch manner. Sometimes this has resulted in a tamer page than we might have hoped for.

In the champagne days of San Francisco—the pre-earthquake years of the glorious century past—when you had done all the bars and restaurants in the golden crescent of downtown, met all the movers and shakers and been caught up on the latest gossip, you were said to have "seen the elephant." Herewith, paragraphs of random intelligence and social notes gained from a stroll along the city's boulevards.

COURTESY NAMES PROJECT

AIDS quilt moves nation

The three-and-a-half-football-fields-long San Francisco quilt embroidered with AIDS victims' names is drawing somber crowds as it moves across the USA . . . Observers say the impact of the quilt's pilgrimage to 20 cities is equal to the famous American Freedom Train's tour during the Bicentennial, displaying the Constitution and other national treasures.

EXAMINER FILE PHOTO

Where the ladies are

Margo St. James, superstar ladies-of-the-night union organizer, is now gainfully employed as a construction worker in the south of France . . . She opted out of San Francisco a few years back, but is still carrying on the Good Fight as co-director of the International Committee for Prostitutes' Rights. She says she's doing construction work (and enjoying it) for subsistance, while renting out to tourists the attic in the old house she shares with her lady friend in picturesque Montpeyroux.

Tom Wolfe's topic A

Legendary writer Tom Wolfe's plan to make San Francisco the topic of his next blockbuster has old friends here both gushing and worrying . . . Wolfe was big pals with Washington Square Bar & Grill co-owners Ed and Mary Etta Moose when he lived here for years with one of Mary Etta's closest lady friends. Moose is being deluged with inquiries from mutual friends about whose ox might get gored locally . . . Wolfe's latest bestseller, *The Bonfire of the Vanities*, tore the stem right off the Big Apple.

D. FINEMAN : SYGMA

Only-in-SF prayer vigil

Each Saturday morning at 10 a.m. a small band of Catholic men recites the rosary in front of famous atheist attorney Vincent Hallinan's office . . . Hallinan's Eddy Street office is next door to the Planned Parenthood clinic where abortions are performed, and the confluence of locations is too much for the Catholics who show up rain or shine.

EXAMINER FILE PHOTO

Plumbers plot to get *Missouri*

Vigorous plumbers' union boss Joe Mazzola is launching a big-money union campaign to land the USS *Missouri* for San Francisco . . . "Can Do" Joe promises a general strike if that's what it takes to get the battleship homeported here in the face of environmentalists and peaceniks.

DOGS ARE FUNNY   *by Mick Stevens*

DOGATHON

SWIM 2 MILES

SHAKE 8 SECS

RUN X MILES

MICK STEVENS

COVER: KATY RADDATZ - EXAMINER

San Francisco Examiner EDITOR AND PUBLISHER: William R. Hearst III • EXECUTIVE EDITOR: Larry Kramer • IMAGE DESIGN & EDITORIAL DIRECTORS: Roger Black, Warren Hinckle • EXECUTIVE PUBLISHER: Pamela Brunger • EXECUTIVE ART DIRECTOR: Bill Prochnow • IMAGE FOOD AND WINE EDITOR: Jim Wood • SENIOR EDITOR: Sara Frankel • ASSOCIATE EDITORS: Jo Mancuso, Catharine Norton, Michael O'Loughlin • EDITORIAL ASSISTANT: Robin McKenna • ART DIRECTOR: Dian Azza Ooka • ASSOCIATE ART DIRECTOR: Josephine Rigg Park • PICTURE EDITOR: Bob McLeod ■ ADVERTISING MANAGER: Linda Rotelli • SPECIALIZED PRINTING MANAGER: Glenda Jackson • VICE PRESIDENT, ADVERTISING: Ralph Hanes • GENERAL ADVERTISING MANAGER: Ray McManus • RETAIL ADVERTISING MANAGER: Frank Flood ■ EDITORIAL OFFICES: 110 Fifth Street, San Francisco, CA 94103 (415) 777-7905 • ADVERTISING OFFICES: San Francisco Newspaper Agency, 925 Mission Street, San Francisco, CA 94103 (415) 777-7594 Represented nationally by Sawyer-Ferguson-Walker • For information on foreign representation, call (415) 777-7402 ■ IMAGE (incorporating **California Living**) is a publication of the **San Francisco Examiner & Chronicle**, edited by the **San Francisco Examiner** • © 1988 San Francisco Examiner, Box 7260, San Francisco, CA 94120

Figure 11-2
"Seeing the Elephant"

"Seeing the Elephant" generally follows a simple box-lines format from issue to issue. Everything is rectilinear over one or two columns—in a four-column grid. It's just a question of working with the photos and making it all fit. Mick Stevens, a *New Yorker* cartoonist, and originally from San Francisco, regularly does a cartoon for the bottom of the page. At first he tried a multipanel strip, but decided that the tiny space forced him into doing a single-frame sight gag.

A typical design is the page from the May 1, 1988 issue. We had four items, the cartoon, and the masthead. The masthead and logo are "standing" in the template. We put initial text into the Mac network from the paper's main editorial system, but typically this text arrived almost in note form. We had text for some items and photos for some, but not necessarily ones that worked together. First, we scabbed in the pictures. Two were file pictures, one was from the Sygma photo agency, and one was furnished by the AIDS Quilt organization. The only color picture was the one of Tom Wolfe. Since the *San Francisco Examiner* only had a black-and-white desktop scanner, we sent any transparencies to the newspaper darkroom to have a conversion print made. (A Xerox or Canon color copier would work just as well.)

Eventually, the *Examiner* is planning to implement a complete desktop color system for the magazine, and will get a high-quality color scanner. For now, the color is produced conventionally, and the halftones are all "For Position Only."

Templates

The page template for "Seeing the Elephant" (in this case built in QuarkXPress) included all the necessary grid and style sheets—specifications for every standard typographical configuration. The style sheets are in place for the headline style, subhead style, a photo caption style, and a normal (text) style. The grid was ready to use with margins and four columns in place. Part of the format was hairline column rules between items but not within items. This left a lot of room for playing to make the specific copy fit.

As for most magazine layouts, the design starts when the text is ready (but is probably too long) and is in the system—on the server or on a disk.

The first thing to do for almost any page is to flow all the text onto the basic page, and apply the style sheets to see how much there is. For a layout like this, we needed at least a ratio of about 50-50 of art to text—it is better at 60-40. The art included the cartoon, which was almost always the same size, though it could go on either side of the page. Once the text was trimmed to a reasonable length (either by an editor, or arbitrarily by the designer to indicate just how much would fit), different items were put into separate text boxes, which helped in moving them around on the page.

We set up the template with five little one-column text boxes along the bottom, making sure in QuarkXPress that "Text indent" (in the Item modify window) was set at 0.

Once we copied all of the items into their separate boxes, the underlying page did little more than act as a grid. I found it better to keep all the elements sitting within a basic text box to enable quick moves of the whole page up or down—or even off to another page, if the folios changed (as they frequently did to work around the ads.) In QuarkXPress, there was no Shift-select feature to allow selection of more than one element at a time. Instead boxes and rules, if created within another box, became "children" of the original, "parent" box. This was incredibly annoying until we learned how to make use of it. If we thought of a page as a collection of generally rectilinear components, then this parent-sibling box control became quite useful to gather everything up and move it around.

I tend to use the basic page on the screen as a background, something akin to the little blue boxes on pasteup boards. Using separate boxes makes them easier to move around and adjust later.

To figure out how to play each of the items at *Image*, we discussed the relative importance with the editors and decided which had the best pictures. The AIDS quilt was probably the most important story, but the art work just couldn't do justice to the subject in a small space. We decided to lead with Tom Wolfe in the end since he was the biggest celebrity and was planning to write a book about San Francisco. We also didn't think anyone else had this item yet.

Once the priorities are set, the layout becomes a kind of massage game. I am fairly intuitive about how I work at this stage. I'll pull in some of the elements that are sitting on the template, like horizontal rules with the requisite amount of space around them. Then I start playing with the column rules, covering them up as needed when the text boxes are put in place and sized.

Since we wanted to make Tom Wolfe the biggest item in "Seeing the Elephant," with the best picture, we put him on the outside, upper-right part of the page. We put the AIDS quilt on the upper-left so that it was literally the first item but not necessarily in the most dramatic location. The quilt is a wonderful thing, but AIDS is a serious and difficult subject, and the point of this page is to have fun.

The Margot St. James picture ran very small since it didn't add much. The *Image* design stylebook called for a "tabloid crop," meaning we crop tightly, usually shearing off a bit of the forehead, but always leaving a little space under the chin. The mug shot for the plumbers' union leader was treated in the same way, but run a little bigger. For these two black-and-white photos, we later instructed the printer to make a blue tint, blue duotone. This made the photos less dull next to the full-color shot of Wolfe.

The only type on the page that couldn't be handled in QuarkXPress was for the vertical picture credits. In QuarkXPress you could not rotate text, so we used a desk accessory utility called SmartArt, which allows (among other things) text rotation. The lines were set, and then saved to create a little EPS file for each credit (this can be done in advance or on the fly). The credit text was copied onto the clipboard and then into SmartArt, to another template, where the text was already styled and rotated. It was then brought into QuarkXPress using the Get picture function.

When it was all done, we sent the page file, minus the four-color illustration to the L-300 printer for the four-color passes onto film. The halftones were handled conventionally, and stripped into position according to the original LaserWriter proofs of each layout. QuarkXPress separated the color for its own rules and graphics. The "Seeing the Elephant" logo was done in Adobe Illustrator, and it was also automatically separated.

Inside: Features

The one-page front-of-the-book section leads immediately into the feature section, allowing a typical issue of *Image* to get off to a fast start.

The headlines for the features are typically set in Cheltenham Old Style or Franklin Gothic Condensed. (These fonts are now available in PostScript, but at the time of this design they were ordered especially from The Font Bureau.)

Looking in hindsight at the secondary spread of our main feature, "Keeping People Out of Nursing Homes" (see Figures 11-3a and 11-3b), it might have been smarter to repeat a little headline at the top of the pages because the focus is lost. In this case, we got rid of the Scotch rule border (which is required for departments, but is optional with features), and started with some big text type—12-point rather than the normal 9.

THE CUTTING EDGE

Keeping people out of nursing homes

An old-fashioned
doctor's crusade to find
alternative ways for
the elderly to enjoy
their last years

Figure 11-3a In features, start off with a bang

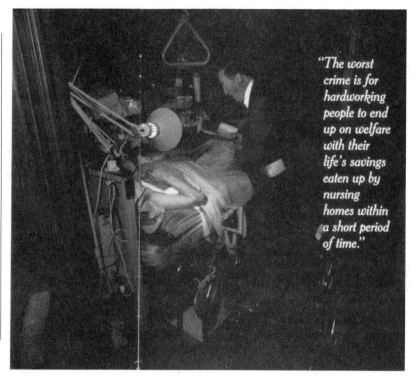

"The worst crime is for hardworking people to end up on welfare with their life's savings eaten up by nursing homes within a short period of time."

Figure 11-3b
Visual impact from running a second huge photo

than the normal 9. Although we removed the Scotch rule, the text stays indented to standard margins. This gives ample, if not luxurious, open margins to separate the editorial from the ads and to give some white space—and thumb room to hold the magazine. Wide margins may be the best way to handle white space. Maintaining classical proportions for the margins—with the narrowest on the inside, top the next, then the outside, and the widest at the bottom—gives the magazine a pleasantly traditional feel.

We decided that it would be a good idea to label each of the feature stories as a section with a little ribbon or snipe that cuts into the page from outside. The ribbon serves almost as an artificial editorial device. Some readers like their magazines very organized and others don't care. The ones that don't care won't notice the labels, but the readers who like organization will appreciate the definition.

At the very least, in a world with increasing clutter of advertising, labeling like this gives people a chance to tell the editorial from the ads.

The pictures for the features were extremely important because we skipped most of the usual preliminaries to start out the magazine with a bang. This bang has to be planned with great care, or the magazine will tend to fall back into being conventional. We wanted *Image* to be more than a conventional, small-format, "Suburban Desk" product. When the editors remember to start with something arrestingly, challengingly visual, the magazine works. Surprise is the key word.

One way to make sure you start big is to use a full spread right at the beginning. The magazine doesn't have an enormous number of spreads to play with because of the small size and number of partial ads. If you put two spreads together at the very front, you get off with a big hit. Then, it's back to the shoe ads, the furniture ads, and little jewelry ads.

On partial pages we decided to run the Scotch rule only along the top, to make the text columns wider and eliminate the fussiness of too many rules, and to remind you that you are in an editorial section.

In the example, "The Wine Country," shown in Figure 11-4, we have a classic San Francisco, Dugald Stermer design. It has a Scotch rule, a big headline, a big photo, a big drop initial, and it starts out with big text. You would know it was an Image page if you ever saw the magazine before.

Inside: Departments

Despite the eclectic quality of the magazine—and the desire to mortgage the minimum amount of space to standing departments—we wanted to include a few staples. Readers had gotten attached to the "Whole Bay Catalog," and as Frank McCulloch, the *Examiner's* managing editor kept reminding us, "Ignore the habits of readers at your own peril."

Whole Bay Catalog

So there is always a "Whole Bay Catalog" (see Figure 11-5), which is essentially a "best bets" page of fun items you can buy in the Bay Area. We actually had a hard time with the design of this page and finally

The wine country

By Jim Wood / Photographs by John Storey and Katy Raddatz

Now's a lovely time to visit the fog-cooled valleys and terraced vineyards of California's wine country. The area has been likened to Brigadoon, Camelot and a Hollywood golf course, but even the most jaded observer will concede it's one of the most beautiful areas on earth. Easily overlooked in the scenic splendor are the people who make the wine and must face the realities of a tough business combining hard work, enological sciences and a fair degree of luck.

In the capital-guzzling wine industry, where fortunes are invested with little immediate return other than enormous satisfaction, the past two decades have been a time of especially dizzy change.

The growth has been extraordinary: Napa Valley land that sold for less than $3,000 an acre now fetches $30,000-45,000 an acre. Growers have sharply increased their quality table grape acreage. Ten years ago, California had 12,000 acres planted in Chardonnay; the most recent figure is almost 35,000 acres. The 4,000 acres of Sauvignon Blanc planted in 1977 is now 14,000.

Blush wines, all but unheard of 20 years ago, are a major part of the market, making wineries like Sutter Home and Fetzer among the state's largest producers of table wines.

U.S. wine exports, with California producing 95 percent of the wine sent overseas, have increased 526 percent since 1977.

And the change in quality has been enormous. Almost every winery of any size enjoys the services of a trained enologist. Very little bad wine is made. That statement could

WOODCUT ILLUSTRATIONS IN THE TRADITION OF THOMAS BEWICK.

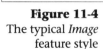

Sunday, October 23,1988 * I M A G E * 3

Figure 11-4
The typical *Image* feature style

decided the best way to bring some focus to this feature was to run one item bigger than the others, preferably with a person silhouetted.

Figure 11-5
"Whole Bay Catalog"

Every time it was possible to get human beings into the layout, we did. They tended to be real people—either people on the staff, or in one case, the mail carrier—rather than models.

This page does not follow any grid. It is a collage. The designer fits the pieces together. Typically, there are photos-versus-text arguments between the editors and designers.

After working with this section for a few months, we changed the format slightly to make it look more like an editorial feature. We added the column rules that butt up to the Scotch rules.

Fashion

Fashion typically is not very constrained editorially. The emphasis is on bigger pictures. This can be a real hassle. To get a big fashion picture, we even turned the picture on its side once, as shown in Figure 11-6. Of course, doing fashion with the staff photographers at a daily newspaper is always risky. These photographers tend to be trained

Figure 11-6
The emphasis is on
big pictures in fashion

journalists, not studio photographers or people who are particularly in love with fashion. It takes a fashion editor who knows what he or she is doing to bring it off. In a way, fashion editing is photo editing. If the fashion editor takes responsibility for selecting the clothes, styling the clothes and working with the photographer in order to get the fashion message across—whatever it is—it works. If it is all up to the photographer, particularly in a situation where you are not dealing with a top fashion photographer, the results are much riskier.

Typically, on a local magazine, you don't cover the new collections. You usually do what is available in local stores, or you have to find a local angle. One very successful spread (see Figure 11-7) was a real stretch. We had to point out that five years ago Issey Miyaki had a show in San Francisco and the illustrator, *Image* fashion editor Gladys Perint Palmer, is from San Francisco. She is quite a good fashion illustrator, who gives a bit of variety, texture, color, sense of reporting, and personal involvement to the show. Her drawings are great. This is a good example of using terrific local resources. We knew she did these sketchbooks and had published books of her sketches so we arranged for her to bring back her notebooks to publish. Since it was a San Francisco reporter, it was appropriate for the magazine.

Figure 11-7
Finding the local angle

Figure 11-8
"Fast Forward" evokes the scrapbook feel

Another department, "Ten Best" was a quirky list of ten good things on one subject each week. It served as a bit of relief in the middle of the magazine. The first logo for it was a stylized version of the regular logo, since we knew it would always run across two inner columns and so couldn't bleed to the outside as the other story labels did. This just serves as an interpretation of the style. Later, we discarded the numeral because it didn't really fit with the rest of the magazine, and we bled a new label into the Scotch border.

Food

The "Food" page posed an interesting problem. The quality of the photography either makes or breaks food stories in general. In the previous incarnation of Image, the editors were spending a lot of money on the styling and photography, yet very often the food was so small you could barely see it. We wanted to bring the image of the food to the front, but we did not have space for a full-page picture. The opening had to get the story started, and then it could continue in some partial space for recipes. Obviously, the recipes take up a certain amount of space and are very difficult, if not impossible, to cut.

Parties

The department which was hardest to produce on the Mac is called "Fast Forward," which covered parties. We tried to get more pictures into a smaller space by cutting them into little rhomboids and parallelograms. See Figure 11-8. This way, you get the sense that the pictures are bigger and run off the page. This section also feels like a scrapbook or a dormitory wall bulletin board. The informal design also reflected our intention to cover not just rich peoples' parties. We also wanted more normal, middle-class events like a tailgate party for the Giants. It turned out pretty well. You get a real sense of what is going on.

For the final department—and to many, the most important department—we kept the crossword puzzle at the end. We put it on the last page where all the crossword fans could easily find it.

Desktop *on the Desktop*

ITC Desktop (now named *Desktop Communications*) was created by International Typeface Corporation (ITC) as a way to introduce desktop publishing to people unfamiliar with both design and computers. It is not another computer magazine or a professional design magazine, but something for normal human beings who've gotten into DTP because it was an interesting new solution to a problem they may never have known they had.

In the classic scenario, management realizes the potential of desktop technology, and quickly passes off responsibility to secretaries with PCs or to midlevel managers, with the instructions to put out the next issue of a newsletter in a hurry. The expectations are unreasonable. Most people are at first afraid of computers (or at least mystified by them), and they have no experience with design and publishing. And while there seemed to be several magazines that help publishing professionals adapt to the new technology, and countless publications for those who seem to have been born knowing the difference between ROM and RAM, nothing existed for the real novice. In 1989, *Desktop* arrived to help them. The message was no longer, "Don't try this at home."

It started as a controlled circulation magazine with a mailing list of corporate users and decision makers. By "controlled," magazine circulation people mean "free." To obtain a second-class mail permit, which separates magazines from junk mail, the recipients have to "qualify" for subscriptions by filling out a card and sending it back in. This gives the publishers even more specific demographic information about readers. And in specific or "narrow" markets, controlled circulation can be very effective. The approach is becoming popular in consumer magazine marketing, due to the steadily increasing flood of publications.

Getting Started

You obviously can't learn desktop publishing in one issue of one magazine, so there had to be a cumulative effect in the editorial content. Our most difficult challenge was not to insult people who already knew something about desktop publishing. If we made it too basic, they would write us off as patronizing jerks.

An especially important aspect of *Desktop* was that since we were producing the magazine itself with DTP tools, we wanted to provide a good, and not-too-complicated example of what readers can create. For that reason, we consciously held ourselves back from doing anything too complicated with the layout, so they could see how we did it on the system.

We broke some new production ground with this magazine. DTP allowed the launch staff to work from three different sites—something that would have been foolish to attempt before lightweight computer technology, modems, and E-mail. Figure 12-1 shows our production setup.

Writers were scattered all over the country. The editors had their own office on Long Island, an hour away from the publisher in

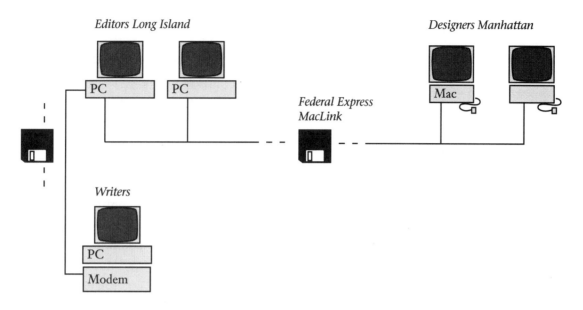

Figure 12-1
Launch staff worked from three different sites

midtown Manhattan. The art department was in lower Manhattan, about 20 blocks away from the service bureau that handled all the text pages and a good deal of the four-color. Jon Houston designed the basic format. Ann Pomeroy and Pam Vassil served as art directors of the first issues. We kept each other up-to-date with Fax, MCI Mail, Federal Express, and messengers carrying larger files on disk.

Sometimes it would seem like a three-ring circus, but for the most part it worked. The new technology meant that the publisher could reduce the startup risk by not having a proper office complement of full-time employees. Every magazine launch is volatile, and this one was no exception. Major editorial changes were made, and ultimately the magazine was sold to another publisher, without the usual agony of firing people.

The copy flow started when the editors on Long Island received copy from writers, sometimes over the modem, and sometimes on disk. Most of *Desktop*'s writers work on computer, as you might expect, so very little had to be keyed in. The editors worked with the copy using PCs and WordPerfect. They also wrote headlines, subheads, possible pullquotes, the author's biographies, and they put everything together in one PC file.

Using MacLink (and a card installed in the PC), they transferred an ASCII file into MacWrite or Microsoft Word because the designers used Macintoshes. Once it had safely bridged that gap, they sent us the disk by Federal Express. We just stuck it in our machine and we were ready to go. (Later, Apple introduced a file conversion utility and a DOS disk was "ready to go.")

With late copy or last minute changes, the editors sent files by electronic mail—MCI Mail in this case, which is much easier to use than attempting a direct modem-to-modem transfer.

Once the disks hit the art department, we brought the text into QuarkXPress files. Regular columns flowed right into templates. For the features we made new layouts, working on a basic grid.

Obviously, this wasn't an instantaneous process, but right from the beginning we got a feel for how long the text was going to run. When layouts were done, the QuarkXPress file was sent to the publisher's office for final copy editing and proofreading. The ITC production office coordinated copy flow. They were aware of when copy came to us from the editors, and they coordinated the issue with the printer and the color prepress house (which handled some color separations and the stripping together of the negatives).

The Type

Since the publisher of *Desktop* was International Typeface Corporation, their products—typefaces—were featured in the design. Also, since it's a desktop-publishing magazine, we stuck to typefaces that have been released for the desktop. Two years ago this was something of a limitation, but now virtually all ITC faces are available in PostScript format on the Mac and the PC. One ITC licensee, The Font Company, gets out the new releases for the desktop before most of the conventional typesetting vendors.

So, of the initial design decisions to be made, type was one of the most important. To showcase the ITC wares, we decided to change typefaces every third issue, but to keep the same basic layout grid.

I decided on ITC Berkeley as the text type (see Figure 12-2), because

INTERVIEW

Doing it Right

There's been a lot of travel through uncharted territory for Frankfurt Gips Balkind (FGB), the New York firm that has helped a number of corporations, including MCI Communications, produce desktop publications. FGB's Aubrey Balkind advises executives thinking of embarking on the desktop publishing odyssey to beware of four potential pitfalls:

THE DESIGN-IT-YOURSELF SYNDROME

With the advent of desktop publishing, powerful graphic design tools are placed in the hands of editors who probably lack the talent and certainly lack the training professional designers bring to their jobs. As a result, many desktop publications are produced without the benefit of a designer's eye, and it shows in the final product.

"Most corporate people get involved with desktop to save time and expenses for typography, design and paste-up," Balkind says, "but to reap these benefits, a new work flow must be set up, appropriate training undertaken, and a template created so that a large part of the process becomes automated."

Desktop editors use professionally designed templates to guide them through the page-design process. But even with the help of a template, users must make critical design decisions. For this reason, Balkind recommends that the desktop novice have a professional review their work at least twice—before a mock-up of the publication is presented to management, and again before the publication is ready for the printer.

FLOGGING THE OLD WARHORSE

Balkind believes that organizations considering desktop publishing should update the design of their publications to take full advantage of what desktop systems can do. Since most page-layout software allows increased flexibility, it makes sense to rethink the basic design in light of desktop capabilities. For example, most page-layout software allows the user to flow copy around pictures and other graphics with ease. This was

rarely done before the advent of such programs, due to the time and high expense involved in creating the effects by hand.

THE INCOMPATIBLE COUPLE

The production of a quality desktop publication requires the marriage of a design firm's creative and technical capabilities with the client's own resources and vision. The two sides must work together smoothly in order to produce the best product. With desktop publishing, compatibility issues extend beyond the ability of the personalities involved to work together. The machines and software must be even more compatible than the people.

Currently, most business information is computed in the MS-DOS environment, while the graphic arts and design communities are solidly in the Macintosh corner. Getting these different systems to work together can be difficult.

Aubrey Balkind, your guide to desktop design.

Balkind says that a client who wants to work with a design firm that relies on a microcomputer should be willing to invest in at least one unit of the same system and appropriate software. "It's not a lot of money when you look at the savings these systems can bring," Balkind says. "The difference in typography costs alone will often justify the expense."

INADEQUATE TESTING AND BACKUPS

Every desktop publishing system should be fully tested before being applied to real copy, graphics and deadlines, Balkind warns. Even systems that seem fully compatible may produce problems that would not be apparent without testing. One FGB designer for example, recently found strange typefaces and column lengths in a page-layout document prepared by a client. The client's own printout of the same file showed no abnormalities. The problem, it turned out, was incompatible software. Even though both FGB and the client used the same version of the software, the two packages were different enough to cause a glitch.

A method of keeping adequate data-file backup systems, to avoid loss of critical documents, must become routine for anyone who works with personal computers. Those who fail to establish good backup systems will learn to regret their overconfidence. One hard-disk crash or electrical problem will convince the most skeptical desktop editor that backing up is more than a good idea—it's essential! ▲

Figure 12-2

Text type is ITC Berkeley

it is a very elegant, readable type. It is based on Frederick Goudy's superb Californian type, designed in the 1930s for the University of California Press. The type designer, Tony Stan, captured a good deal of the original spirit, added a few other Goudy touches, and fleshed out a full family of typefaces, with three weights and Italics.

One important call here is the point size of the text. We made it big (11 on 12-point leading), in part to suggest to DTP users that big text is an option in business communication documents that should always be considered. As we all get older, bigger type is more and more inviting. This decision received some criticism—that it made the magazine look too much like a grade-school primer, but what the heck, it's still vastly easier to read. The elegance of ITC Berkeley helped dispel this impression, while Century Schoolbook at this point size might truly have looked like we were aiming at kids rather than at baby boomers.

A caveat about body type that is worth repeating: it is impossible to generalize much about legibility and readability for body type. So much depends on individual production considerations—the kind of paper and press work a publication gets effects the decision about body type as much as the actual letter form design. The best way to decide is to try a number of alternatives, both in typefaces and in size-leading combinations. If possible, get some samples produced and printed using the exact technology and system that the publication is going to use. Show the samples to a few typical readers. Then decide.

The big headlines were also in ITC Berkeley. (We used Bitstream fonts, the first to be released in PostScript.) The writer biographies were in ITC Berkeley Italic. Column headings (which run in little tabs at the top), bylines, pullquotes, and subheads within running text—all were in ITC Stone Sans Bold. Figure 12-3 shows the Stone Sans Serif family. Stone was designed by Sumner Stone and was initially released by Adobe Systems. It's an interesting typeface because it has three different complete styles—an extended family, if you will. There are three weights in each family, with Italics, so there are a total of eighteen different typefaces. The three groups are Stone Serif, Stone Sans, and Stone Informal. The last was an attempt by Mr. Stone to come up with a typeface that would be good for correspondence and other uses

Figure 12-3
The Stone Sans Serif
family of typefaces
that were used in
Desktop magazine

ITC Stone Sans

A B C D E F G H I J K L M N
O P Q R S T U V W X Y Z
a b c d e f g h i j k l m n
o p q r s t u v w x y z
1 2 3 4 5 6 7 8 9 0

ITC Stone Sans Bold

A B C D E F G H I J K L M N
O P Q R S T U V W X Y Z
a b c d e f g h i j k l m n
o p q r s t u v w x y z
1 2 3 4 5 6 7 8 9 0

ITC Stone Sans Italic

*A B C D E F G H I J K L M N
O P Q R S T U V W X Y Z
a b c d e f g h i j k l m n
o p q r s t u v w x y z
1 2 3 4 5 6 7 8 9 0*

where more typographical letter forms might seem too impersonal, and, well, formal.

An essential issue to resolve was column justification. While American custom tends toward justified text for magazines, we decided on ragged right for the columns and for most of the other articles, except with really wide settings (for example, in two-column pages). We wanted this magazine to set an example to the newcomers, and most newcomers assume that all you need to produce justified text in desktop publishing is to push a button. Sadly, it is not yet that easy. All DTP programs automatically justify columns of text, adding hyphens to break words, but in narrow measures there are invariably many "loose lines." There can be excessive word spacing, or, worse, ghastly letter spacing, to make the line fill out.

The spacing is determined by a justification algorithm, the logic that lets a program find natural breaks between the syllables of words. You need a program that has a good one; none are perfect. The algorithm is a set of rules, and is supplemented by an exception dictionary. The one in QuarkXPress is only 20,000 words, compared to a professional Atex system found at big newspapers, which has something like 200,000 words. Bigger dictionaries would slow down the h-and-j on the Mac.

Important note here: if you are planning to use justified text, make sure that the command for "allow hyphenation" is turned on in the appropriate dialog box. It's easy to forget, and you end up getting justification but no hyphenation.

When type is hyphenated but set flush only left or right, any extra space is pushed to one side, but with justification, the space has to be absorbed in the middle of the line. DTP programs are getting more sophisticated about the controls over hyphenation with each new release. Most now permit you to set limits on the number of hyphens in a row (typographers call more than two a *stutter.*) The best programs let the user set some relative values for word spacing (minimum, optimum, and maximum), and for letter spacing. There is no standard approach, but in any case, it is best to experiment with the typeface you are using.

The default word space is part of the design of type, and is a matter of taste and legibility. Smaller type needs bigger word spaces. You may wish to set optimum somewhat narrower than the designer of the type specified. I usually crank up maximum to 300 percent or more, and then turn off letter spacing altogether. American typesetting is full of lines where the letters have been spaced out to give a hideous gap-toothed effect. Europeans can't believe this, and the folks at ITC, who are fanatics about typography, have near heart palpitations when they see their faces set badly. They opt, in narrow columns, to set everything flush left. Some designers say that ragged right should never have hyphenation.

When justifying, the point is to crowd as many syllables as possible onto each line to minimize white space.

Say you have seven lines in a paragraph, but when you cram as many syllables as fit in each line, you create an ugly gap on the fifth line and you're left with only a partial word on the last line—a widow. To rectify the situation, you need to go into lines two, three, and four, and push some syllables down to the next line. This takes some thinking by the operator because most of the current hyphenation programs aren't capable of going back and fixing for the typographical problems they create. In the old days when experienced craftspeople were setting type by hand or on the original Linotype machine, there was a kind of intuitive interaction between the typographer and the text.

A good desktop typographer always scrutinizes the text and tries to eliminate the loose lines. (Ventura Publisher can highlight these lines to make them easier to spot.) But for newcomers, it may be smart to stick to ragged right.

As for ragged left, I avoid it altogether. It seems hard to read and unnatural.

Contents Page

Most magazines have started to make their contents pages extremely complicated. Sometimes they use two pages, often they're not facing pages. They use all sorts of text wraps, type sizes, inset pictures, and silhouettes. A good example is *Self* magazine. Theirs is well-designed, but if it got much more complicated, you would need a contents page for the contents pages.

We wanted the *Desktop* table of contents (see Figure 12-4) to be something that a reader could produce.

There are a number of style sheets used on the page. After we poured the text onto the page using QuarkXPress, all we did was apply the styles to the headlines and the text. We then went in individually to change the point sizes of the numerals.

One look at the contents page shows the structure of *Desktop* magazine to be blatantly straightforward. This is not a bad thing; every contents page should reveal the underlying structure of its magazine. In *Desktop*, there are columns, features, and departments. The editors felt that readers were most interested in the features, so, they are listed first.

Columns

One of our first design decisions was to choose a four-column grid to use throughout the whole magazine. This is a basic decision you have to make. If your magazine is not going to be interrupted by partial advertising (ads smaller than a page) you can use any grid you want. Magazines that have a lot of partial advertising and a conventional rate card, like *Time* and *Newsweek,* have to use three-column pages because ads come in standard sizes, based on a 7-by-10-inch nonbleed page.

Increasingly, however, ad salesmen will take any size offered. No longer do advertisers even look at the size requirements on rate cards. In the competitive world of magazine advertising, they know they can get virtually any size printed. This would have been a heavy production burden before desktop tools, but now text can be made to flow around virtually any size or shape.

This new trend is bad for the continuity of a magazine, and many seem to be a jumble of checkerboard ads, bottle-shape ads, and floating island ads. But it is good if you want to break out of the traditional three-column strait jacket.

For *Desktop*, we figured that most of the ads in the beginning were

ITC
Desktop
Vol. I, No. 1: March-April 1989

Desktop presentations: An invaluable tool at Dun & Bradstreet, page 39

Cover photograph by George Lange

Give your people time to master their new tools, page 58

ITC DESKTOP (ISSN 1042-1923) is published bimonthly by International Typeface Corporation, 2 Hammarskjold Plaza, NY, NY 10017, (212) 371-0699. Entire contents copyright © 1989 INTERNATIONAL TYPEFACE CORPORATION. All rights reserved, reproduction in whole or in part without permission is prohibited. ITC DESKTOP is a trademark of International Typeface Corporation.

ITC DESKTOP : No. 1

3

Figure 12-4
The structure of the magazine is blatantly obvious from the table of contents

going to be full pages, so the decision to go for a four-column grid was perfectly practical. It is a natural choice to use for business documents as well, so it is appropriate for *Desktop's* business communications audience. When you put four columns on an 8.5-by-11-inch page, you get enough columns for design variety, and the option to go to double-width two-column pages while staying on the grid.

Though we used a four-column grid, we used an underlying guide, rather than a rigid container. It is hard to see it with the column layouts. As shown in Figure 12-5, we divided the inside three columns into two, something extremely easy to do in DTP. Gone are the days when you had to calculate column widths to the nearest point.

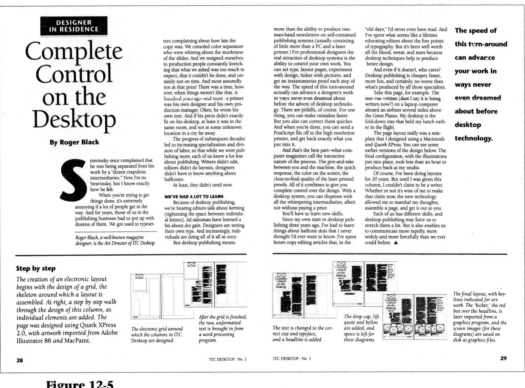

Figure 12-5
The four-column grid for columns provided a number of layout options

For *Desktop* we had set up an underlying (called the "default" in QuarkXPress) three-column page. For the columns, we made a new default page by going back and drawing a new text box three columns wide on the four-column grid; then we set it for two columns in the

Item Modify dialog box. The remaining outside column (part of the four-column page) was left for captions and pullquotes.

The most interesting part of the layout was the way we centered the column heading, the headline, the by-line, and the drop initial on the left side of this new text box. These elements are centered on the gutter between column one and two of the old four-column grid. In the end, we had to nudge the headline box a little bit, because strict centering didn't look quite right. Most readers would not be aware of the grid after we were through with it, which is just as well. Informality can be achieved by playing with this geometry, but by working with the grid you hope to give a feeling of structure and organization.

This column needed a sidebar, so we needed to figure out how to set it apart from the main body of text, without going to the obvious thing and putting it in a box. I don't know why, but I don't like boxes around sidebars, perhaps because I've seen so many of them. Using a rule would have been the most obvious solution. However, if you aren't careful, a rule can cause blocks of type to fill in rather than to be distinct. If you run a rule down the middle of a 1-pica wide white gutter, for example, it may fill in the space. For the sidebar (see Figure 12-6), we opted to widen the gutter, go back to the four-column grid, and a radically different typeface. It worked.

Features and Departments

We wanted the columns to be identifiable, so we kept the same basic design for each one. But we didn't want to constrict the features to a repetitive design treatment. We allowed a certain amount of variety in the headlines and the type layout.

In the feature shown in Figure 12-7, we resorted to an old trick—using cartoons to get attention. We wanted to make sure to communicate some of the fun that people find in desktop publishing—the video game quality of playing around on the screen. If you treat desktop publishing simply as a boring mechanical tool, without mentioning the fun and zeal, then you haven't captured the spirit of the thing. So, we hired a very good cartoonist to illustrate the story and to pick used EGA (Enhanced Graphics Adapter) screens. Moreover, while the EGA screen you may use now supplies you with graphics based on sixteen colors, the 82786 expands this to 256!

With a system packing one of these little IC gems (regardless of which) graphics possibilities include three-dimensional drawing and imaging—indeed, actual visualization of designs—limited only by the skill and imagination of whoever writes the software. In fact, the Texas Instruments chip is so powerful as a stand-alone microprocessor, that it's expected to find even wider application, popping up in laser printers, scanners, and copiers—systems which will more and more frequently rely on graphics.

A look through an electron microscope shows the tiny transistor switches within a typical computer chip. The width of each wire is less than one micron—about the amount a fingernail grows in an hour.

Motorola Semiconductor

Microscopic Electronics: A Primer

The integrated circuit chips which lie at the heart of microcomputers are tiny electronic circuits, cast in minuscule pieces of silicon. The miraculous engines that power our desktop publishing systems contain tens of thousands of transistors which manipulate digital data by acting as electrical switches, opening and closing millions of times each second.

Through the use of advanced photolithographic techniques, integrated circuit manufacturers are packing more and more transistors into a given area to produce "bigger" circuits on smaller bits of silicon. The dimensions of the "components" of these circuits are now measured in units less than a millionth-of-a-meter in size.

Smaller circuits can work faster, opening and closing their switches more rapidly, making a microcomputer act and react almost instantaneously. Computer designers call this capability real time processing. It means that if you tell your computer to make a change in page layout, the image on your screen reforms almost immediately.

We are currently in the era of VLSI—Very Large Scale Integrated Circuits. The first Integrated Circuits contained perhaps ten or twenty individual transistors on a chip. Next came ICs with a few hundred transistors, and Large Scale Integration, LSI, produced devices packing thousands of transistors. Today's chips often cram 200,000 transistors or more onto a bit of silicon one-third of an inch square!

Although there's been talk about still further miniaturization, with Ultra Large Scale Integrated

24   ITC DESKTOP : No. 1

THROW 'EM A CURVE

One of the most striking things you'll notice on your screen when using a desktop publishing system running one of these devices is the lack of jagged lines. Computer scientists and engineers refer to the process of creating a curved display line from a series of small straight lines aliasing. These ICs eliminate the effect by mathematically number-crunching the pixels involved and smoothing the rough edges.

And these devices produce images almost instantaneously, drawing lines at the rate of 1 or 2 million pixels each second! Letters and figures are produced at rates ranging from 7,000 characters per second to as fast as 40,000-plus. Simple text, proportionally spaced characters, and kerning with selectable right and left justification can be easily accomplished.

Windowed environments and paint programs also are enhanced, running algorithms—the steps the computer uses to perform the required calculations—that have been known for a long time, but have been too complicated for the microprocessors previously available. For example, outlines of objects aren't enough for today's graphics, so these new ICs let you fill in outlines and shade them, producing intersecting and overlapping shapes never before possible.

MORE TO COME

As if such advances were not enough, T.I.'s next graphics processor, already named the 34020, will include provisions for working in tandem with a full floating point co-processor. This means the two-chip set might run as much as 100 times faster than the 34010 and be specifically tailored for three-dimensional processing, while maintaining software compatibility with the 34010 predecessor!

New graphics chips also are being developed by National Semiconductor, Advanced Micro Devices, and other companies. These IC makers are readying products that will spell an exciting new era of interactive graphics for desktop publishing users.

In the meantime, watch for plug-in boards and software packages that can make use of the new Intel and Texas Instruments devices. Vendors of boards with either of these graphics processors are offering you capabilities at the leading edge of today's video display technology! ▲

Why care about good graphics? Because your message needs a life beyond the moment.

Circuits (VLSI) discussed as a possibility for the next generation of chips, technical constraints probably will prevent their production in commercial quantities. For example, when circuits are so small, contaminants—like smoke and dust particles—become a major problem during manufacturing. Also, the more complex a tiny circuit, the more difficult it is to test it, since determining the cause of a malfunction might require detection of just one faulty transistor among millions!

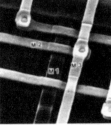

GE Micro-Electronics

Very Large Scale Integration (VLSI) packs as many as 20,000 transistors onto one-third of an inch of silicon.

ITC DESKTOP : No. 1   25

Figure 12-6
We looked for something other than a rule to set off this sidebar

up the writing. Then, we took the section headings, used different ITC typefaces for each one (which the publisher obviously appreciated) and decorated them a little bit with Adobe Illustrator.

In general, there was large type at the start of almost all the feature stories. This brought readers into the story, by calling their attention to the beginning, and by reducing resistance. Big type is simply easier to read. It also shows off the type design (pleasing the publisher again). And there is a practical reason: the size and length of this big lead are flexible, making it easier to fit pages. With PostScript you can make type any size—limited, if that is the word, in most programs to increments of a tenth of a point.

We didn't want all of the features in *Desktop* to have a how-to focus. We also wanted to include a healthy dose of "what is possible" and "what's good, what's bad." In one feature, a variety of design approaches to the same project was presented. We took an existing brochure and redesigned it three ways. (See Figures 12-8a–12-8b.)

Figure 12-7
Communicating
the fun

I had the chutzpah to ask my brother-in-law (who is a DTP enthusiast from the point of view of a journalist, but not a full-time designer) to allow three designers to rework a brochure he had produced on his own desktop-publishing system.

His solution for this particular brochure—using a stop sign—is very graphic. The yellow he used all over the page is a little frightening—it attracts attention—though the work is clearly not a professional's. We asked two professionals, David Taub and Howard Mandel of New Media Design Group to take the same idea and make it a little more arresting graphically. They created a new brochure with Adobe Illustrator and QuarkXPress that incorporated the original stop sign, but made the overall look more sophisticated.

Doug May, a designer in Dallas, went for a more new-wave approach, but he maintained the highway sign feeling and used tools in the page-layout program. In the explanation of how he did it he said, "What's fun about these programs is that they allow you to be very

Pulling Out All The Stops

FOUR APPROACHES
TO THE SAME GRAPHIC
DESIGN PROBLEM

W e at *ITC Desktop* asked four designers to take an existing brochure and redesign it. We set no limits on what could or could not be done. Our only request was that it be executed exclusively with desktop technology. Here is the existing brochure. With the permission of Indumar Products Inc. and ProGraf Inc., the modified versions appear on the following pages.

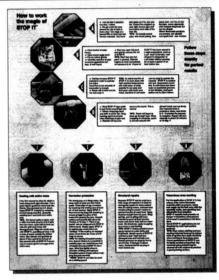

Derrick Booth, ProGraf Inc., Houston, Texas

Booth designed this brochure for Indumar Products Inc. using Xerox Ventura Publisher 2.0.

Figure 12-8a
Redesigning
the brochure

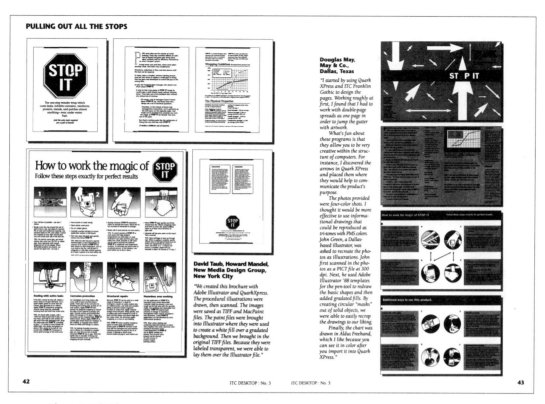

Figure 12-8b
The professional solution

creative within the structure of computers. For instance, I discovered the arrows in QuarkXPress and placed them where they would help communicate the product's purpose." It wasn't hard to do.

In "Templates: Flexible Consistency," as shown in Figure 12-9, we made the lead page very simple to try to balance a very complicated page on the right. A hindsight criticism is that this does not let the pages tie together well enough, and perhaps we could have picked up some colors or tones from the illustrations. There is a big text intro with a headline in Berkeley that is flush left.

We hired a talented designer, Marjorie Spiegelman, to interpret the templates that were available off-the-shelf. She took the same text and used the two major products, Quark Style templates (which also work with QuarkXPress) and one from the PageMaker template packages, which include a number of templates, to see how a corporate report or memo, or a newsletter could be interpreted using the different formats.

They actually came out quite well. They look corporate, they're

Figure 12-9
A simple lead page, to balance the complicated facing illustration

clean, and I don't see anything wrong with them. The extra bonus is the time saved by not starting from scratch. If I were a newcomer, my first question would be, "where do I start with this template thing?" So, this article and its design has to serve as a kind of tutorial. To get the templates off the ground you obviously have to know the basics of your page-makeup program because they only exist in the world of these programs.

Type Is All You Need—Three Type Design Rules of Thumb

"Brochure Basics" is a somewhat different typographical effort. (See Figure 12-10.) We did an all-type story, which is something *Desktop* readers can do with small publications. We didn't want to get too fancy, but show what type alone could do without illustrative

BROCHURE BASICS

Practical Tips For Creating Effective Promotional Pieces

By Steven Brightbill

The advertisements suggest that all you need to produce top-notch brochures is the right desktop publishing system. After all, why pay for professional marketing, graphic design, and production services when you can do it all yourself?

Well, as any seasoned veteran of advertising, design, production or desktop publishing can tell you, there's more to doing an effective brochure than learning a few keystrokes and mouse-clicks. Producing a brochure is a complex communications task that requires both creative and technical skills—concept development and planning, writing and editing, layout and design, graphic arts production, to name just a few. The process requires an understanding of basic advertising principles and the skillful application of appropriate writing, design and production know-how.

BASIC QUESTIONS

To create an effective brochure you must clearly identify what you want it to accomplish. Before you begin writing copy or developing a design, ask yourself some basic important questions: What is the brochure's objective? Are you entering a new market by introduc-

Steven Brightbill operates Betagraph Design Associates, a Denver, Colorado design studio.

38

ing a new product, or is the goal to remind existing clients of what you have to offer? Do you want to build or reinforce name recognition and reputation, or are you making a specific offer of a particular product or service?

Be as specific as you can about your brochure's objectives. Avoid vague generalities such as "I want my brochure to help me sell more products." If you don't know what you want your brochure to accomplish, the reader won't know either and won't know how to respond.

Who is your target audience? Your brochure cannot appeal to everyone, so clearly identify who you are trying to reach and address them in your copy.

For example, if you are marketing financial services, do you want to reach young families who have limited resources to encourage them to start a regular savings program? Or do you want to target middle-aged, financially secure professional people who have large sums of money available for both short-term and long-term investments?

It is impossible to reach everyone with a single brochure. Since each audience has different needs and interests, your message must be tailored to a specific target group you are trying to attract. If you are trying to reach several targets, produce a series of brochures, each directed to a specific group.

How does the customer benefit? Why should a customer choose your product or service instead of someone else's? Every product or service benefits

ITC DESKTOP : No. 3

someone. Think about what makes yours special, a good buy, something that will satisfy the customer's wants or needs.

When identifying customer benefits, focus on the single most important advantage to your target audience. Let's return to our financial services example. If you are trying to reach the young family with limited resources and you want to appeal to the need for security and stability, you could point out how long your company has been serving the community: "ABC Financial Services: We Were Here When Your Grandfather Needed Us." On the other hand, the middle-aged professional might want a diversified investment strategy. Your customer approach might read something like this, "Multiple Options to Meet Your Changing Investment Requirements."

How is your advertising message best supported? What can you say that will assure customers that what you are selling will truly benefit them? Considering the gimmicks and questionable claims of many marketing efforts, customers rightfully want and need a reason to believe that your product or service is worth their investment. Whatever your message says, it must be well substantiated.

What is the tone and personality of your product? Make sure what you have to offer is in tune with your intended market and sufficiently set apart from similar products or services.

For example, compare the Ford Escort with the new Ford Probe. Both have four wheels, an engine, and carry people from point *A* to point *B*. But the personalities of these two vehicles are different. The Escort is designed for and marketed to people who want solid, dependable, economical transportation. The Probe, on the other hand, appeals to people with sportier interests and larger wallets.

The answers to these basic, essential questions become the road map that will guide the brochure writing and design process. Write them down and refer to them often.

THE CREATIVE PROCESS

After you've identified your objective, target audience, product benefits, support, and personality, it's time to begin the creative process. Here are seven specific tips to help you write and design your brochure.

Spend lots of time on the cover. A brochure's cover is like an ad's headline—it's looked at for perhaps three seconds or less. What's more, four out of five people never get beyond the cover.

The importance of the brochure's cover cannot be overemphasized. Some advertising experts suggest that as much as 50 to 75 percent of your creative energy should be spent on cover development.

Don't skimp on copy. If your cover managed to capture the reader's interest, don't shortchange his curiosity by skimping on copy. People don't mind

ITC DESKTOP : No. 3

reading a lot of copy if they value the message. Therefore, make sure that what you have to say is easy to read, well written, logically presented and worth reading. Avoid long sentences, technical terminology and jargon. And when appropriate, simplify the reading process by using lists and bulleted information.

Highlight important benefits and facts. Go back to your road map and pick out your customer benefits. Draw attention to those benefits and other important facts. Make them stand out from the rest of the text by using lists, bullets, boldface type, color, boxes, and other typographic and design techniques that will attract the reader's eye.

Use testimonials when appropriate. It never hurts to have a satisfied customer sell your product or service by way of a testimonial or endorsement. Prospective customers feel reassured when someone who has bought the product or service says nice things about it. When using a testimonial, make sure you get permission from the endorser.

Be honest. Apart from the legal and ethical reasons for avoiding misrepresentations, your brochure will be effective only if it tells the truth. It is impossible that a single product or service can do everything, so don't try to stretch the truth and imply otherwise. People can spot dishonesty and deception a mile away.

Request a response. You're creating a brochure because you want its readers to do something. But don't assume they will automatically know what you want them to do. If you want them to call your 800 number, say so. If you want them to return a postage-paid response card, invite them to send it back.

Use meaningful graphics and photos. Too many novice desktop publishers try to use all sorts of graphic tools simply because they're available and easy to handle. Yet some of the best graphic treatments you'll ever see are simple and direct.

Select graphics that reinforce the message and help tell the story. Let's suppose you are trying to sell young families on the idea of putting money into a savings account to pay for a future college education.

CHECKLIST FOR BETTER BROCHURES:

1. Spend lots of time on the cover.
2. Don't skimp on copy.
3. Highlight the important benefits and facts.
4. Use testimonials when appropriate.
5. Be honest.
6. Request a response.
7. Use meaningful graphics and photos.

39

Figure 12-10
An all-type effort

material. So, we cut the large type lead into a three-on-four measure so that it hit the underlying grid under the page. The type at the top of the page was designed carefully using only three fundamental type rules.

The Three Type Design Rules of Thumb

Stat to Width

Make Everything Line up with Something Else

Follow the Theory of Invisible Descenders

The first, "Stat to Width," is named for the days when you had to send out for photocopies to enlarge or reduce type to exact sizes. It means that instead of taking an arbitrary size like 48-point type, you take the whole line, or the widest, longest word and make it the width of your grid so that it fits exactly. We had a little subhead, so we made "BROCHURE BASICS" fit as large as possible, flush left, all caps. It was natural to do something with the space beside "BASICS."

This comes to the second rule of thumb, "Make Everything Line Up With Something Else." In this case, the far right lines up with the right column. The top of the cap height and the bottom of the baseline align with the cap height and the baseline of the other line. These two rules usually work well in tandem.

Finally, the third design precept involves the "Theory of Invisible Descenders." An example is headline. I like to put extra space under typographical elements. It is too easy in the plastic age of computer type to jam everything in. Since aesthetics (like ethics) are conditioned by practical realities, typographical aesthetics are to some extent determined by the past 500 years of production constraints in printing.

My invisible descender principle is built on the hard fact that in metal type every letter had to be cast in a given point size. The capital letters would not occupy the full face of the piece of metal, only about two-thirds, to leave room for the descenders on small letters in the same font. If you set a line of big caps in regular type, or even a lowercase phrase as in Figure 12-11, which happens to have no descenders, there would always be a gap between the baseline and the top of the next line because the metal would keep it away. This is the invisible descender!

Figure 12-11
The Rule of Invisible Descenders: always leave a gap between the baseline and the top of the next line

admit it is

----
hard to tell

I somehow feel that the principle doesn't apply to the lines within a big headline (which can actually be set with negative leading). All the space can go below the headline when you leave space for the descenders in a headline.

Every designer has rules or tricks like these. Cumulatively they become a style, and with this style in mind it took only about fifteen minutes of fooling around on the screen to finish the layout.

Departments and Templates

This is the utility section of *Desktop*, pretty straightforward, as is the editorial content—product reviews and analyses of newsletters. As shown in Figure 12-12, we let the base structure of the magazine show through—the four-column grid—and ran fairly conventional column headlines along the top of each page to hold the section together. There are times when simplest is best. There is no reason why *Desktop* should not remind people of a magazine!

We used templates as the basis for the department design. The text was poured into the text box shell, and manipulated to make it fit. The template is the contemporary equivalent of the old layout sheet, with the grid ruled out in blue.

The advantages to having a template over designing a page from scratch in QuarkXPress or PageMaker are *first,* a blank page is very daunting if you are not an experienced designer. The template offers a jumping-off point. The grid offers some automatic guidelines. *Second,* by conforming to a basic template a publication has a better chance of tying together. For a professional, the template provides the standard pieces to get a layout started. Besides the grid, the template might contain samples of headlines, pullquotes, drop initials, captions, and other reader devices.

Someone like Jan White, the well-known corporate designer, will go into a corporation and set up design guidelines for all corporate communications.

More and more, publication format design consists of making specific DTP templates. Then, anyone can fill in the text and produce

DESKTOP PRODUCTS

A brief look at selected hardware and software products for your desktop publishing and design system

Apple Mac IIcx: Conveniently small, with the power of bigger Apples.

Edited by Peter O.E. Bekker Jr.

Computers

UNISYS PW³ SERIES 800/25A

This 25-MHz. system is targeted at desktop publishers as a local area network (LAN) server for group design and publishing tasks. The system is offered in a variety of configurations that range from diskless to an impressive 640Mb of hard disk storage. 2Mb RAM, MS-DOS 4.01 and Windows/386 are standard. Graphics card and video monitor are optional.

Price: $7315 for basic diskless system. Unisys

Unisys PW³: Share the desktop, split the bills.

but there are plenty of ports and connectors including an SCSI socket that can control up to seven devices. A math coprocessor is standard, as is Apple's 1.4Mb Superdrive. Combined with Apple File Exchange software, this drive will read MS-DOS, Prodos and OS/2 disks.

Price: $5370 with 1Mb RAM, and 40Mb hard drive. Keyboard, video adapter and monitor not included.

Apple Computer, 20525 Mariani Ave., Cupertino, CA 95014, (408) 996-1010, (800) 538-9696.

Publishing Programs

PAGESTREAM 1.5 (Atari)

This upgraded rendition of Publishing Partner provides users of Atari ST machines with heavy-duty desktop publishing capabilities. However, it differs so significantly from its predecessor that the old program's documents and fonts are unusable. Conversion programs are supplied but users report only limited success. Pagestream is GEM-based and includes a full range of layout and word processing capabilities, including a spell-checker with definable dictionary. Typographical control is very good for the 10 built-in fonts. However, text will not bind directly to a path and, therefore, routing text around a curve is a tedious manual process. The software offers color and monochrome support, macros, snap-grids for posi-

Corp., Blue Bell, PA 19424, (800) 547-8362.

APPLE MAC IIcx

A diminutive version of the Mac IIx built around the same 15.7-MHz. Motorola 68030 chip that powers the IIx and SE/30. Sits flat or on its side, occupying a space of only about 1' x 1' x 6". It has only three Nubus expansion slots, one of them filled by the video adapter.

tioning, a nice selection of importable text formats and good printer support.

Price: $199.95. Soft-Logik Publishing Corp., 1131-F South Towne Square, St. Louis, MO 63123, (314) 894-8608.

Illustration Software

ADOBE ILLUSTRATOR (DOS)

This DOS version of the popular PostScript-based Mac drawing tool lacks several features of the Mac version. There is no color support and typographical functions are weak, with no outlining, fill patterns, or drop-shading. However, a very good autotracing feature imports images from MacPaint (.PNT), PC Paintbrush (.PCX) and Tag Image File Format (.TIF), Auto

Pagestream 1.5: Good typographical control.

CAD and other files. A fast AT-class or 386 computer is a must. Requires at least 256K of expanded memory, a hard disk, and DOS 3.1 or better. Includes runtime Windows.

Price: $695. Adobe Systems Inc., 1585 Charleston Rd., Mountain View, CA 94039, (415) 961-4400, (800) 344-8335.

ITC DESKTOP : No. 3

DESKTOP PRODUCTS

ALDUS FREEHAND 2.0 (Mac)

A first-rate illustrating tool that has bridged every gap in the original version. There is PostScript-based full-color support including the Pantone set, personalized RGB, CMYK, HLS (hue lightness saturation), and spot and process colors. It also supports color separations. FreeHand 2.0 offers a full complement of drawing tools, along with typography and font manipu-

Adobe Illustrator (DOS): Better on the Mac.

lation features second to none in its class. It works with FreeHand version 1 files and files from Adobe Illustrator 1.1. Imports Mac-Paint, PICT and TIFF files. Full PostScript output. Requires a Mac II, 2Mb RAM, System 4.3, and Finder 6.0 or better.

Price: $495. Aldus Corp., 411 First Ave. South, Seattle, WA 98104, (206) 622-5500.

CORELDRAW! (DOS)

A spectacular Windows-based drawing program with many unique and thoughtful features. For example, each of the program's 50 or so fonts appears in its own face on the selection menu so there's no more guessing what fonts look like. On the downside, CORELDRAW! typefaces are proprietary

and the program cannot use fonts from vendors such as Bitstream. CORELDRAW! is not as speedy as some other illustration programs, mostly because Windows isn't very agile. But the package includes many of the features missing from similar programs. For example, the drawing pen adjusts thickness proportionally depending on the drawn angle. CORELDRAW! also provides "fountains" that apply color or shading in a smooth progression either linearly or outward from a fixed point, a macro language, autotrace of bit-mapped images without extended memory, and a simple curve-drawing capability. Requires Windows and therefore, at least an AT-class machine.

Price: $695. Corel Systems Corp., 1600 Carling Ave., Ottawa, Ontario, Canada K1Z 8R7, (613) 728-8200.

MICROGRAFX DESIGNER 2.0 (DOS)

An onslaught of newcomers now breathes down its neck, but this granddaddy of PC draw programs remains competitive. It is especially well suited for technical illustrations because of exceptional features such as automatic dimensioning, the use of layers, and its ability to import the .DXF file format used in Computer Aided Design (CAD) software. Another big plus is its customizable tool selection that allows the user to define which of the program's many tools to keep handy and which not to display on

the icon menu. Fountains, autotrace, color separations, a superb help system, and a burgeoning clip art collection all enhance Designer's stature. But this classic has lost the typography edge. Type handling is awkward and not at all up to the program's graphics capabilities. Includes runtime Windows. An AT-class machine or better is strongly recommended.

Price: $495. Micrografx, 1303 Arapaho St., Richardson, TX 75081, (214) 234-1769, (800) 272-3729.

Graphics Software

CRICKET PRESENTS (Mac)

Text enhancement is the only soft spot in this otherwise exceptionally powerful presentation package. Not much typography control but otherwise a blockbuster. It includes a fine selection of templates and an excellent outliner for preparation. Supports color and black-and-white. Offers very good drawing capability, including polygons and rounded rectangles. Produces Area, Line and Stacked Bar charts. Generates handouts and note pages. Strong on graphics

Cricket Presents (Mac): Mostly a blockbuster.

importing including PICT, PICT2, EPS and MacPaint. Service bureaus can quickly create 35mm slides from Cricket's output. Requires a Mac Plus or better.

Price: $495. Cricket Software, 40 Valley Stream Parkway, Malvern, PA 19355. (215) 251-9890.

IMAGESTUDIO (Mac)

A splendid image retouching program with many unique features such as the "waterdrop," "fingertip" and "charcoal" retouching tools. Black-and-white only. Supports 265 gray levels at resolutions of from 10 to photographic 2000 dots per inch. Direct import from most popular paint and scanner programs. No image scrolling; work is done a screenful at a time. Image rotation possible only in 90 degree increments. Otherwise, ImageStudio has it all: sophisticated image analysis, graymap editing of brightness and contrast in all or part of an image, filters for many special effects, user-configurable tool selection, customizable pens and fill patterns. An extraordinarily complete package.

Price: $495. Letraset USA, 40 Eisenhower Drive, Paramus, NJ 07653, (201) 845-6100.

PHOTOMAC (Mac)

A professional prepress color retouching program at a midrange price. Imports eight-bit and 24-bit scanned color images for enhancement. Can use PICT, PICT2, TARGA, VISTA and 24-bit TIFF files. Prints to TIFF or PICT2 format or directly to a

ITC DESKTOP : No. 3

Figure 12-12
Back-of-the-book, where we let the structure show

something that conforms to the bigger design goals of the company. A newsletter may not even go outside the company, or it may go to only one small market of the company, but with the use of design templates, it still definitely looks like it comes from that company. For smaller companies who might not be able to afford a professional designer to set up guidelines, there are a number of canned templates on the market that work with specific page-layout programs.

Newsletters

Many people initially get into desktop publishing with the idea of putting out their own newsletter. Without much marketing information, it's my theory that people start out with an IBM PC running a spreadsheet, and then realize they have the power to get information out to customers.

The first move might be something as simple as creating a standard information sheet or graph, then dolling it up with an editorial explanation, or using DTP tools to make the information look more professional or important.

Self-Publishing

Most of the heat and publicity generated by desktop publishing is in the professional area. People see the results, and experience increased sales and the huge savings in time and money. *Publish* and other computer magazines focus on the advances of desktop publishing for professionals who are already in the publishing world, and who are already producing publications by traditional means. I feel that the real excitement of the technology is what Paul Brainerd was originally talking about when he was working with the initial concepts for desktop publishing—self-publishing.

The real excitement is putting the means of production into the hands of people who have previously not thought of publishing anything. They might have been put off by the cost, the time factor, and the hassle of having to deal with editors, production people, typesetters, photo service bureaus, and printers. The beauty of desktop publishing is that in the ideal situation, they could do the whole project from beginning to end—even cutting out the printer if they only needed to laser print a small number of copies. It is a return to the world of Benjamin Franklin, except anyone can print his or her own propaganda and tracts.

As individuals and organizations begin to realize the power they have, this is the role that newsletters will begin to play in the modern world. It is unlikely that a rocket scientist or a school principal will decide to put out a full, slick magazine with his or her PC. But, that person could decide to produce a newsletter.

The biggest hurdle for the independent publisher is figuring out how to do a layout. Everyone who contemplates putting out a newsletter will be familiar with words and writing. The articles are easy to envision because we are aware of communicating with words on a daily basis. Design may be something new. Of course, we all have had design in our lives as long as we have had words. They just don't teach you about typefaces along with your ABCs. You may never have been aware of all the elements of a page which can make an article into a "must read" or a "quick miss."

Why a Newsletter?

Newsletters bring together the writing and correspondence of you and a few friends or colleagues who work for the same company or cause. This is the newsletter that you might put out for your local PTA, your church, a local branch of a computer user group, a small company, or your Big Chill group of college friends. We're not talking about an IBM newsletter or the mammoth trade newsletters like *Media Industry News,* which tend to have professional staffs or are designed by outside professionals.

A newsletter can be an interesting communications tool for a business and its customers. It's not really advertising, but in effect, it keeps your company in the front of your customers' minds. Essentially, you can provide some information for your customers and then hope they will like you more.

Obviously, the impetus to starting a newsletter is to make a connection that sometimes you can't make by phone or in person—often because there is not enough time in the day. Everybody leaves a trail of dozens of people they meet over the course of a year, people they meet at trade shows or people they meet sitting on a plane. In a business of any kind, you start to wonder how you can keep in touch with all of those people. In general, 75% of them are worth keeping in touch with. So a newsletter is not a bad way to do this without too much effort. If you give them something that is either interesting, informative, or entertaining, it could help them to understand what you are trying to do and what you have to offer.

Think of a newsletter as a long letter. Aunt Martha, for example mails you such a letter at Christmas that is mimeographed down at the school. (Your Aunt Martha, of course. Mine would never do such a thing.) This is probably a hideous example of design. She probably drew something resembling a wreath at the top. But Martha has the same impulse, the same incentive—not writing all those Christmas cards.

Historical Basis

Newsletters are similar to early magazines and journals. Figure 13-1 shows an example of a newspaper of 1723. The first newspapers were not unlike a modern newsletter. *The Pennsylvania Gazette,* Benjamin Franklin's newspaper was larger than 8.5-by-11 inches, but not by much. It was two columns on a page without pictures. The text started in the upper-left corner and just went to the end. These early newspapers would start with a letter and continue on, serially through

THE [N° 85

New-England Courant.

From MONDAY February 4. to MONDAY February 11. 1723.

The late Publisher of this Paper, finding so many Inconveniencies would arise by his carrying the Manuscripts and publick News to be supervis'd by the Secretary, as to render his carrying it on unprofitable, has intirely dropt the Undertaking. The present Publisher having receiv'd the following Piece, desires the Readers to accept of it as a Preface to what they may hereafter meet with in this Paper.

*Non ego mordaci distrinxi Carmine quenquam,
Nulla venenato Littera mixta Joco est.*

LONG has the Press groaned in bringing forth an hateful, but numerous Brood of Party Pamphlets, malicious Scribbles, and Billingsgate Ribaldry. The Rancour and bitterness it has unhappily infused into Mens minds, and to what a Degree it has sowred and leaven'd the Tempers of Persons formerly esteemed some of the most sweet and affable, is too well known here, to need any further Proof or Representation of the Matter.

No generous and impartial Person then can blame the present Undertaking, which is designed purely for the Diversion and Merriment of the Reader. Pieces of Pleasancy and Mirth have a secret Charm in them to allay the Heats and Tumors of our Spirits, and to make a Man forget his restless Resentments. They have a strange Power to tune the harsh Disorders of the Soul, and reduce us to a serene and placid State of Mind.

The main Design of this Weekly Paper will be to entertain the Town with the most comical and diverting Incidents of Humane Life, which in so large a Place as Boston, will not fail of a universal Exemplification: Nor shall we be wanting to fill up these Papers with a grateful Interspersion of more serious Morals, which may be drawn from the most Judicrous and odd Parts of Life.

As for the Author, that is the next Question. But tho' we profess our selves ready to oblige the ingenious and courteous Reader with most Sorts of Intelligence, yet here we beg a Reserve. Nor will it be of any Manner of Advantage either to them or to the Writers, that their Names should be published; and therefore in this Matter we desire the Favour of you to suffer us to Hold our Tongues: Which tho' at this Time of Day it may sound like a very uncommon Request, yet it proceeds from the very Hearts of your Humble Servants.

By this Time the Reader perceives that more than one are engaged in the present Undertaking. Yet is there one Person, an Inhabitant of this Town of Boston, whom we honour as a Doctor in the Chair, or a perpetual Dictator.

The Society had design'd to present the Publick with his Effigies, but that the Limner, to whom he was presented for a Draught of his Countenance, descryed (and this he is ready to offer upon Oath) Nineteen Features in his Face, more than ever he beheld in any Humane Visage before; which so raised the Price of his Picture, that our Master himself forbid the Extravagance of coming up to it. And then besides, the Limner objected a Schism in his Face, which splits it from his Forehead in a strait Line down to his Chin, in such sort, that Mr. Painter protests it is a double Face, and he'll have Four Pounds for the Pourtraiture. However, tho' this double Face has spoilt us of a pretty Picture, yet we all rejoiced to see old Janus in our Company.

There is no Man in Boston better qualified than old Janus for a Couranteer, or if you please, an Observator, being a Man of such remarkable Opticks, as to look two ways at once.

As for his Morals, he is a chearly Christian, as the Country Phrase expresses it. A Man of good Temper, courteous Deportment, sound Judgment; a mortal Hater of Nonsense, Foppery, Formality, and endless Ceremony.

As for his Club, they aim at no greater Happiness or Honour, than the Publick be made to know, that it is the utmost of their Ambition to attend upon and do all imaginable good Offices to good Old Janus the Couranteer, who is and always will be the Readers humble Servant.

P.S. Gentle Readers, we design never to let a Paper pass without a Latin Motto if we can possibly pick one up, which carries a Charm in it to the Vulgar, and the learned admire the pleasure of Construing. We should have obliged the World with a Greek Scrap or two, but the Printer has no Types, and therefore we intreat the candid Reader not to impute the defect to our Ignorance, for our Doctor can say all the *Greek* Letters by heart.

His Majesty's Speech to the Parliament, October 11. tho' already publish'd, may perhaps be new to many of our Country Readers; we shall therefore insert it in this Day's Paper.

His MAJESTY's most Gracious SPEECH to both Houses of Parliament, on Thursday October 11. 1722.

My Lords and Gentlemen,

I Am sorry to find my self obliged, at the Opening of this Parliament, to acquaint you, That a dangerous Conspiracy has been for some time formed, and is still carrying on against my Person and Government, in Favour of a Popish Pretender.

The Discoveries I have made here, the Informations I have received from my Ministers abroad, and the Intelligences I have had from the Powers in Alliance with me, and indeed from most parts of Europe, have given me most ample and current Proofs of this wicked Design.

The Conspirators have, by their Emissaries, made the strongest Instances for Assistance from Foreign Powers, but were disappointed in their Expectations: However, confiding in their Numbers, and not discouraged by their former ill Success, they resolved once more, upon their own strength, to attempt the subversion of my Government.

To this End they provided considerable Sums of Money, engaged great Numbers of Officers from abroad, secured large Quantities of Arms and Ammunition, and thought themselves in such Readiness, that had not the Conspiracy been timely discovered, we should, without doubt, before now have seen the whole Nation, and particularly the City of London, involved in Blood and Confusion.

The Care I have taken has, by the Blessing of God, hitherto prevented the Execution of their traytrous Projects. The Troops have been incamped all this Summer; six Regiments (though very necessary for the Security of that Kingdom) have been brought over from Ireland; The States General have given me assurances that they would keep a considerable Body of Forces ready.

the publication, in order, laying out each letter as it came off the boat. There was no editing. They would just add the next letter to the bottom of the last, often without individual headlines.

Later the editors started highlighting the main items by putting them at the top of a column or by drawing some big bars next to them.

Even when the paper got bigger, the concept remained the same. With a four-column layout, the most important story would be placed at the top of the third column. For the same reason that Aunt Martha's letter was not a real joy to behold, it became evident that publishers would have to put more emphasis on design. Everyone isn't going to be a doting nephew.

Starting

A good model to use when you are planning your newsletter is, of all things, the letter. When I was planning a big conference for the Type Directors Club a few years ago, a newsletter sprung out of an unrealistic amount of correspondence. When I figured out that it was literally impossible to keep everyone up-to-date with a personal letter—even with a computer mail merge program—I moved to a newsletter. (See Figure 13-2.) When something came up, I just put it in the newsletter and printed it when it was full.

This is actually an example of a second-level newsletter (a step above Aunt Martha's). Like its early-American predecessors, it is a series of letters in a linear, orderly fashion. If you want to get a little more complicated, the next evolution is to interrupt the stories with something else—put some raisins into the pudding. In other words, have a little picture or box with other text. This is very easy with desktop publishing because you can easily snake text through columns of your newsletter until it fills. You just continue to add text to the end of the previous story until you reach the end. This is basic DTP Layout 101.

In all high-end DTP programs the necessary number of pages will be automatically created. With some of the other programs, you have to continue to create pages as long as there still is text. Once all of the

Figure 13-2
When you have to get the information out and don't have time to write personal letters, try a newsletter

text is flowed solidly onto the pages, you have a good idea of how long your newsletter will be. It's a good idea to flow all of your text into pages before you think about a layout.

A typical rule of thumb for publications of any sort is that if you have two pages of solid text (when you've flowed all the text into pages), you need at least a four-page newsletter. The ratio of "raisins" to "pudding" should be 50-50.

Columns

Though there are many options for setting up newsletter columns, most newsletters take one of two forms. They are open-column wide—like most investment newsletters—and are almost impossible to read. This hearkens back to the days when the letters were typewritten. The other predominant form is three columns as an homage to *Time* magazine. This form is also hard to read because of the thin columns. The professional designers at *Time* can pull it off. Many newsletter designers have a harder time of it. I find the little-used two-column format of the old *Pennsylvania Gazette* to actually be more relaxing and readable than either of the two most used. If you use the simple two-column format, you can use a fairly large text size—13- or 14-point—for readability. The broad columns allow it.

If you feel constrained by two columns, try four instead of three. This offers a lot more flexibility and you can revert to two-column measure (two double columns over four) for certain articles. Short news items can run 11-point ragged right and down small columns, and longer items can run across two.

Another format that we are seeing more of is a wide, single column with a narrower, marginal column on the side. Most computer manuals and other forms of technical documentation use this style, which was derived from military manuals. The effect is a one-third, two-third split of the page. See Figure 13-3. Below the design is a three-column base (like *Time*). On the first page the right column runs across two of the three, and the left, marginal column is used for peripheral or supplemental material which relates to the main body of the text. Another device is to number the elements like the U.S. Army and IBM, using large numbers for sections and a period denoting subsections.

Figure 13-3
A two-column format on a three-column base

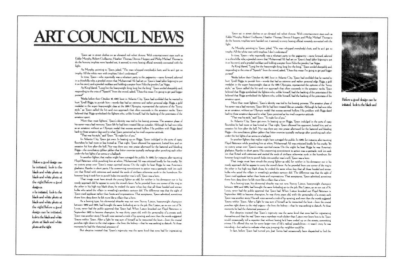

People see this style in computer manuals and adapt it to newsletters. Ventura Publisher even includes this style as a template. If you have things to put in the margins, and if you use a more interesting typeface than the U.S. Army does, this is not necessarily a bad typographical style.

I like the idea of *not* trying to pattern a newsletter after a magazine, or even more difficult, a newspaper. Picking up the manual style offers different connotations and can be very effective.

Size Is Important...For Paper

The problem with using newspapers as models is their size. Most newsletters are one-quarter the size of a newspaper. With six columns and 21 inches of depth on a newspaper, there are a lot of design options. With a smaller sheet of paper, you are severely constrained if you try to fit together a tight newspaper design. Unless you really have malleable copy, it's very hard to make a miniature newspaper. Your newsletter doesn't have to square off all the articles to be successful.

On the other hand, why not challenge the paper size? Why does it have to be 8.5-by-11 inches? You can change the size for a different effect or more flexibility.

Of course, in the business world, people get very upset if you don't use standard sizes which they can photocopy and put neatly in their little filing cabinets. This is more or less a valid concern. So, if you are doing something like *Idaho Re-Insurance News,* or another business interest—particularly one on the conservative side—you may not want to try a different size. You have to live with 8.5-by-11 inches or something easily folded to this size.

Many paper sizes are multiples of 8.5 by 11. Tabloid is two times the standard, for example.

You should explore your options if you are not doing a conservative business newsletter. Say you are doing a newsletter for your neighborhood cultural group, or for an association of amateur zoologists—people who are not planning on filing the thing in the end. Then you can do something else.

Talk to your printer about options. Find out the sizes his presses can handle. If you have received bids on an eight-page newsletter, check on the cost of doing a four-page tabloid. It should cost the same. Also, check what size paper he has on hand. There might be something interesting.

If you have a relationship with a printer and you are doing a folded 8.5-by-11-inch newsletter, consider running the whole page 11-by-17 inches. If it's going to be an 11-by-17-inch piece of paper, run it as a tabloid.

Other options to check are paper grade and color. People get set on a certain kind of paper. They think they need the one they saw in their favorite magazine. That's okay, and printers can order any kind of paper that you want, but it is worth a try to see if there's anything cheap or interesting lying around the print shop. Sometimes they will give it to you or offer a good price just to get it off their hands.

In 1976 I did a newsletter for the LA Bicentennial Committee—a rather under-funded segment of the national celebration. We wanted a local angle on the bicentennial. We had high school printing students doing the printing and we were able to get paper donated by going around to local printers. So, all the paper was different colors. We ended up with a lot of very pulpy, newsprint paper and I designed a newspaper based on an early-American style. It was one of the best things I ever did.

If you are a charity or a worthy local group, maybe you can get paper donated. You might get luckier than if you spent hours choosing just the right one. Have fun and exploit the different thicknesses and textures.

There are always other options. The Type Directors Club newsletter moved to an 11-by-17-inch broadside, and it opened options for different type elements, as well as more and bigger pictures. For a change, think of your newsletter as a poster—do it with all the text on one side and a poster on the other. Use a little imagination. You don't have to model your newsletter after the local gas company's. The local gas company has its own problems.

Make It Easy

If you are going to be doing your newsletter on a regular basis—weekly, monthly, or every six months—you don't want to make it so complicated that each issue is a major project to design. It is much easier to just flow the text into a basic design (a template) and then decorate it, than it is to redesign each issue, treating each article as a separate item. Keeping your design consistent also helps readers recognize your publication and feel comfortable with it.

In the same vein, you don't want to redesign your newsletter very often. If it is doing what you need it to do, it should be redesigned no more than every three or four years. You can make occasional improvements, like updating the caption style, while remaining within the same general framework. Readers like the familiar, which is another argument for finding a design and sticking with it.

Of course, you can put some items in boxes and then flow the rest of the type around them. Make the size bigger or add a picture to make it fit. If you have a little space left at the end of the last page, make a picture box exactly that size and move it anywhere in the flowed text. It won't look like you are just filling the space left at the end. Flowed text is an exact volumetric measure. Before desktop publishing, designers spent hours figuring out how long text would flow. Of course, it wasn't exact, and we spent a lot of time finessing to make the text fit. In desktop publishing, everything is exact and can be manipulated through trial and error.

Typography

There isn't an enormous difference between the typography of newsletters and other publications, but a good rule of thumb is to stick to two typefaces, a bold and a light. With production constraints, you can't express a broad tonal range.

The primary concept to remember when designing your newsletter is to keep everything structural. Don't go totally freeform. If you are a professional designer, you can "wig out" and do a collage that looks good. Don't try to do a collage as your first newsletter. Try to get the basic columnar structure and control of the other elements down first.

The Logo

Perhaps the most important typographic element is the logo. It's critical because it determines how people are going to think about the rest of the content. It can keep your newsletter from looking amateurish if done right.

The word that comes to mind when people start working on their logo is "fancy." They decorate it and doll it up too much. For example, the *Seybold Report on Desktop Publishing* used to have a Swash Bookman logo like the old Friendly Skies of United typeface. In addition to looking very 1960s and dated, it looked out of place on a newsletter. The natural instinct of a nondesigner is to say, "Hey, it's my name. Let's put some inlay in here, some filigree, some little doodads. I want to show what control I have of the desktop toys."

Instead, consider setting the name in straight type. For example, if you are doing *Art Council News,* take your text face, whatever it is, and set the words "Art Council News" in huge size. Try it stacked flush left on three lines; try it all on one line, as big as possible. Try tracking the lettering tightly and then combine it with a thick bar at the top or the bottom. It will even look better if you leave some space on the top or the bottom. See the examples in Figure 13-4. Then stop. Often, this is all that it takes to put together a good-looking newsletter logo.

White Space

I can't emphasize enough the value of judicious white space. In books, each chapter title starts with a sink—a lot of white space at the top of the page—to tell you it is the start of another chapter. Add another inch of white space at the top of the first page before you even start your logo, so that readers realize that there is something there.

To draw attention to the number one item in the page, run it all in big type or use one of the other type devices in Chapter 3, "Reaching the Reader." Figure 13-5 shows the lead story introduced with big type.

Figure 13-4
Keep newsletter logos
simple

*Try forming your
logo by setting it
on two columns...*

ART COUNCIL NEWS

*...by setting it large
running across...*

ART COUNCIL NEWS

...or tracked tightly...

ART
COUNCIL
NEWS

*...with a bold
line beneath*

ART
COUNCIL
NEWS

Figure 13-5
Draw attention to the
lead story with type

Photos

Photos should get the same treatment as type—tread lightly because of the small tonal range. When you scan in pictures and use graphics made on the computer, remember that halftone reproduction quality decreases with the size of the picture. You can usually get enough information with a good desktop scanner to reproduce a small picture well. The bigger a picture is, the more trouble you are going to have.

Editorial Considerations

Since many newsletters are standalone amateur products, it is not outside the scope of this book to mention the editorial considerations. If you are doing it as an amateur designer, you may not have any editorial help. It is essential that you present the editorial material in as clear and simple a manner as possible. The writing must be lucid and all elements should have headlines and captions so that nothing is standing alone.

Stories should be as short as possible. Edit them down to the nibbon. I've usually discovered that if the editorial content is thought out, structured, and has some reason to exist, the design becomes easier and is itself, more purposeful.

The other idea to keep in mind from the editorial standpoint is your personal reason for putting out the newsletter. The reason should be readily obvious to anyone who picks up your publication. Are you doing this to have fun or to entertain your readers? Are you doing it to present straight information? Even if you are only offering straight information, you don't have to present everything in just 8-point type.

Desktop Design Power

People tend to sum up the impact of desktop publishing with the fulsome phrase, "the biggest thing since Gutenberg." This is a big claim, and it is hard for us today to appreciate the explosive change caused by the introduction of printing 500 years ago. Literacy is taken for granted now, and we are shocked when we hear about how many cannot read in our supposedly civilized world. Myopically, we imagine that the arrival of television was just as important as the invention of the press.

In the last 50 years the electronic media seized our imagination, our lifestyle, and our business world. Since the pronouncements of Marshall "The Medium Is The Message" McLuhan in the 1960s, it has been popular to assume that the printed media were inevitably giving away to the electronic. Computers seemed to hasten this trend. But the facts are contrary. Desktop publishing gives the power of the printed medium to everyone with access to a computer.

The initial impact is in offices. Business people have always published things, but it was a struggle. The tools just were not there. Manual typewriters and spirit duplicators gave way to IBM electrics and Xerox machines, but everything still revolved around letters.

Even with the advent of word processing, the goal of the manufacturers was still letter-quality printing.

Now any alert office worker knows about fonts and halftones. Letter quality has taken off into an unexpected direction. It no longer seems weird to get a letter set in Galliard; indeed it seems that by the year 2000, everyone will have a favorite typeface.

Meanwhile, traditional publishing has changed enormously, but instead of going extinct it is more robust than ever. There are twice as many magazines as there were 20 years ago, and although a few huge consumer titles perished in the competition with cheap TV advertising, many big publications have survived—*Time, McCall's, Reader's Digest, Esquire,* and many other familiar names still have millions of readers and make more money than ever. Using DTP tools, newcomers are effectively challenging the old titles, but it seems that there will simply be more and more specialized publications for every interest and subculture, every industry and market channel.

The tide has turned, and now, thanks to cable, public access, satellite dishes, and VCRs, it is television that is in trouble; the old U.S. networks are languishing, the audience is splintering. Funny, TV has become a lot like print.

The Joy of Printing

What is happening is that the distinction between print and electronic media is dissolving. Desktop publishing is a phenomenon that proves the point. Electronic mail is tying print to the global communications network. Digital photography is putting images on pages as quickly as they can be broadcast. The promise of "multimedia" is that it will all blend together in wonderful megadocuments, combining type, graphics, video, and sound.

This fusion contains much hype and many buzz words ("multimedia" is one of them). Talented and well-funded groups may be putting together the corporate equivalent of rock videos in the near future, but the amount of effort involved in multimedia is staggering.

There is a reason why there are all those names in the credits of a movie, or even after the evening news. Even assuming that we will soon have at our disposal enormous libraries of video clips, sound bites, still photos, and reference libraries (and clear and inexpensive rights to use them), individuals will still turn to print as the best way to get a point across without having to hire an army to help.

However historians judge its importance, DTP has put publishing into the hands of millions of people. And however well we can judge the revolutionary changes caused by Gutenberg, we can now feel some of the emotions of the early printers who found themselves in complete control of the publishing process. For newcomers there is the feeling that they now have some ownership of a medium that used to belong to a kind of priesthood of professionals.

These professionals (writers, editors, and designers) now find they can take control of publishing—or more links in the chain—without a lot of people in the way. Igor Stravinsky once complained that he was being separated from his work by a "dozen crapulous intermediaries." Now I'm no Stravinsky, but I and most designers know exactly how he felt.

And for years, those of us publishing anything—from a glossy, high-budget magazine to the low-budget newsletter—had to put up with typesetters complaining about how late the copy was. Color separators whined about the murkiness of the slides.

We had to hear them ask with mock innocence, "Why would you want to do that?" We resigned ourselves to production people constantly mumbling that what we asked was too much to expect, that it couldn't be done, and certainly not on time. And most assuredly not at that price! There was a time, however, when things were simpler. A few hundred years ago a printer was his own designer and his own production manager. Indeed he often wrote his own text. And if his press didn't exactly fit on his desktop, at least it was in the same room, and not in Winnebago, Wisconsin.

The "progress" of subsequent decades led to increasing specialization and division of labor, so that while we now may be publishing more, each of us knows a lot less about publishing. Writers no longer edit, editors don't do layouts, designers don't have to know anything about halftones—and production and manufacturing managers are separated from the editorial process altogether.

Come the Revolution

Now, because of desktop publishing, we're hearing editors talk about kerning. Ad salespeople know a bit about dot gain. Designers are setting their own type. And increasingly, individuals are doing all of this at once. For me, desktop publishing means more than the one-man-band newsletter produced by a zealot on self-contained publishing systems (usually consisting of little more than a PC and a laser printer.) For me, the power of desktop publishing is the control of my own work.

I can set type, layout pages, experiment with design and pictures, and at each step get an instantaneous proof. The speed of this turnaround actually advances my work in ways I could not have predicted before I got my hands on the technology.

For one thing, I can make mistakes faster, and get rid of them faster, if I want, although some of the mistakes inspire even better ideas. Then, when it's done, I can send a PostScript file off to the high-resolution printer, and get back exactly what I put into it.

And that's the best part—what computer magazines call the "interactive" nature of the process. The give-and-take between me and the machine, the quick response, the color on the screen, the close-to-final quality of the laser-printed proofs. All of it combines to give me power over the design that I never had before.

I have dispensed with all the whimpering intermediaries, albeit not without paying a price. We all have to learn new skills. Since my own start in desktop publishing in 1986, I've had to learn things about color that I never thought I'd ever want to know. I've spent hours copy editing articles that, in the "old days," I'd never even have read. And I've spent what seems like a lifetime educating editors about the fine points of typography.

The computer skills we've had to learn are child's play compared to all this craft.

Has it been worth it?

Without the slightest doubt!

The new understanding from having to deal with all the steps in the process once left to others has sharpened my skills. I've become more of a generalist. I have come to realize that it is the specialization that slows down the publishing process and promotes larger, more inept organizations. Not only is DTP faster; I'm convinced that it results in better design.

And even if it doesn't, who cares? It's cheaper, more fun, and certainly no worse than what's produced by all those specialists. And the result is tremendous satisfaction.

I am reminded of my first job as an art director, in Houston for the legendary advertising man, Adie Marks. At the interview, he asked me why I wanted to be an art director, and I explained the great satisfaction I derived from designing things and seeing them printed and distributed in quantity. I was pretty passionate about it. Adie looked at me and said, "That's funny. I'm in it for the money."

Well, I got the job, but a few months later, when I realized that my salary was just about covering the cost of keeping my automobile filled with gas, I went back and tried to negotiate a raise. Adie said, "Gee, Roger, I thought you were in it for the joy of the printed page."

I still am, but it is always good to remember that the reason for the success of desktop publishing relates to the bottom line. The rest is gravy.

Working in Groups

The solitary pleasure of the desktop really is not where the action is. Standalone PCs and Macs have been linked with networks, and a new concept has emerged: groupware. Publishing of any size is done in collaboration. And here the power of desktop publishing is more apparent. With the troublesome intermediaries—assistants and messengers—absent, the key people at a publication are able to work together more efficiently, and with greater inspiration.

The payoff is described in the chapter on *Smart,* where the editor, Terry McDonell and I conspired to put out a cover by ourselves in a matter of hours. This kind of effort called for a simple network so that text and pictures could be quickly brought to my workstation. And we needed a big color monitor, so that we could both see what was going on. When we were ready, we invited others to come take a look.

The next step would be to get a really big monitor hanging from the ceiling, or maybe a projection monitor so that work in progress could be shared easily with colleagues. The notion of letting it all hang out would never work in a traditional, hierarchical publication, but this technology is promoting a more horizontal, even a democratic structure for magazines and newspapers.

In Spain, at the new daily newspaper *El Sol,* which is entirely produced on the Macintosh, the traditional structure for newspapers didn't seem appropriate for the new system. The usual desks, like the city desk, never appeared. In their place are workgroups, each devoted to putting out specific pages in the paper. One workgroup might be working on national news pages, and consist of an editor, five writers, an art director, and a photographer. A financial news workgroup might add a couple of graphic artists working on Macs to produce business charts.

The groups are collaborative, but at the same time they are self-contained and independent. At the end of a day, literally, they publish. Group members can pick up the paper and get the satisfaction of seeing their work come to life. A very thin layer of editorial management at the top makes sure that all the groups are working in the same style and in the same direction. Of course, there is a team of staffers devoted to tasks that are newspaper-wide (such as color correction and other specific production jobs). But even they are grouped into teams.

The plan is to rotate the reporters, designers, and editors so that everyone gets to know everyone else, and picks up some new skills. Time will tell if this experiment will work. The staff may tend to go back to the old desk system that is more familiar to them. Or they may create a richer environment and a dynamic way of working—the desktop publishing way—that gives the paper a great competitive advantage.

Where We Are Going

Desktop publishing has just begun to influence the big companies that now dominate the business. At virtually all of them, in the U.S. and in Europe, experiments are under way. Recently Time Warner came out with *Entertainment Weekly* and Hearst with *Victoria*—both produced with desktop tools.

There is some resistance to changing big existing publications to DTP, mainly because of huge investments in mini-computer front-end systems, the previous technology that "revolutionized" publishing. Now these Atex (and other) machines are called dinosaurs. Yet they still work, they are paid for, and they do things that desktop publishing systems do not. The main thing is file management. An Atex system tracks the work of numerous writers and editors, provides automatic backups of files and an "audit" trail of previous versions of each story, and handles the codes to drive typesetting machines with complete kerning controls and a superior hyphenation dictionary.

What none of the "dinosaurs" provide is a design interface as good as QuarkXPress, PageMaker, or Ventura Publisher. In the last two years the DTP programs have taken on virtually all of the typographic sophistication of the big, and costly front-end systems, but Atex and the others failed to develop a page-layout capability anywhere near as good as the shrink-wrapped desktop software. Now the established publishing system companies are struggling to make links with QuarkXPress, PageMaker, DesignStudio, or Ventura Publisher, rather than build their own.

It seems to me that DTP has already won, and a good indication is the attitude of production managers and art directors at rival publications. In 1988 they were skeptical, if not condescending, toward anyone trying to put out a first-rank publication with desktop publishing tools. Now they are trying to catch up, and those who have not made moves toward the new technology ask questions with a new sheepishness, urgency, and a little fear.

To replace the dinosaurs, desktop publishing must offer solutions to the file management problem—some kind of adaptable publishing database software. This is not a trivial thing, and there are likely to be a number of offerings, not all of them off-the-shelf. But people are working at it, and already weeklies, big monthlies, and even a few dailies are publishing in an all-electronic environment—managing either by the old-fashioned human method (often easier), or by writing some code.

With resolve, publishers are adapting to standard computer platforms and running shrink-wrapped software. For text and page layout, these "fourth-wave" solutions, as Jonathan Seybold called them, are virtually in place. The next step is color. And if we think that the craft of typography was hard to learn, the art of color separation is much harder. It is technical, and it is subjective at the same time.

There are a few interesting pieces of the color puzzle that have already been put in place. Nikon makes an excellent scanner; Adobe Photoshop offers a fast color retouching; and Anaya Systems has announced a superior color separation technique to be used on existing PostScript imagesetters.

At every level more work must be done. We need better scanners, better, more intuitive color-retouching software, better control for color on the output side. Huge files must be managed, and it all must be done in a common "color space," where scanners, monitors, and printers are automatically tuned to the same color values.

It's all about to happen. And we'll go on to bigger, high-definition monitors, as sharp as a proof. Computers in 10 years will be five times as fast, and a twentieth of the cost, and our worries about moving big files through tiny cables will seem trivial.

We'll see an endless parade of new products, and these will be updated with .1, and then .2, and on and on. It is actually the relentlessness of the new technology that will be the most difficult part.

It seems that you have barely mastered new technology before something better comes out. And yet it is easier each time, and there is a satisfying convergence in the way DTP programs are handled. The PC has begun to act like the Mac, and vice versa; the Unix workstations already look familiar. Even the vexing font issues of the past two years are being resolved by a willingness on all sides to convert formats and allow compatibility.

It is all getting hooked up. The learning curve will not flatten out, but as you climb it becomes less steep. It's worth learning all the arcane technical stuff, because it puts the designer in control. It gives us a degree of desktop design power.

Permissions

Page 6, Figure I-2a, reprinted with permission of Abel Quezada.
Page 6, Figure I-2b, reprinted with permission of *The San Francisco Examiner.* Copyright 1898 San Francisco Examiner.
Page 6, Figure I-2c, reprinted with permission of Metropolitan Life Insurance Company. Design, Corporate Graphics Inc.
Page 15, Figure 1-2, reprinted with permission of *Vogue.*
Page 16, Figure 1-3, reprinted with permission of *Esquire.* Photography, John Stewart.
Page 18, Figure 1-4, reprinted with permission of *Esquire.*
Page 20, Figure 1-5, reprinted with permission of Bob Ciano.
Pages 21 and 126, Figures 1-6 and 6-4, reprinted with permission of *Psychology Today.*
Page 23, Figure 1-7, reprinted with permission of *Rolling Stone.* Photography, David Gahr.
Page 73, Figure 3-9, reprinted with permission of *Novedades.*
Page 77, Figure 4-1, reprinted with permission of *Smart.* Design, Rhonda Rubenstein.
Page 80, Figure 4-2, reprinted with permission of *Smart.*
Page 92, Figure 5-1, reprinted with permission of *Smart.*
Page 93, Figure 5-2, reprinted with permission of *Walking* and Frank Siteman.
Page 99, Figure 5-3, reprinted with permission of Banana Republic and Hokan Ludwigsson.
Page 107, Figure 5-4, reprinted with permission of *Desktop Communications.* Illustration, Patrick McDonnell. Copyright 1989.
Page 110, Figure 5-5, reprinted with permission of *Newsweek.*
Page 111, Figure 5-6, reprinted with permission of *Schweizer Illustrierte.*
Page 113, Figure 5-7, reprinted with permission of Norman Mayskopf.
Page 116, Figure 5-8, reprinted with permission of Norman Mayskopf.
Page 121, Figure 6-1, reprinted with permission of *Desktop Communications* and Nancy Moran.
Page 122, Figure 6-2, reprinted with permission of *New York* and Hiro.
Page 124, Figure 6-3, reprinted with permission of *New West.*
Page 130, Figure 6-5, reprinted with permission of *Rolling Stone.*
Page 133, Figure 6-6, reprinted with permission of *Smart.* Photography, Kazumi Kurigami.
Page 189, Figure 8-4, Courtesy Linda Nardi.
Pages 199 and 205, Chapter 9 opener and Figures 9-1g—9-1i, reprinted with permission of *Smart.* Photography, Jon Gardey and Greg Gorman.
Page 204, Figures 9-1a—91f, reprinted with permission of *Smart* and Jon Gardey.
Page 211, Figure 9-3, reprinted with permission of *Smart.*
Pages 216-217, Figure 9-6, reprinted with permission of *Smart.*
Page 219, Figure 9-7, reprinted with permission of *Smart* and John Howard.
Pages 221 and 229, Chapter 10 opener and Figure 10-2, reprinted with permission of Banana Republic. Illustration, Abel Quezada.
Page 232, Figure 10-3, reprinted with permission of Banana Republic.
Pages 235 and 236, Figure 10-5, reprinted with permission of Banana Republic.
Page 237, Figure 10-6, reprinted with permission of Banana Republic.
Page 239, Figure 10-7, reprinted with permission of Banana Republic.

Index